I0901594

IMAGES
of America

WAH-TUT-CA SCOUT RESERVATION

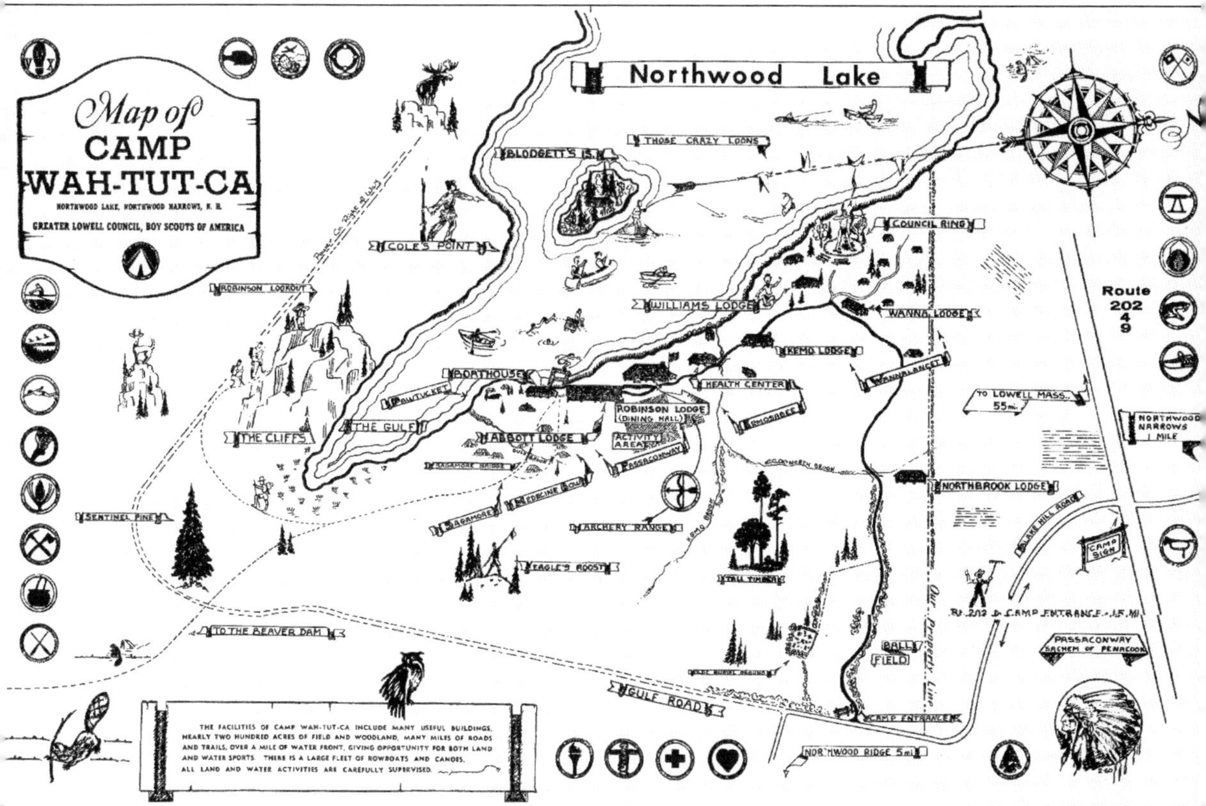

Wah-Tut-Ca is a place for adventure, as can be seen in this 1950s map created by Alexander A. Vervaert. Like its creator, the map is both legend and legacy. Although Vervaert died in 1991, portions of the text of this book were taken from letters he wrote and documented speeches he made during his lifetime. He is in every respect an author of this work.

On the cover: The Wah-Tut-Ca waterfront is shown in the postwar era. Boats tied up on the dock wait to take Scouts on a "voyage of discovery." Aquatic staff members watch over boys swimming in Northwood Lake. Although taken half a century ago, the scene is timeless and perfect. (Charles F. Emerson collection.)

IMAGES
of America

WAH-TUT-CA SCOUT RESERVATION

The Key Foundation Inc.

ARCADIA
PUBLISHING

ISBN 978-0-7385-4978-1

Published by Arcadia Publishing
Charleston SC, Chicago IL, Portsmouth NH, San Francisco CA

Printed in the United States of America

Library of Congress Catalog Card Number: 2006938408

For all general information contact Arcadia Publishing at:
Telephone 843-853-2070
Fax 843-853-0044
E-mail sales@arcadiapublishing.com
For customer service and orders:
Toll-Free 1-888-313-2665

Visit us on the Internet at www.arcadiapublishing.com

To all of our friends and brothers who wait for us in the stockade.
The fire they tend will "glow the brighter" when they,
at last, welcome us home.

CONTENTS

ACKNOWLEDGMENTS

Most of the pictures in this book come from The Key Foundation Inc. archives, a collection made up of records and photographs from individuals such as Charles F. Emerson, Alexander A. Vervaert, Harold R. Stevens, Blake M. Watson, John A. Goodwin, and Brian J. Lobao. The Key Foundation Inc. would also like to recognize the following for supplementing our collection and helping us along our quest: Penny Lacroix of the Westford Museum and Historical Society; David H. Brow and the *Lowell Sun*; Joanne Bailey of the Northwood Historical Society; Harvard University Archives; Chesley Memorial Library; Judith Balomenos and Robert McKittrick; Harry and Loretta Graves; Chelmsford Historical Society; Spar and Spindle Council Girl Scouts of America; St. Anne's Episcopal Church, Lowell, Massachusetts; and the Northwood Lake Association.

The research of this book has been quite an adventure, and we would like to thank everyone who shared their story with us. Special thanks to John A. Goodwin, who was a staff member at both Camp Chadwick and during Wah-Tut-Ca's first seasons, and Edgar Emerson, who was a camper that first year.

The Key Foundation Inc. owes a debt of gratitude to the editors of this book. They are Kevin R. Dion, Michael T. Fournier, Jonathan J. Keating, George D. Kouloheras, David S. Leonard, Brian J. Lobao, Howard W. Martin, Andrew M. Rubenstein, Daniel S. Smith, and Alexander A. Vervaert.

The editors would like to thank all who offered support, advice, and material throughout its writing, particularly Marc Desgrosiellers, Donald Eckelkamp, Linda M. Lobao, Stephen Marchacos, Charles D. McMurrer, Bennett A. Sawyer, Scott H. Sughrue, and Phyllis Wink.

We would especially like to acknowledge Brian J. Lobao, president and CEO of The Key Foundation Inc. This book exists today due to his vision and dedication.

In 2001, Lobao established The Key Foundation Inc. Archive Program. The foundation took on the mission to collect, archive, and share the grand adventure that is the story of Wah-Tut-Ca. Our goal is to leave a legacy and challenge for those friends and brothers who will follow. We believe that by knowing their past, they will continue to build the future.

—George D. Kouloheras
For The Key Foundation Inc.

INTRODUCTION

The founders of Wah-Tut-Ca Scout Reservation had a particular vision in mind when they purchased a large plot of farmland in 1936. Boys living in the rural Greater Lowell area had ample space to play but little opportunity for the kind of adventure that comes with leaving the surroundings of home. The woods of New Hampshire, although only 60 miles away, held great intrigue. The voyage to Northwood involved multiple modes of transportation and culminated in a place far from familiar neighborhoods and yards. The trip served to emphasize that something special was going to happen—anticipation and nervous energy built as the journey wore on. Are we there yet? What is this place? What is it going to be like?

No matter the year, Wah-Tut-Ca has always been full of potential. For campers, it was adventure, a week or two away from home to learn new skills, make friends, and get away from the bustle of traffic and noise. For the staff, the potential was the chance to lead, to develop confidence and leadership skills at the toughest, most fun summer job a guy could ever have. For old-timers, it was witnessing the cycle begin anew, seeing the campers who might break out of their shy shells, the fresh staff members who have started to become imbued with the spirit that carried Wah-Tut-Ca through all of the years where both budgets and belts were tight.

It is amazing to think about that spirit. Since its inception, Wah-Tut-Ca has endured more than its fair share of crises. The 1940s found the country in the midst of war rationing, which severely taxed both the resources needed to operate a summer camp and the means of getting there. The 1960s brought civil unrest, the likes of which our country had never seen, and the 1970s brought decreased enrollment and monetary hard times. Wah-Tut-Ca survived. Flash floods, fires, microbursts, land development deals, and councils merging did not break us. We carry on, made stronger by the crises. The spirit envisioned by Wah-Tut-Ca's founders not only endured, but flourished, maturing and gaining strength with each passing hardship.

Campers at Wah-Tut-Ca build their own histories year after year. Each summer finds a new staff of dedicated members working tirelessly to inspire and educate the boys who pass through the gates on Blake's Hill Road. Scouts who return for a second summer use their past experiences as a frame of reference—the nice guy at Discovery who talked about trees, the lifeguard who helped with the backstroke. The staff members and campers who moved on become part of the lore. Their stories are told nightly around campfires as mosquitoes drone idly by. The tales traded become immediate, dear, and intensely personal. It is not uncommon for one boy's best story to be borrowed by another. A name here, a "fact" there, the experiences, through repetition, become fact, sometimes even if they did not really happen (the fish was *how* big?).

This book is a culmination of every choice made by all involved in Wah-Tut-Ca. The personal tales would not have a chance to flourish were it not for the efforts of Wah-Tut-Ca's visionary staffs, volunteers, and community leaders. The story extends beyond the camp's inception in 1937, just as it extends beyond the present day. The past and the future tell the tales of the present. It is important to preserve the past so that future generations can flourish and build on both the legacies of those who came before us and those of today.

We hope that this book extends beyond the preservation of a single history. There are stories everywhere, and we are all storytellers. What of your camp, your neighborhood? How did they come to be? Who was involved?

The history of your experience is just as important as its discovery. The process is integral. Dead ends and hours in dusty libraries serve to motivate even further. The digging and sifting become a connection to the past. Through learning your own particular history, you embark on a personal "voyage of discovery," a chance to eagerly search for what is on the other side. You will get a chance to discover and survey what lies beyond, just as Wah-Tut-Ca's founders did when they spent an evening camping on the cliffs.

As you look through the pages of this book, please consider the histories that you hold dear and carry with you. After you are gone, who will cherish them? Who will honor these memories?

Do not let your knowledge be lost. Speak to elders. Comb through old documents. Document your history, your friends. Do not let it be lost.

A great deal of history has passed through Wah-Tut-Ca's gates since they first opened in 1937, a fact that is easily witnessed in the stacks and stacks of archival photographs that were considered for inclusion in this book. Some 20,000 shots were considered, with somewhere in the neighborhood of 200 finally making the cut.

If you happen to be one of the thousands of lucky friends and brothers who had an opportunity to share some time under the great pines, please allow these pictures to bring you back to a simpler, possibly happier time and take this opportunity to wander through time to your own personal experiences during your time spent on Northwood Lake.

If you are one of the many who has not heard of our camp before, we hope you enjoy your stay. By all means, come and see us. Introduce yourself. Welcome home!

One

The Land for Friends and Brothers

In 1774, the Blake family settled on a large hill that borders what was then known as Suncook Pond, renamed Northwood Lake in 1929. The Blakes cleared the land and then built the road and dwellings. This area of Northwood still bears the name Blake's Hill, as does the road that runs up it.

In 1779, Jacob Swain married Mehitable Blake and obtained much of the land that is now known as Wah-Tut-Ca. For the next 138 years, the Swain family farmed the land. Jacob Swain had no children and left the land to his nephew William Swain in 1822.

Wah-Tut-Ca includes another piece of land known as the gulf. This area is a deep ravine, bordered by a high ridge and cliffs that dip down hundreds of feet to the base of the lake. A small section of Northwood is on the far side of this ravine.

By 1783, Theophilus Griffin and Nathan Bartlett owned estates on the far side of the gulf. There was no way to get from their farms to Northwood proper without passing through neighboring Deerfield and Epsom. Northwood granted both men tax-free status if they would build a road to go through the gulf. A crude yet passable town road was completed in 1794, known alternately as the Gulf Road or the Griffin Road. (This area of Northwood was also known as Griffintown). The road now runs through Wah-Tut-Ca and was abandoned by the town in 1930.

"Our mountains are not too high and our soil is not too deep" is how some of its townspeople described Northwood. The rocky soil of Blake's Hill was never optimal for farming. Many of the local farms supplemented their income by making shoes, aided by a dam-powered mill at the end of Northwood Lake. Several of Northwood's farmers became subcontractors, manufacturing pieces of shoes on their farms.

In 1917, Frank Swain, great-grandson of William Swain, sold the family farm to settle the debts of his father, Sibley. The Swain family farmhouse was torn down in 1920. The property was parceled then owned for a short time by the Lynn Country Club, which ran summer outings and picnics on the site.

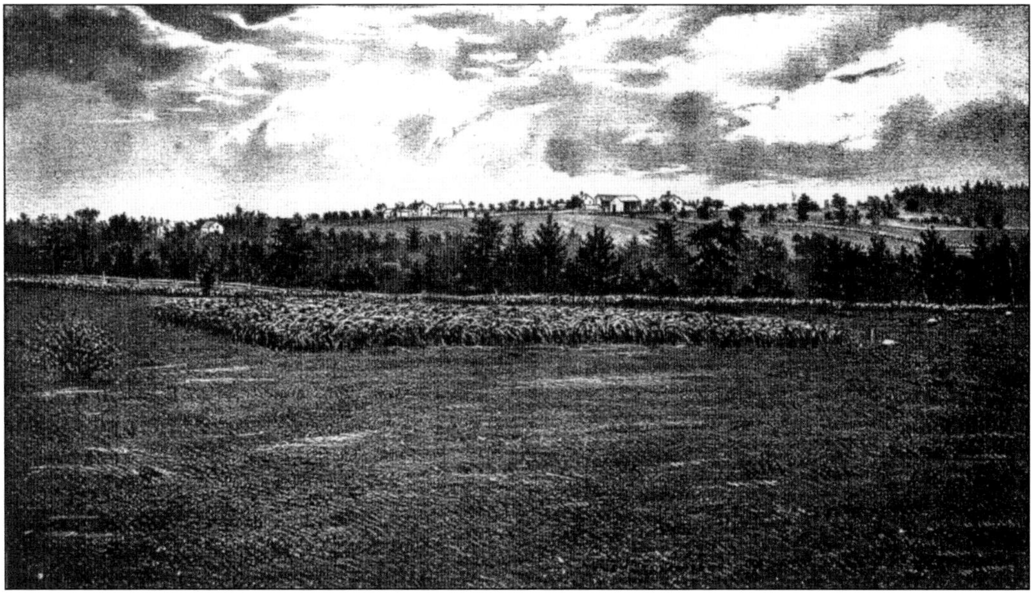

The town of Northwood separated from the town of Nottingham in 1773. Sherburne and Dudley Blake were among the town's 350 early residents and settling one of the highest points in town. The sections of Northwood were identified by school districts. With a schoolhouse on top of the hill, the area became known as Blake's Hill.

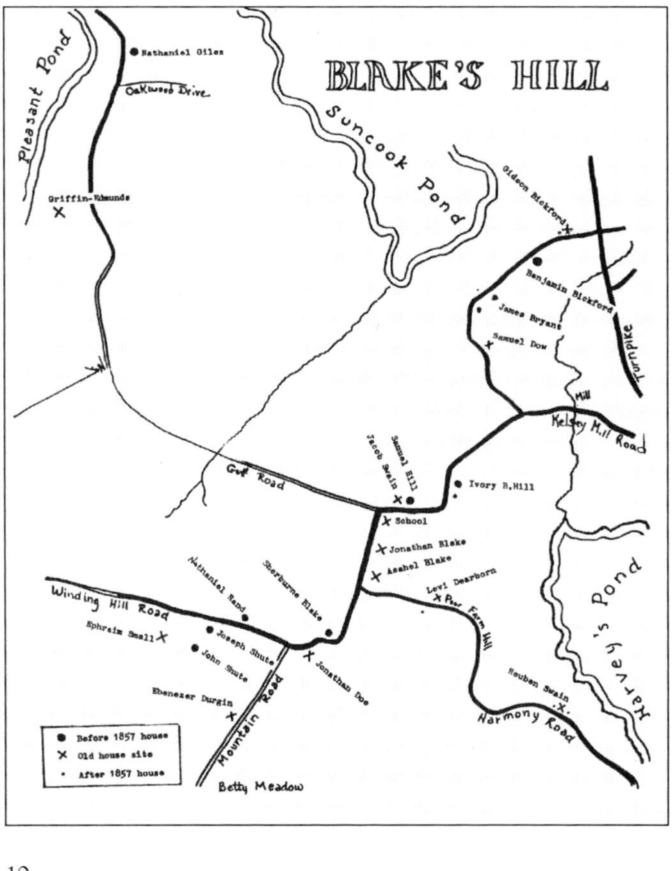

This map of Northwood shows Blake's Hill and some of the early farms and buildings located there, including the schoolhouse. The lake was originally named Suncook Pond but was renamed Northwood Lake in 1929 to avoid confusion with Upper and Lower Suncook Lake in nearby Barnstead.

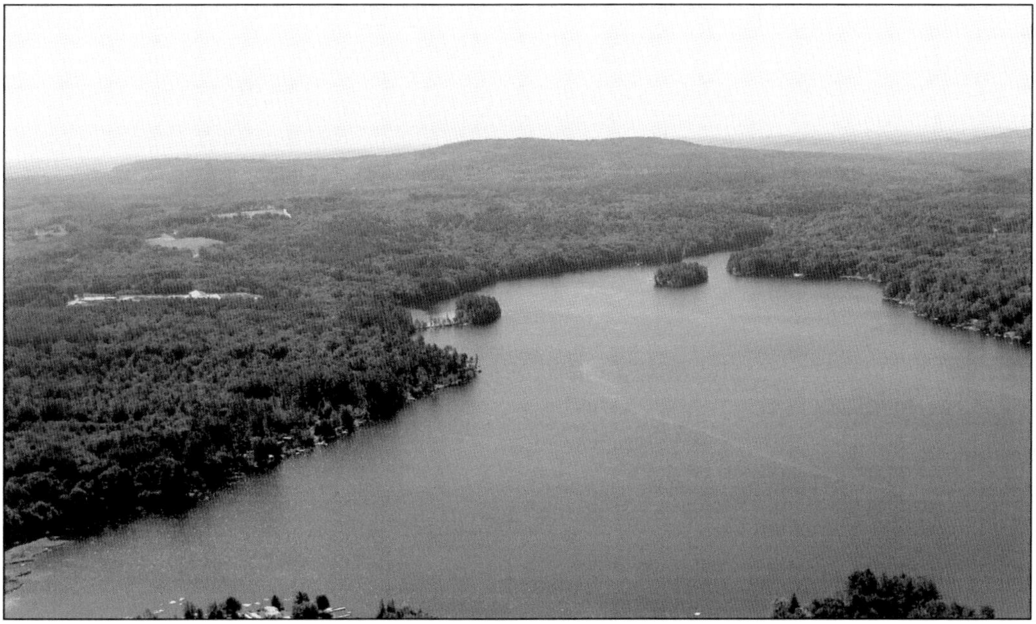

In 2006, the trees stand much as they would have prior to 1773. Many of the trees were removed by the first settlers on Blake's Hill so the land could be farmed. The lumber was used for houses and firewood. With the decline of farming in the late 19th century, the pastures created by Northwood's first settlers slowly disappeared.

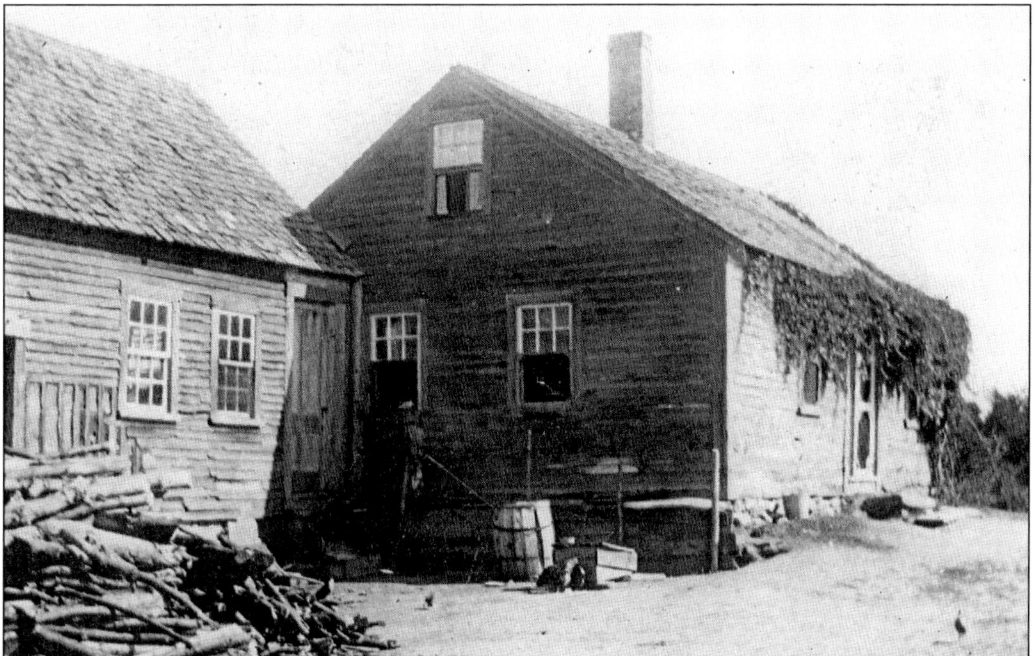

The Rollins-Graves farm was located down the road from the Swain family farm and is typical of the buildings that stood on Blake's Hill. The clapboard-sided dwellings were usually left unpainted because it was cheaper to replace the siding than to buy paint. This building was torn down in the 1960s.

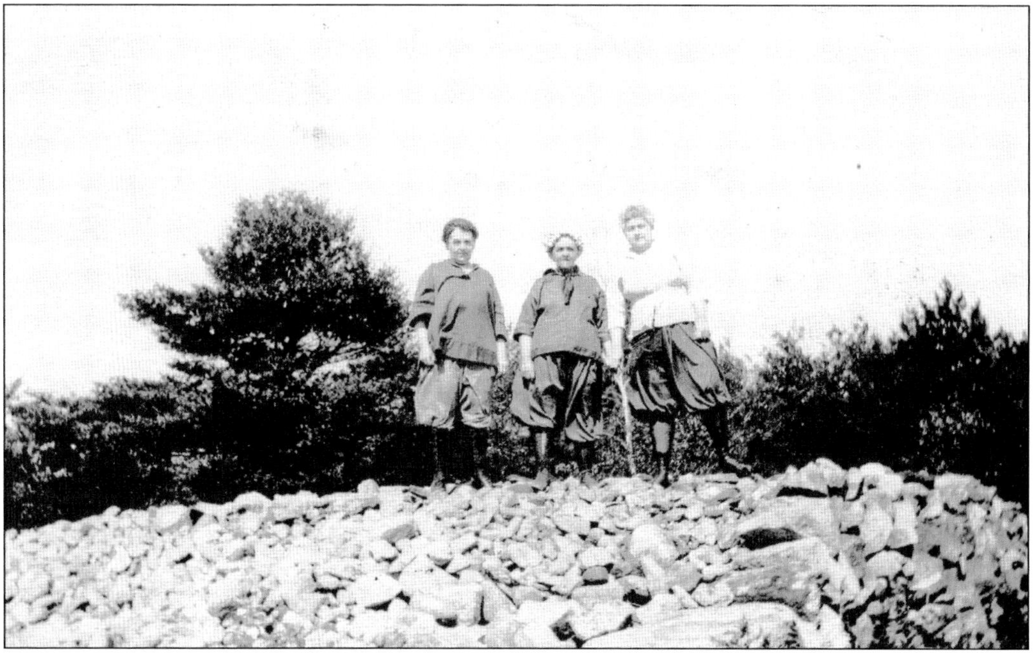

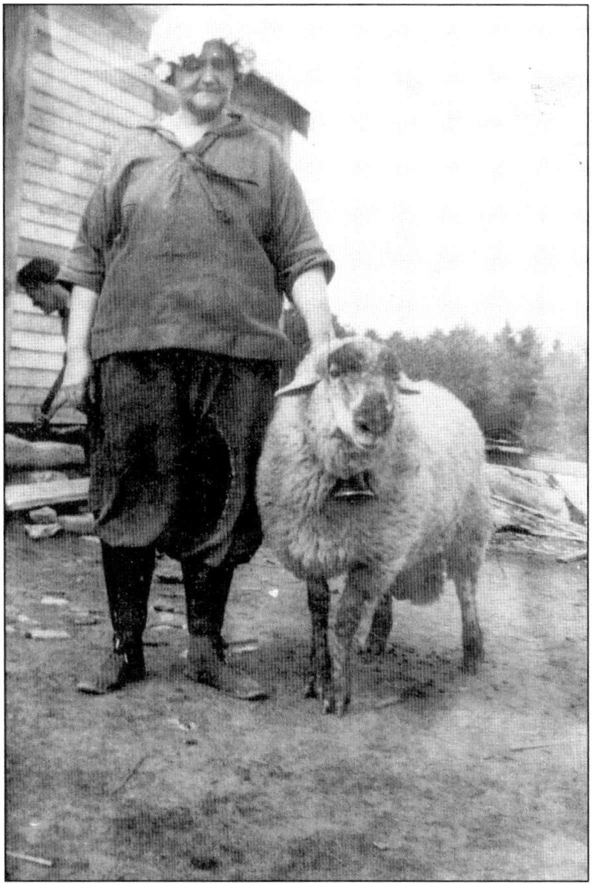

The rolling hills and rocky terrain that give Wah-Tut-Ca much of its character also made farming in Northwood difficult. Rocks that were forced to the surface by the freezing and thawing of the land needed to be removed in order to plow. Many of the rocks were dug out by hand and moved on horse-drawn skids. They ended up as rock walls like the ones that crisscross Wah-Tut-Ca or in the foundations of houses and barns. Excess rocks often ended up in large piles, like this one near the Rollins-Graves farm. Similar but smaller piles can be found in several locations at Wah-Tut-Ca.
Effie Rollins is seen both on the rock pile and with a favorite sheep, Sampson. The hard work needed to run a farm on Blake's Hill required people of both physical strength and strength of character.

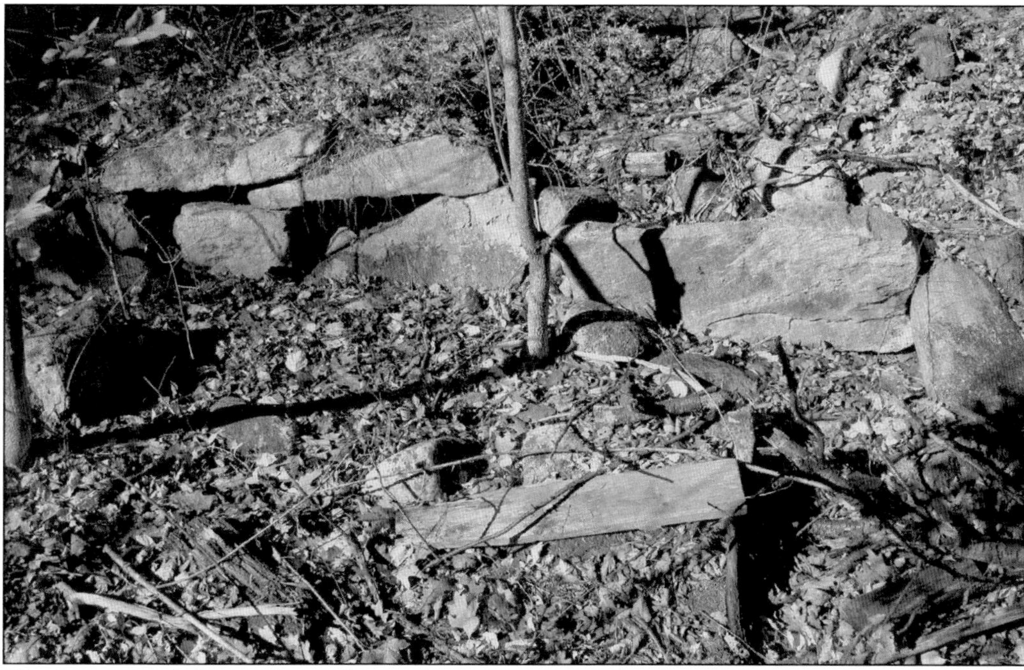

The Swain family house, located near the entrance to Wah-Tut-Ca, was home to five generations of Swains. It was occupied until the early 1900s. Frank Swain sold the property to settle the debts of his father, Sibley, who was a shoe maker. The house was razed in 1920, but the foundation is still visible.

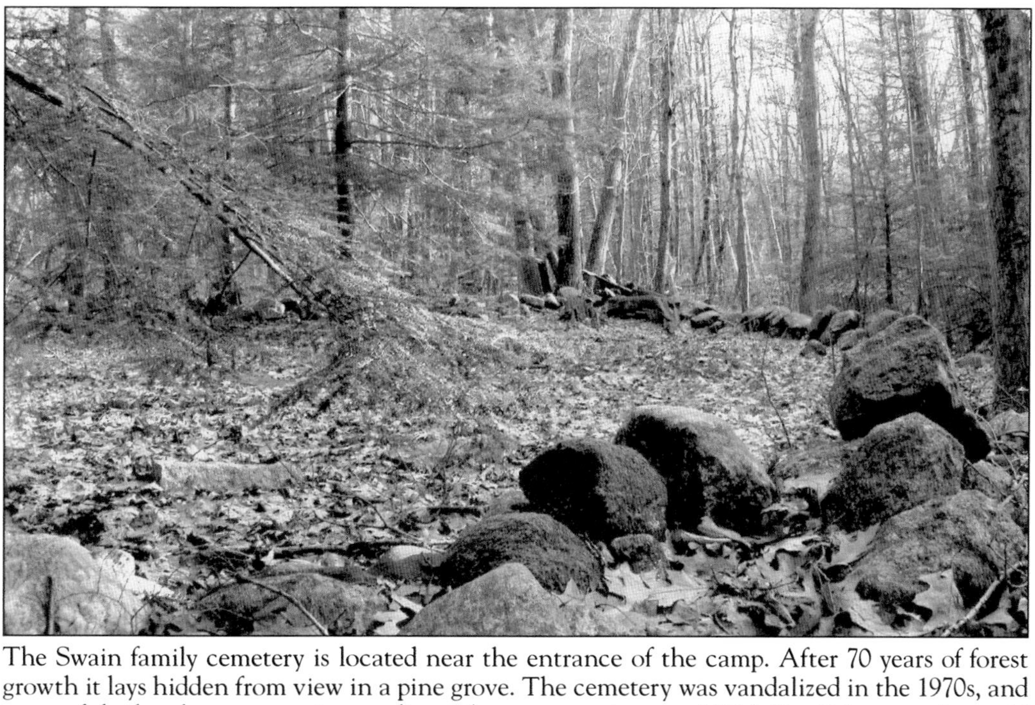

The Swain family cemetery is located near the entrance of the camp. After 70 years of forest growth it lays hidden from view in a pine grove. The cemetery was vandalized in the 1970s, and none of the headstones remain standing. The cemetery is part of Wah-Tut-Ca's most often told campfire tale: the story of the ghost of Wanna Swain.

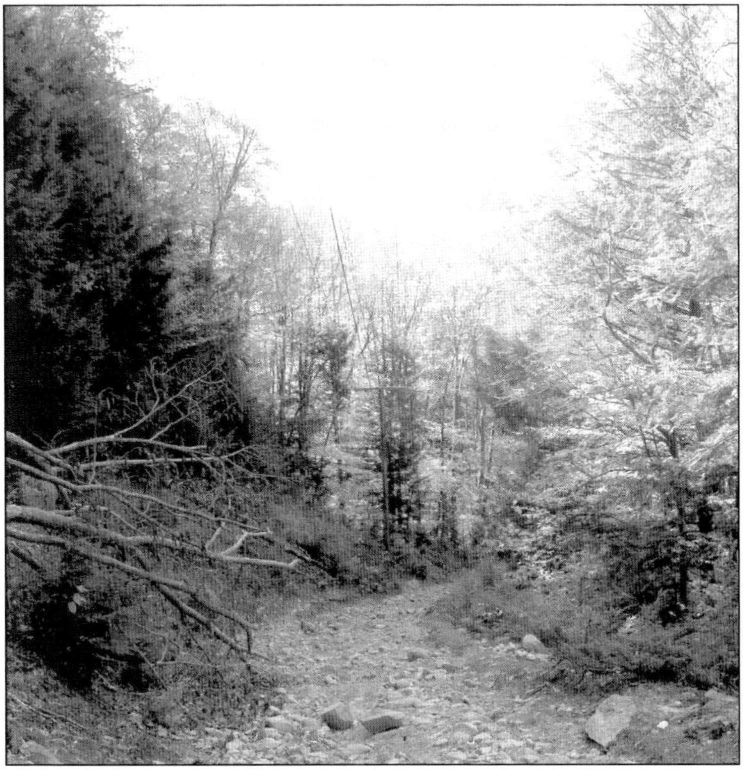

Theophilus Griffin settled on the far end of the gulf in 1771 and started building this road in 1783 in lieu of taxes. It connects Northwood to the Griffin homestead, an area later known as Griffintown. The steep hills and ridges made the road barely passable by horse and wagon, and it was eventually abandoned by the town.

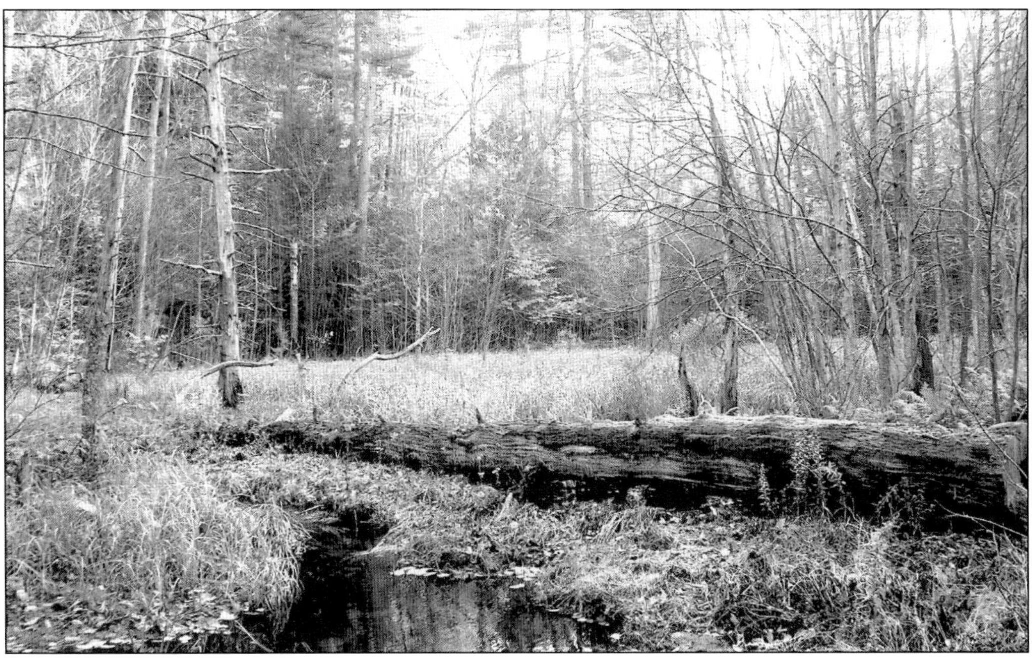

The only way to access the Griffintown area of Northwood is through Epsom and Deerfield. The foundation of a Griffintown house is located next to this stream a few hundred yards from Griffin Road, where it starts to climb out of the swamp. On the other side of the road, the land climbs steeply to a set of spectacular cliffs.

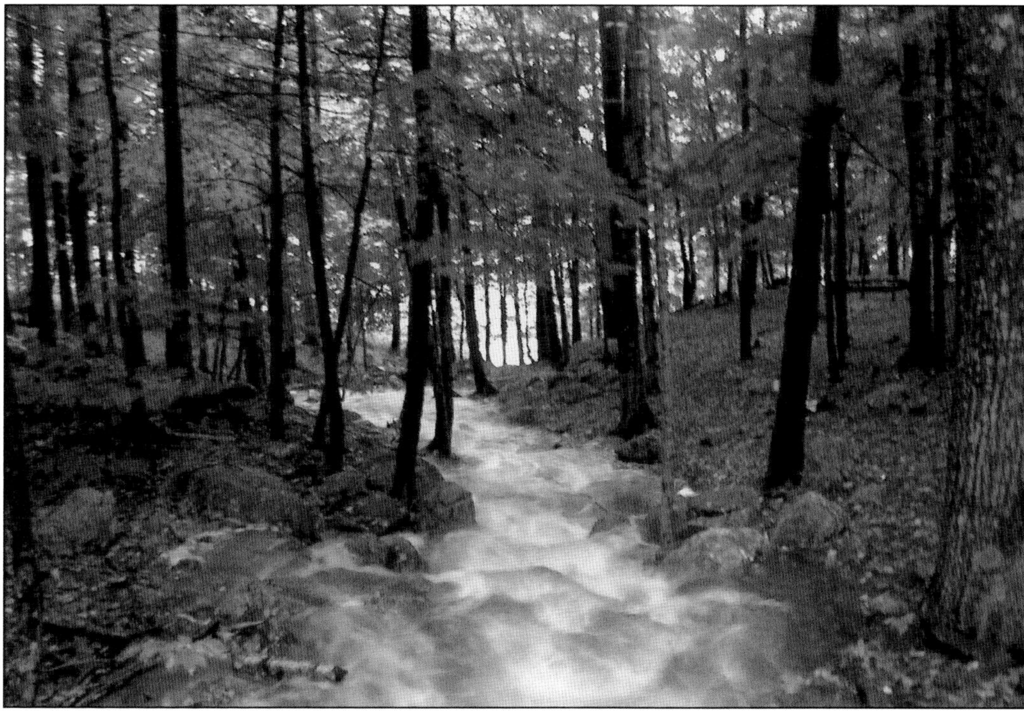

The land of Wah-Tut-Ca captured the imaginations of the first visitors from Greater Lowell just as it has thousands of boys in the years since. Three streams flow through the property and there are many seasonal wetland areas. The rolling hills and curving trails give a feeling of magnified size.

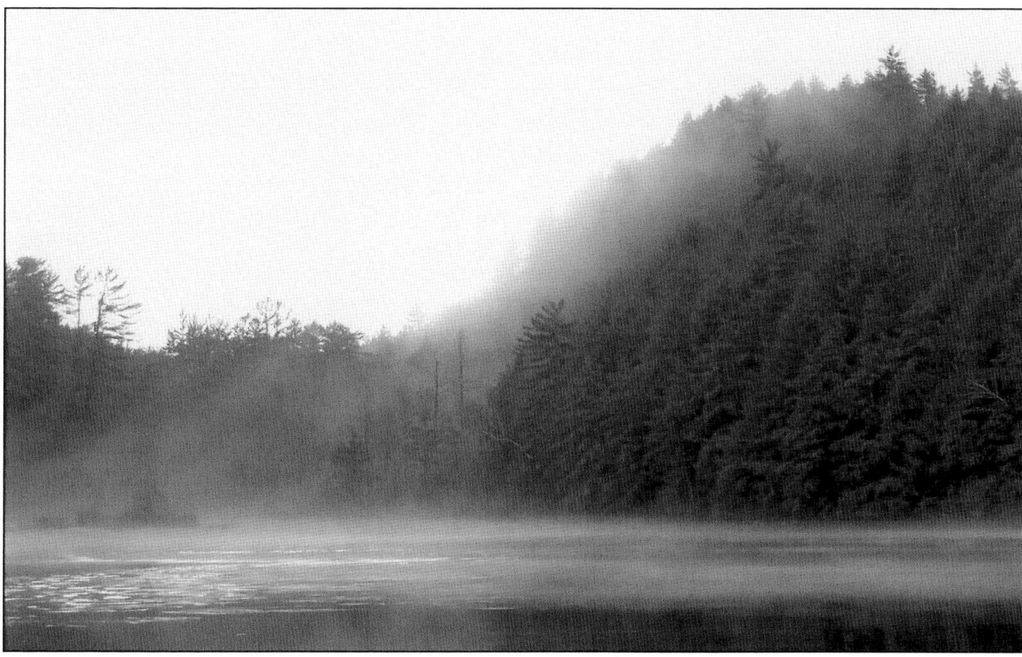

From the top of these cliffs looking out over Northwood Lake, boys can see the entire property that became Wah-Tut-Ca. Today a trip up the steep cliff is a great adventure where awestruck Scouts witness the magnitude and beauty of the New Hampshire wilderness.

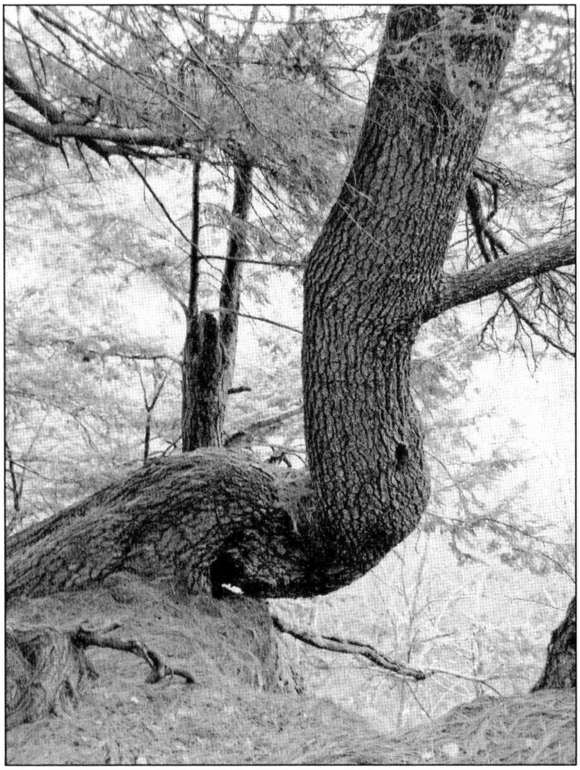

Due to its dramatic geography, the area around the cliffs is known as a wild and wondrous place. There are small caves in the area, and the exposed rock faces provide an area to study geology. When Wah-Tut-Ca founder Charles A. Robinson first visited the site in the fall of 1935, a hike was made to the top of the cliffs. He was admiring the view when a shouted warning of "Robinson, look out!" prevented him from being hit by a tree being felled to improve the view. After a laugh, it was decided to name the area Robinson Lookout.

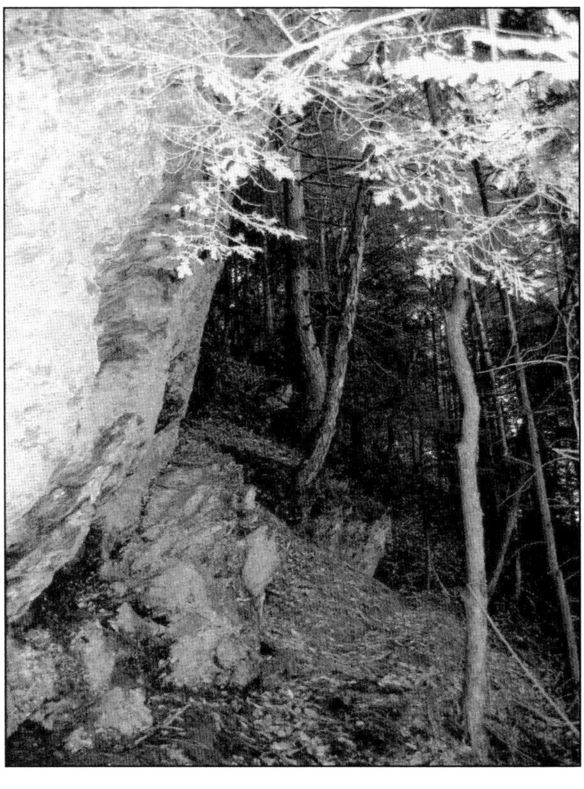

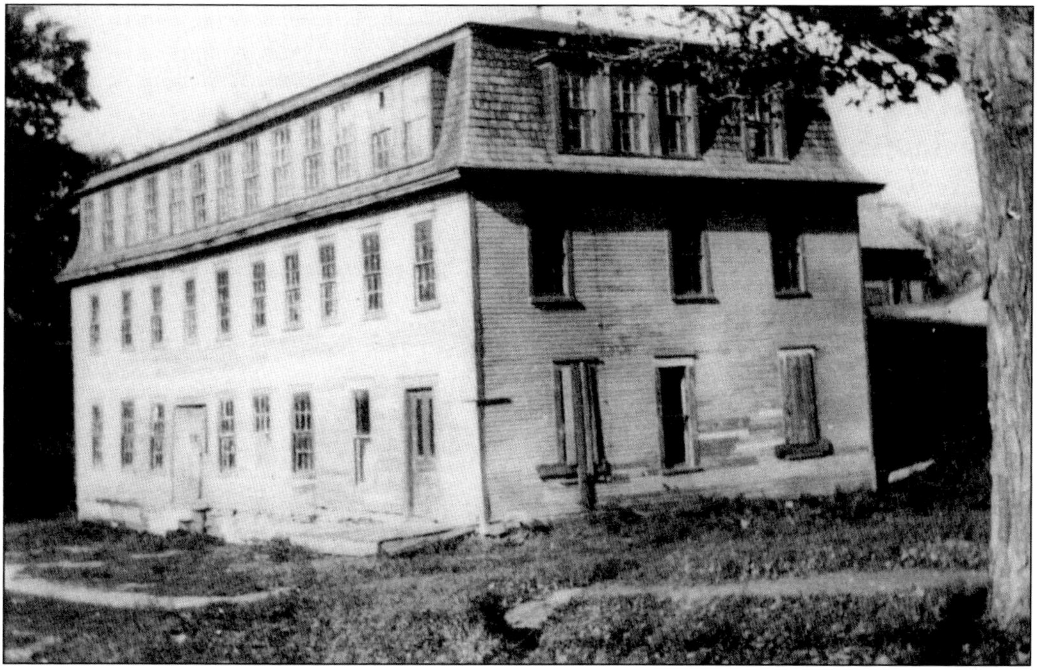

This shoe factory was located near the outlet of Northwood Lake. After the Civil War and the expansion of railroads, grain from the Midwest was abundant and available. Farming on Blake's Hill was no longer profitable. To supplement their income, many in Northwood turned to shoe making. Even as early as the 1850 census, the occupations of several members of the Swain family are listed as shoemakers.

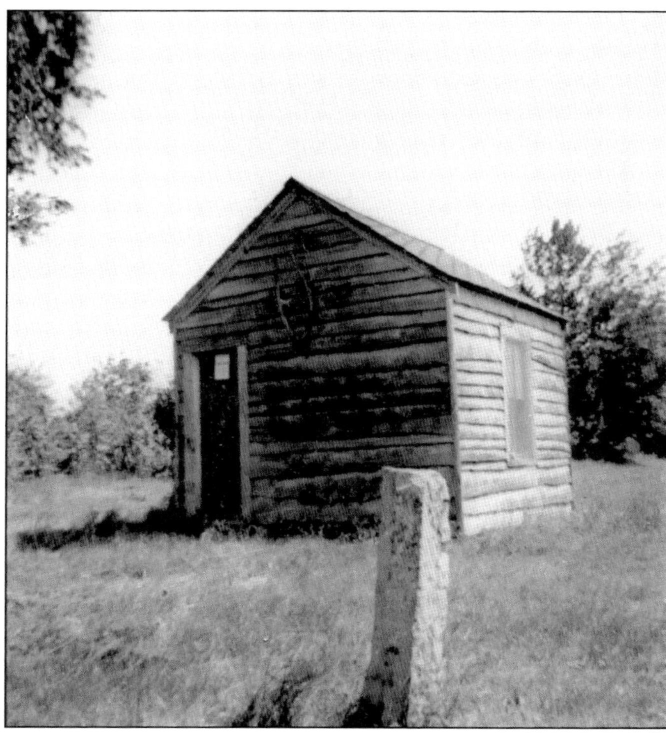

The only building still standing on the reservation when it was purchased by the Greater Lowell Council was this small shack. It was in buildings like this that townspeople did piecework for the Northwood shoe factory. The original building was torn down and replaced in 1967. It was named the Cobbler Shop in 1987 in remembrance of Wah-Tut-Ca's history.

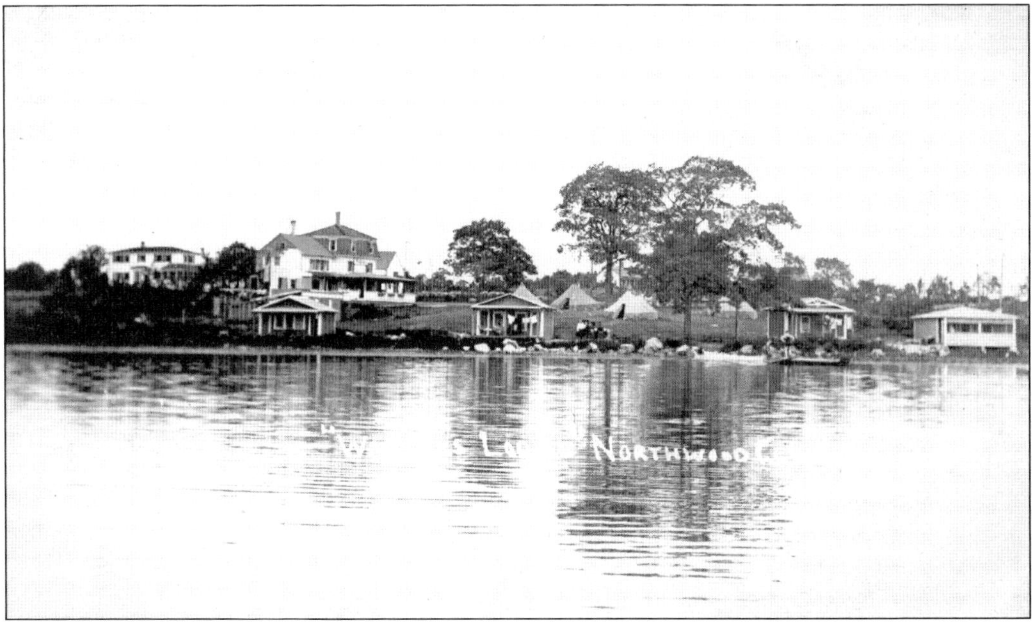

By 1900, with the decline of farming and the shoe industry, the town was looking for ways to use the land. Many of the farms were split into smaller pieces, and the town actively promoted the sale of summer homes and cottages, which soon dotted the lakeshore. This picture shows cottages near the Northwood Narrows section of the lake along Lake Shore Drive.

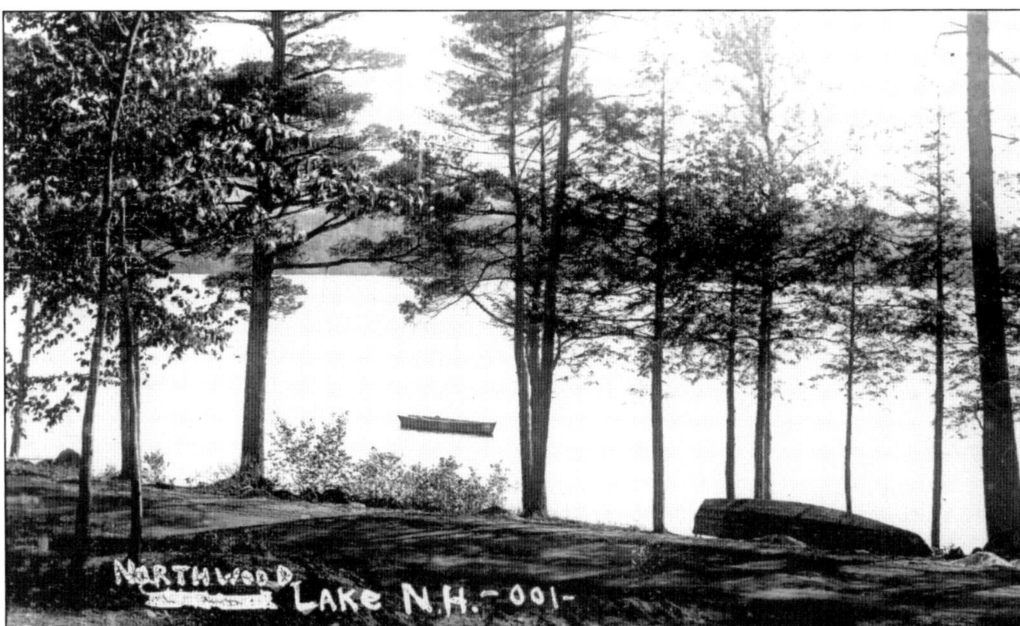

Northwood's natural beauty and numerous lakes were aided by its proximity to Concord, Portsmouth, and Manchester. In the 1920s, a dance hall and a steamboat attracted more tourists to Northwood Lake. Meanwhile the forest was quietly reclaiming the fields of the Swain family farm. Pines, maples, and oaks thrived anew in soil where livestock grazed and potatoes once grew.

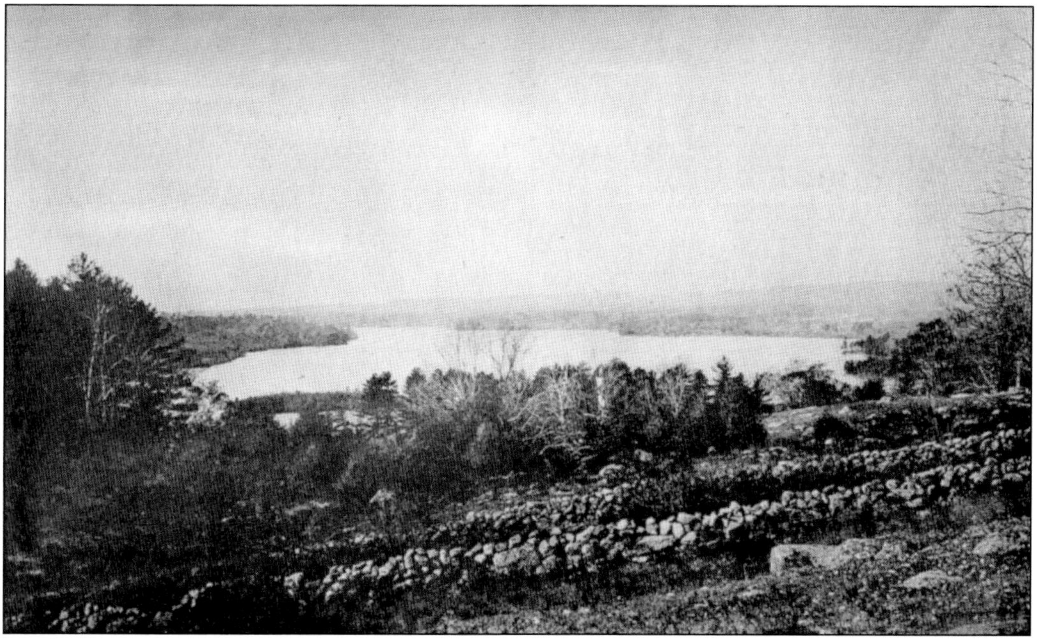

At the time this picture was captured in 1878, nothing remained of the houses of Griffintown but the foundations. The walled road built by Theophilus Griffin is still well defined. Over time the lake was slowly being obscured by the industrious red and white pines. In 2006, the lake was no longer visible from Griffin Road.

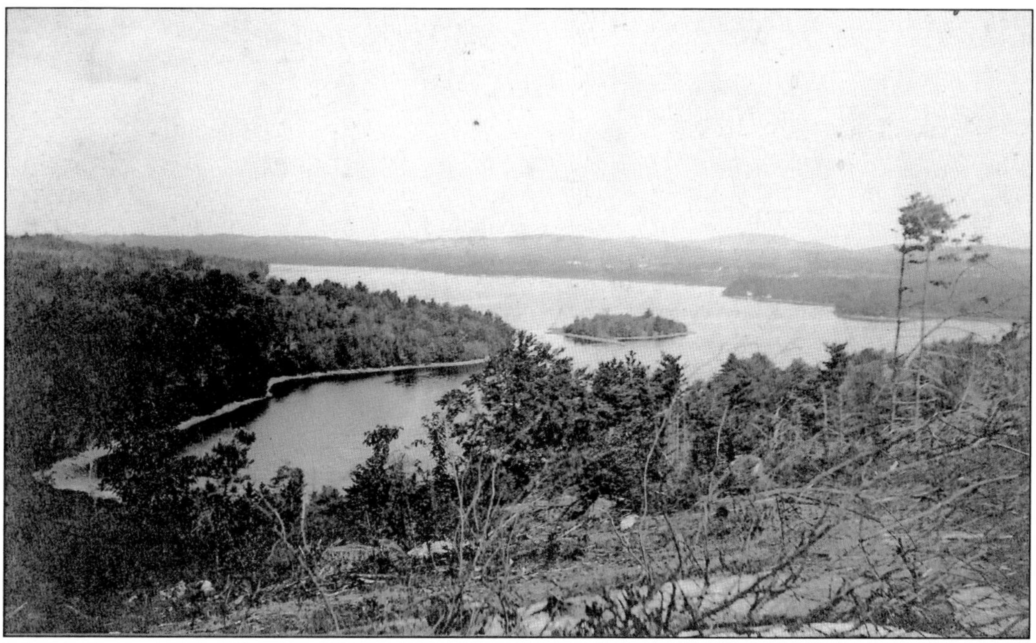

This is the same view from Griffin Road in 1900. It would take several more decades for the forest to fully restore itself. In 1987, Alexander A. Vervaert wrote, "The Northwood site, beautiful and promising as it was, included many acres sparse from generations of farming and lumbering. It would be allowed to heal and thrive. A balance of nature would be restored . . . Wah-Tut-Ca would be the wilderness of every boy's dream adventure."

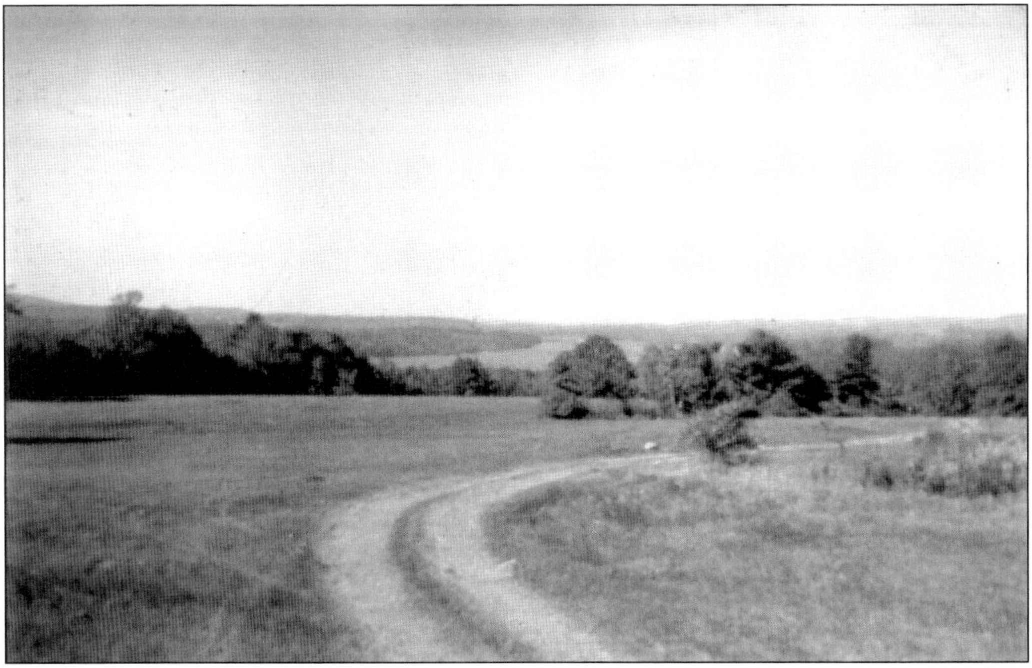

This field is the first impression for anyone who visits Wah-Tut-Ca. The lake was still visible from the field near the camp gate during 1936, a sight that few would recognize today. There were still many storms to be weathered. The trees began to take firm hold of the soil on Blake's Hill.

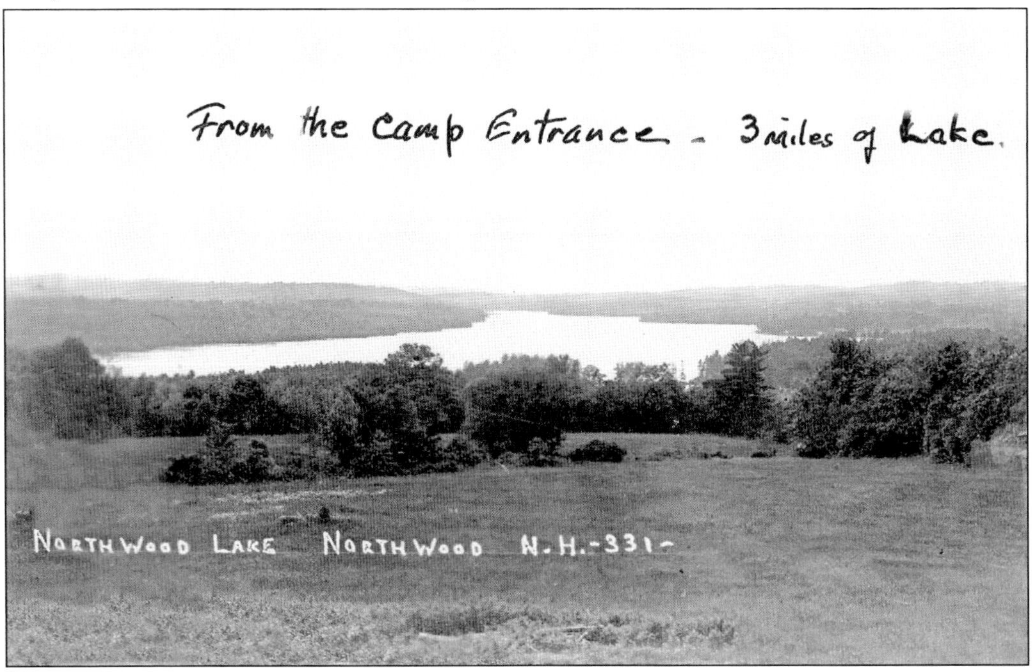

By 1935, the stage was set. Sixty miles to the south, in the cities and towns surrounding Lowell, Massachusetts, the players were getting ready. The land of Blake's Hill that had been difficult to farm and was not profitable for shoe making had been reclaimed by the forest. The land was now ready for its true calling: Wah-Tut-Ca Scout Reservation.

Two

The Road to Northwood

Boy Scouting began in Great Britain when Gen. Robert Stevenson Smyth Baden-Powell published his book *Scouting for Boys* in 1908. Prior to the Boy Scouts of America's incorporation in 1910, many Scout units were started, using Baden-Powell's book for inspiration.

Greater Lowell was home to one of these units. A 29-year-old James Kiberd Sr. emigrated from Liverpool, England, with his family in 1902. He worked as a house painter. Settling in North Chelmsford, he joined the North Chelmsford Congregational Church. In the summer of 1908, he was asked to organize some sports activities for boys in the community. Using Baden-Powell's book as a guide, these activities were expanded into nature hikes and overnight camping trips.

In 1910, the Boy Scouts of America (BSA) was ardently supported and promoted by the YMCA. Thomas R. (T. R.) Williams, director of Lowell's YMCA, organized the first BSA unit in the city of Lowell. The unit he created was Troop 10, purported to be the 10th troop of the BSA.

On April 18, 1910, Rev. E. Victor Bigelow of Lowell's Eliot Union Congregational Church traveled with Kiberd to New York City. Together they attended a national organizational meeting for the BSA. They brought with them a suggestion that would make Scouting a little more American.

Baden-Powell's Scout Law had nine points. The Greater Lowell team successfully lobbied for the addition of three points: brave, clean, and reverent. These additions remain in the Scout Law to this day.

Scouting grew rapidly as America became involved in World War I. As patriotism spread, boys were eager to wear a uniform like their older brothers in the service. Growth continued after the war, as did the development of summer encampments.

Camp Maguncug and Camp Faulkner were early council camp programs held on borrowed or leased land. With each success, the council's camps became more advanced and closer to the camps known today. It took more than 25 years to get there, but Greater Lowell's Scouting community was clearly on the road to Northwood.

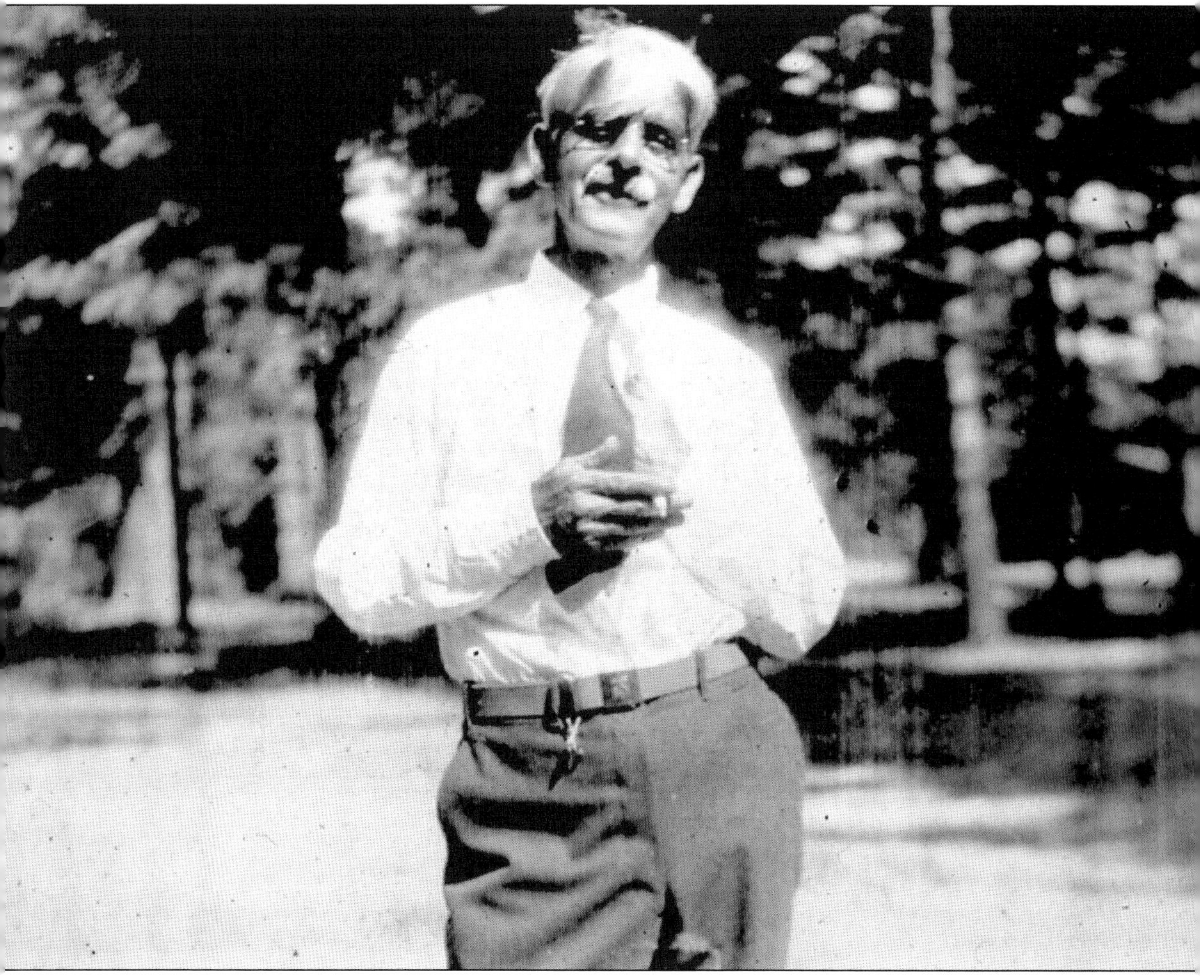

James Kiberd Sr., a house painter from Liverpool, England, would begin Scouting in the Greater Lowell area. Known to the boys as "Uncle Jim," his service would span 40 years. It was said of him that he could change himself from a man to a boy and back to a man again faster than the speed of light. He thoroughly understood a boy's instincts. His personality was winsome and entertaining, although he always emphasized the spiritual aspects of life. From the time he was young he loved books and would read anything he could get his hands on, and although his formal education was limited, his reading allowed him to gain enough knowledge to speak with authority on many subjects.

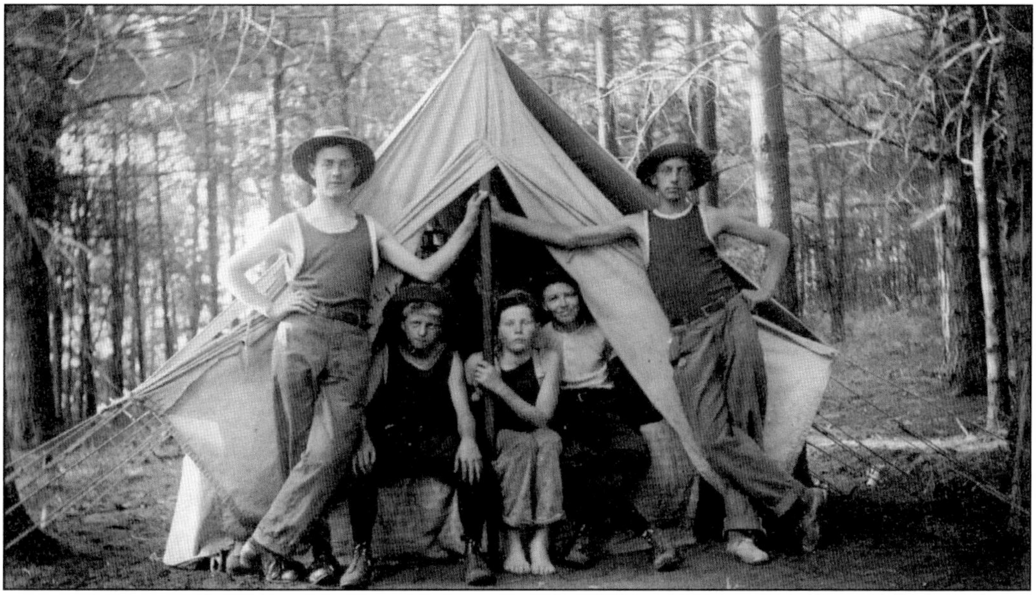

Shown is Uncle Jim's North Chelmsford troop on a camping event in 1914. On the right is Ray Ballinger, and on the left is Jim Jr., Kiberd's son, who was known to his friends as Kibbe. Uncle Jim would be seen throughout the town of Chelmsford with these boys, always trying to find something useful for them to do. He would teach them the laws of nature and the beauties and harmonies of the outdoors.

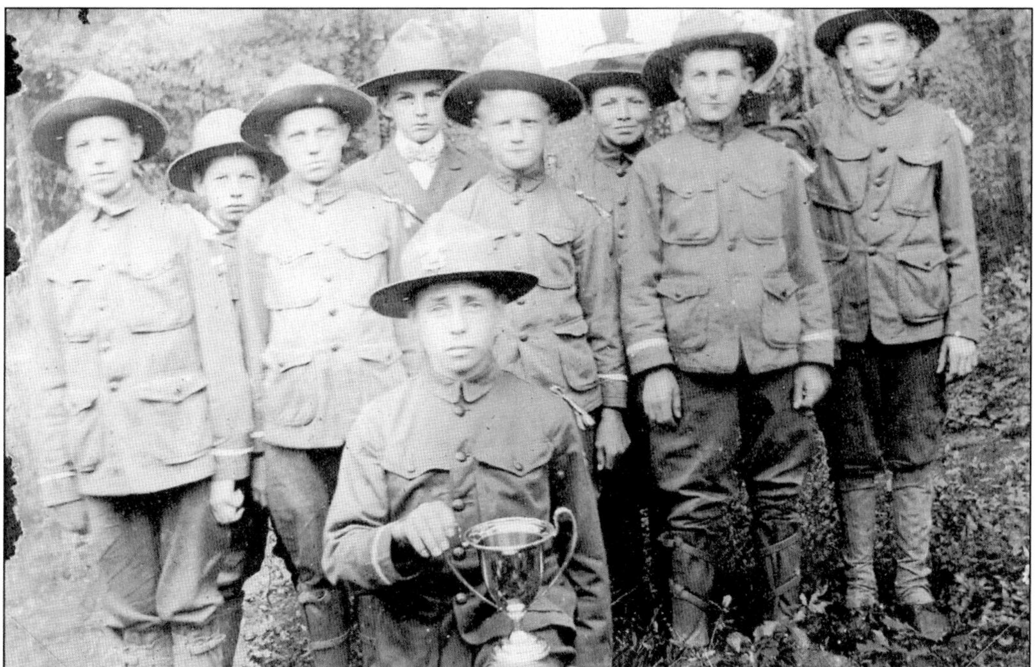

The second weeklong council camp was held at Burges Pond in Westford, Massachusetts, in 1914. Here the Scouts of Uncle Jim's North Chelmsford troop display a trophy earned in an intertroop competition held at the camp. These early heavy Scout uniforms were not well suited for a hot summer day but where worn with pride.

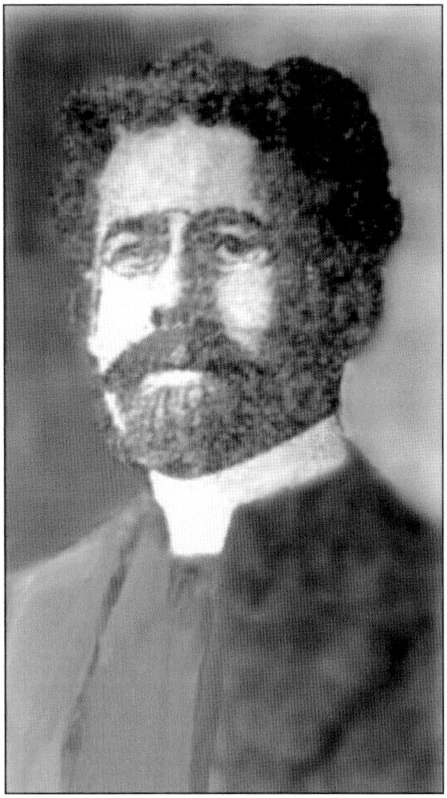

Rev. E. Victor Bigelow of Lowell's Eliot Union Congregational Church was a friend of James "Uncle Jim" Kiberd Sr. and helped organize Scout troops. Both Kiberd and Bigelow attended an early organizational meeting of the BSA in New York City. From Uncle Jim's notes, Kiberd recalls discussions with Bigelow regarding their advocacy for reverent being added to the Scout Law, which caused some debate at the national meeting.

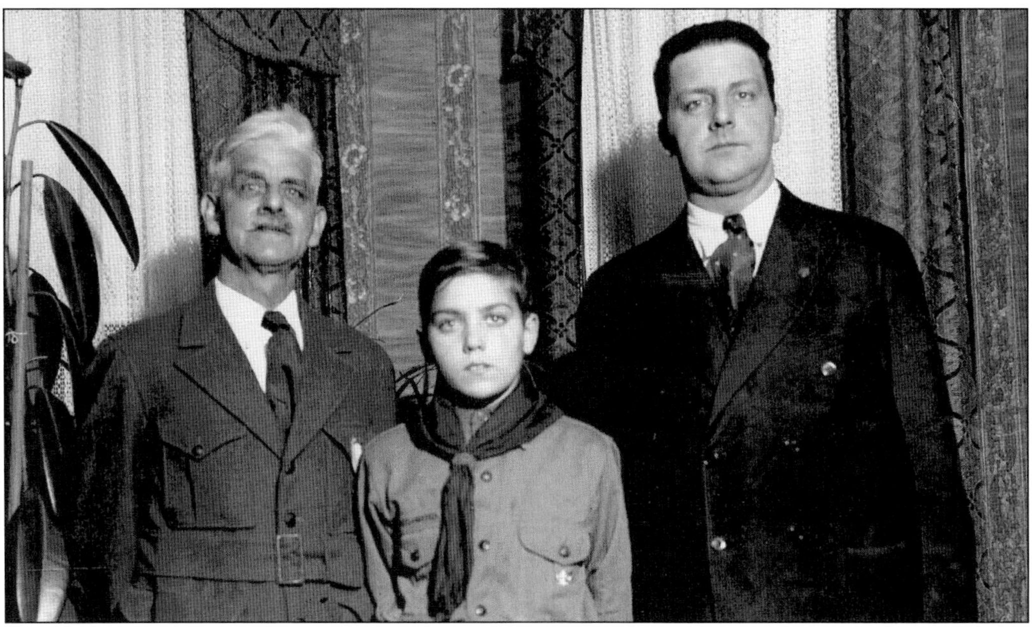

To celebrate the 25th anniversary of Boy Scouting in 1935, Uncle Jim stood for a picture with his son and grandson. James Kiberd III would be noted as the 1,000th Scout of the Greater Lowell Council. Kiberd Jr. would leave his dad's troop to help lead Troop 17 at the Grace Universalist Church in Chelmsford, Massachusetts.

Luther W. Faulkner was born in 1882. He would become Greater Lowell's first commissioner, the leading volunteer in Scouting. Faulkner would organize many of the first intertroop events and activities of the early Lowell Council. In 1923 and 1924, he would run Camp Faulkner, the council's summer camp program held on Robinson Pond in Hudson, New Hampshire.

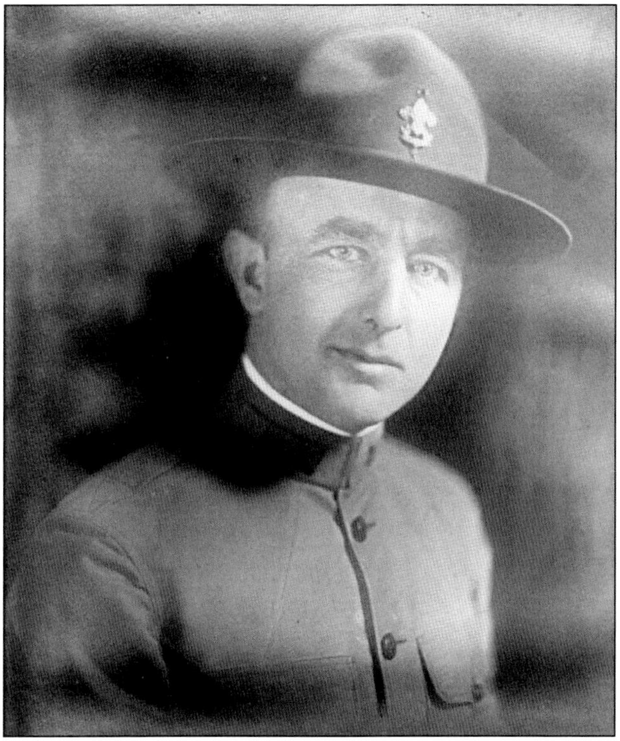

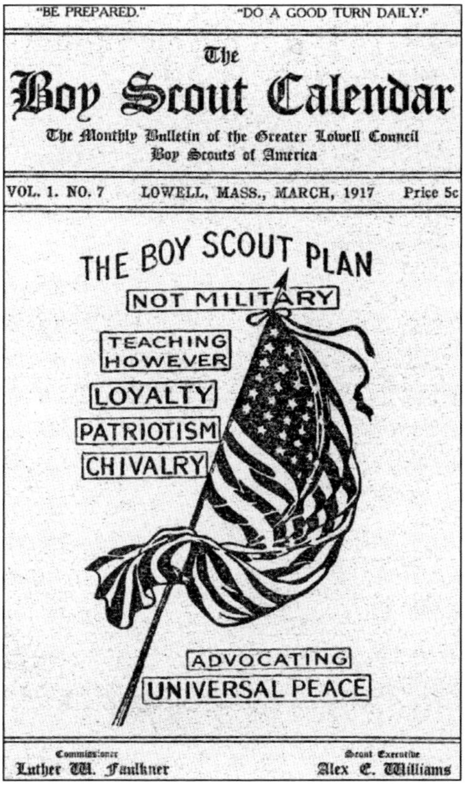

"BE PREPARED." "DO A GOOD TURN DAILY."

The
Boy Scout Calendar
The Monthly Bulletin of the Greater Lowell Council
Boy Scouts of America

VOL. 1. NO. 7 LOWELL, MASS., MARCH, 1917 Price 5c

Commissioner
Luther W. Faulkner

Scout Executive
Alex C. Williams

Under Faulkner, Scouting in Lowell would become organized. The *Boy Scout Calendar* was one of the first Scouting publications in Greater Lowell. The council would run annual rallies and events for troops. A Scoutmasters Club was created to help leaders develop programs and activities for youth. A monthly patrol leaders meeting would be held to train and develop youth leaders.

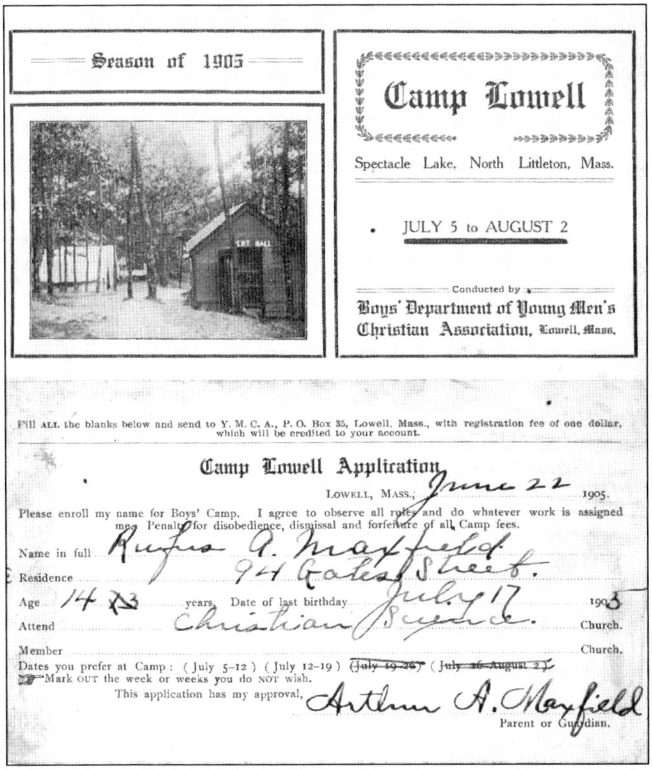
Season of 1905

Camp Lowell

Spectacle Lake, North Littleton, Mass.

JULY 5 to AUGUST 2

Conducted by

Boys' Department of Young Men's Christian Association, Lowell, Mass.

Fill ALL the blanks below and send to Y. M. C. A., P. O. Box 35, Lowell, Mass., with registration fee of one dollar, which will be credited to your account.

Camp Lowell Application

LOWELL, MASS., June 22 1905.

Please enroll my name for Boys' Camp. I agree to observe all rules and do whatever work is assigned me. Penalty for disobedience, dismissal and forfeiture of all Camp fees.

Name in full Rufus A. Mayfield

Residence 94 Gates Street.

Age 14 years, Date of last birthday July 17 1905

Attend Christian Science. Church.

Member Church.

Dates you prefer at Camp: (July 5–12) (July 12–19) ~~(July 19–26)~~ (~~July 26–August 2~~)

Mark OUT the week or weeks you do NOT wish.

This application has my approval, Arthur A. Mayfield

Parent or Guardian.

The YMCA ran the first summer camps for boys of Greater Lowell. Thomas R. (T. R.) Williams came to the city of Lowell, Massachusetts, in 1907 to become the director of boys work for the YMCA. He was a member of St. Anne's Church in downtown Lowell. There he was active in parish work and served as a Sunday school teacher. In 1910, he organized a Boy Scout Troop in the parish, the first in the city of Lowell.

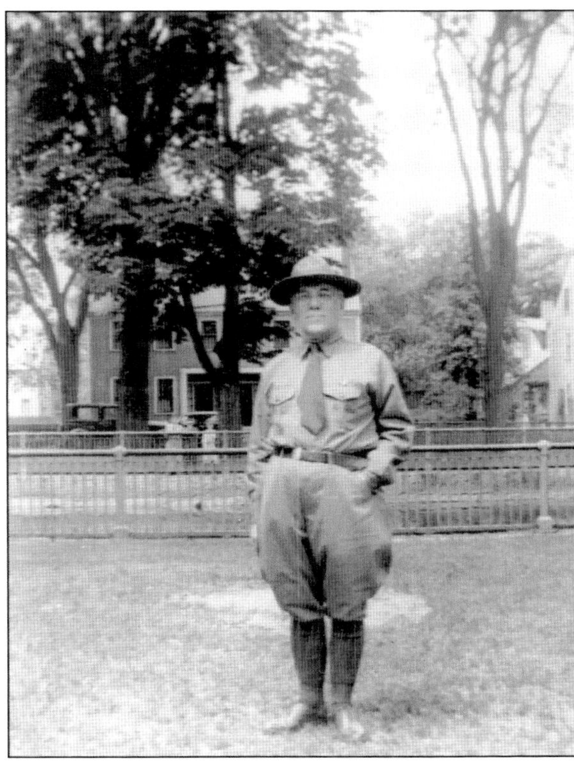

Fred Timmins was another English immigrant from Liverpool, England, who would make his mark on Greater Lowell Scouting. He came to Lowell in 1897 and worked for the Meyer Thread Company. A member of St. Anne's Church, he would become one of the Scoutmasters of Troop 10. Known for his wit and sense of humor, Timmins would lead his troop through the early camps, Camp Chadwick, and on to Wah-Tut-Ca.

Boy Scout Minstrels

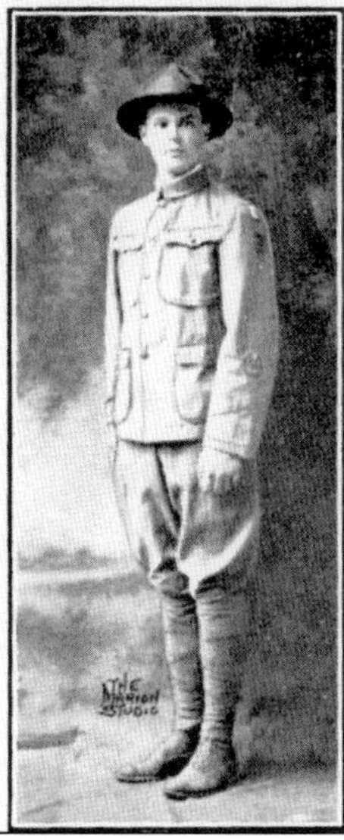

Troop 10 — Lowell, Mass.

MERRY MINSTRELS OF ST. ANNE'S CHURCH, LOWELL
CONGREGATIONAL CHURCH HA[illegible] TEWKSBURY, MASS.
Tuesday Evening, June 12, 1917, 8 P.M.
Under the auspices of Troop No. 1 Boy Scouts of America
Hector Jackson, Scoutmaster
Director, Mr. Fred Timmins — Accompanist, Miss Amy M. Williams

Program

PART ONE

OPENING CHORUS	*"How's Every Little Thing in Dixie"* *"Indiana"* *"Down Where the Black Eyed Susans Grow"*	
INTRODUCTION		Interlocutor, Archibald Campbell
SONG	*"Come Out of the Kitchen, Mary Ann"*	R. Winston Rouse
CORNET SOLO	Selected	Scout Wilbur Roberts
SONG	*"In the Candle Light"*	Misses Lee, Brundin, Black and Dainton
SONG	*"Keep your Eye on the Girlie You Love"*	Iver Johnson
READING	*"The Blacksmiths Story"*	Scoutmaster Fred Timmins
SONG	*"America, Here's My Boy"*	Roland Worth
SONG	*"A Little Bug's Going to Get You"*	Karl Lunnan
SONG	*"Down Where the Daisies Grow"*	Florence Brooks
FANCY DANCE	Highland Fling. In native costume	Greta Pickering

INTERMISSION
Ice Cream For Sale

PART TWO

SONG	*"Little Damozell"*	Clementine Veloove
SONG	*"The Land Beyond the Rainbow"*	Edith Dainton
SONG	*"Way Down in Iowa"*	Albert E. Thurston
CORNET SOLO		Scout Wilbur Roberts
SONG	*"Roamin' in the Gloamin'"*	Wilfred Clayton
SONG	*"Oh! Johnny, Oh! Johnny, Oh!"*	Ruth Dainton
SONG	*"Minstrel Band"*	James Kelley and Leslie Clayton
SONG	*"Let's All Be Americans Now"*	Gardner Collins
SONG	*"The Greatest Battle Song of All"*	Fred Timmins
FINALE	*"America"* With Scout Yell	All Scouts and Entire Chorus
	Call to the Colors	Scout Roberts
	"My Country 'Tis of Thee"	Everybody

Fund-raising to pay for troop activities has always been an activity in itself. For several years, Troop 10 would run minstrels shows at St. Anne's Parish House. In its day these shows were a recognized form of American theater. Clearly racist by today's standards, the shows would include musical performances, dancing, and comic skits.

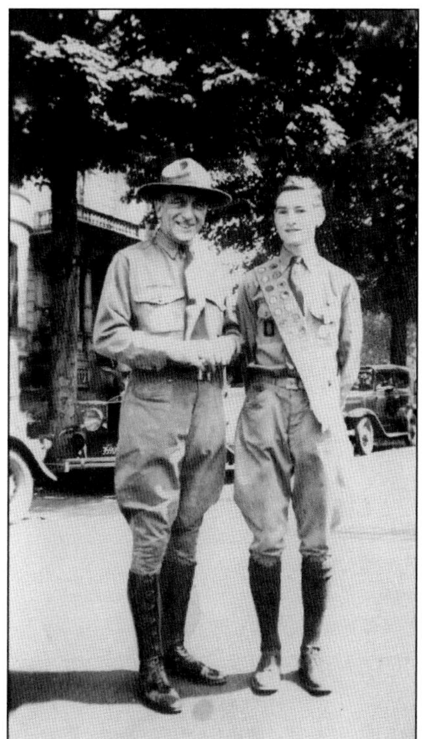

Another one of Troop 10's scoutmasters was Arthur C. Dawes, yet another English immigrant. In Scouting's early days, Troop 10 would become one of Greater Lowell's strongest troops. Dawes is pictured here with Eagle Scout Rawden B. Slater. Known to Scouts as "the Captain," he would direct the So-Kee-Tay program at Wah-Tut-Ca.

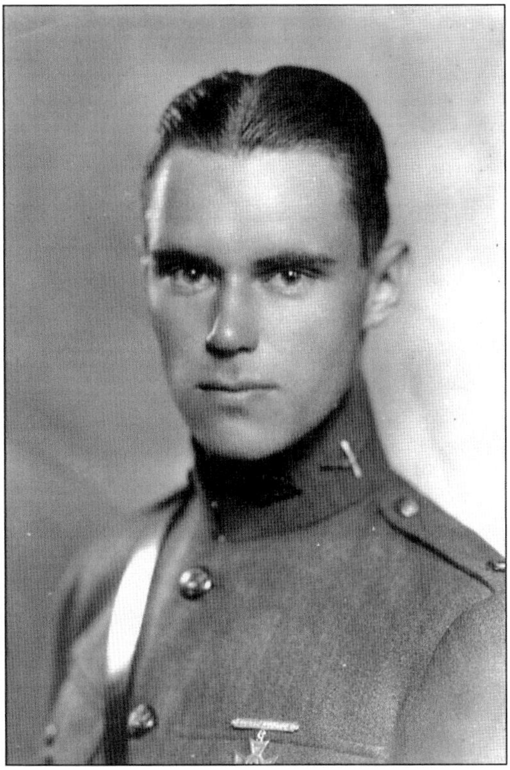

One of the first Eagle Scouts of Troop 10 was Hoyt S. Vandenburg. General Vandenburg would become the second chief of staff of the United States Air Force. In World War II, as a pilot, he earned the Silver Star and Distinguished Flying Cross. In 1952, Pres. Harry Truman promoted him to the position of U.S. Air Force chief of staff. Vandenberg Air Force Base in California is named for him.

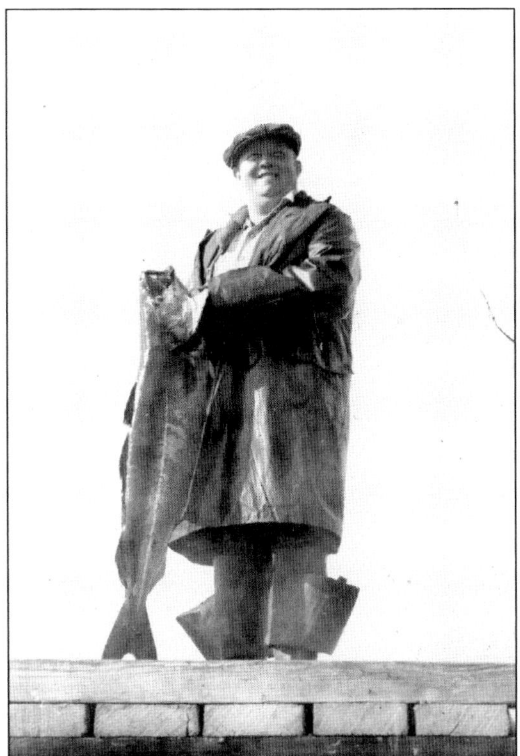

Charles F. Emerson began his Scouting adventures in Lowell's Troop 1. As a boy, he was a senior patrol leader, and as an adult, he became the scoutmaster. An electrician by trade, he would service all of Camp Chadwick's and Wah-Tut-Ca's electrical needs. From the time he was a boy, Emerson collected scrapbooks of photographs, scouting literature, and news clippings. This collection would document the history of Scouting in Greater Lowell.

United States of America

NO CHARGE FOR SERVICE

No banker, trust company, broker, or store, will make any charge for taking your order or delivering your bond. No Boy Scout receives pay for Liberty Loan work. This is their service to the Government.

THIRD LIBERTY LOAN

APPLICATION BLANK

Prepared especially for National Campaign by

PAY MONEY ONLY THROUGH BANK

The Scout will deliver the application, but he is instructed not to accept money. You make your first payment on or before the closing day of the Campaign at your bank or to its certified agent.

BOY SCOUTS OF AMERICA

Banks in all parts of the country are requested to accept this application and cooperate in securing first payment before closing of campaign

Date ...., *1918*.

To the ....
(Insert on above line name of bank or trust company to which the subscription goes.)

The undersigned hereby requests you to subscribe for *his or her* account $.................. face value of United States Government Bonds of the Third Liberty Loan in accordance with the official circular of the Secretary of the Treasury offering the same, and in payment for bonds allotted on such subscription, the undersigned agrees—

Check method of payment.
☐ *1. To pay you in cash*
☐ *2. That you may charge his account with*

the purchase price thereof at or before the times required by such circular as follows:

Check plan desired here.
☐ *1. To make complete full payment at once.*
☐ *2. To make installment payments on dates fixed by United States Government.*
☐ *3. To make installment payments on such dates as may be agreed upon between the purchaser and the bank to which the subscription goes.*

Indicate whether *1. Mr.* *2. Mrs.* *3. Miss* ....
(Signature of subscriber in full)

Address, number and street ....

City or town .... State ....

It is important that Scouts endeavor to assist the banks by giving the following additional information:

$50 ☐ $100 ☐ *Check here*

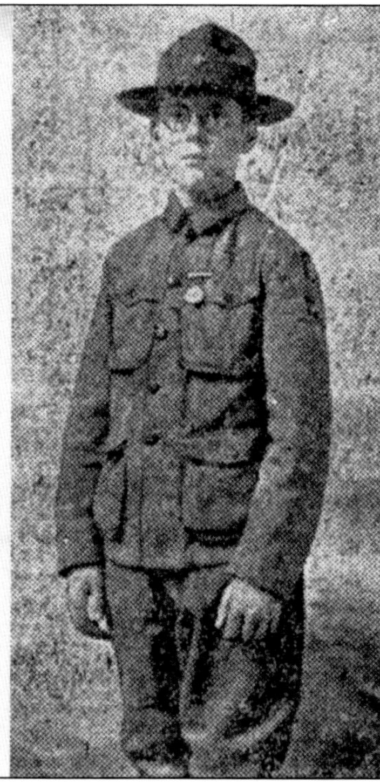

The Liberty Bond was a way that the United States funded its participation in World War I. Using the theme "Every Scout to Save a Solider," Boy and Girl Scouts would go door to door to sell bonds. Scout Guy Butler was Greater Lowell's top seller of Liberty Bonds.

Report of Special Joint Meeting of the Scoutmasters and Executive Committee held on May 13, 1917.

A special joint meeting of the Scoutmasters and Executive Committee of the Lowell Council was held in the Council Chamber to hear the report of the sub-committee authorized to present plans for the proposed Farm Scout Camp. The report as filed was read by Mr. George Stevens, chairman of the committee, and after a lengthy discussion the following motion was presented and passed unanimously:

To the Public Safety Committee.

Copy of resolution passed at the joint meeting of the Scoutmasters and Executive Committee of the Lowell Council, Boy Scouts of America, held Sunday, May 13, 1917.

Moved by Mr. Arthur T. Safford, seconded by Mr. J. A. Hunnewell, and carried unanimously.

That we recommend to the Lowell Public Safety Committee a Central Boy Scout Camp, consisting of from 30 to 50 boys, for the raising of food stuffs, to be conducted under the direction of Commissioner L. W. Faulkner and Executive Committee of the Council, with the understanding that any nett loss resulting from the operations of the camp be made good by the Public Safety Committee.

Signed.
Alex E. Williams.
Scout Executive.

Moved that Commissioner L. W. Faulkner present the report to the Public Safety Committee at their meeting to be held on Sunday, May 13, 1917.
Moved to adjourn.

#2.

Cost of above for 15 weeks	$1035.
Farm implements	105.
Cost of feeding 32 boys for 15 wks. @ 50¢ per day	1680.
Ploughing ten acres	100.
15 Tons fertilizer	600.
Seeds for ten acres	300.
Board of Horse	50.
Incidentals	50.
Total	$3921.

Sub-camp

Camp leader---$10 and what he can earn.	
15 weeks for above	$150.
Farm implements	50.
Total	$200.

Ten camps established.......................$2000.
Boys and leaders to pay their own way, tentage to be borrowed.

Since the above meeting, Scoutmaster Stevens reports the offer of 13 acres of land within a five cent car fare, suitable for the above plans.

****

5-10-17

In 1917, instead of conducting a Boy Scout camp, the Lowell Council decided to run a Scout farm. With the goal that every Scout participating could "feed a solider," Luther Faulkner organized the program. The original plan called for a 15-week program for 30 to 50 Scouts. Faulkner's budget included provisions to feed the Scouts and board for the horses.

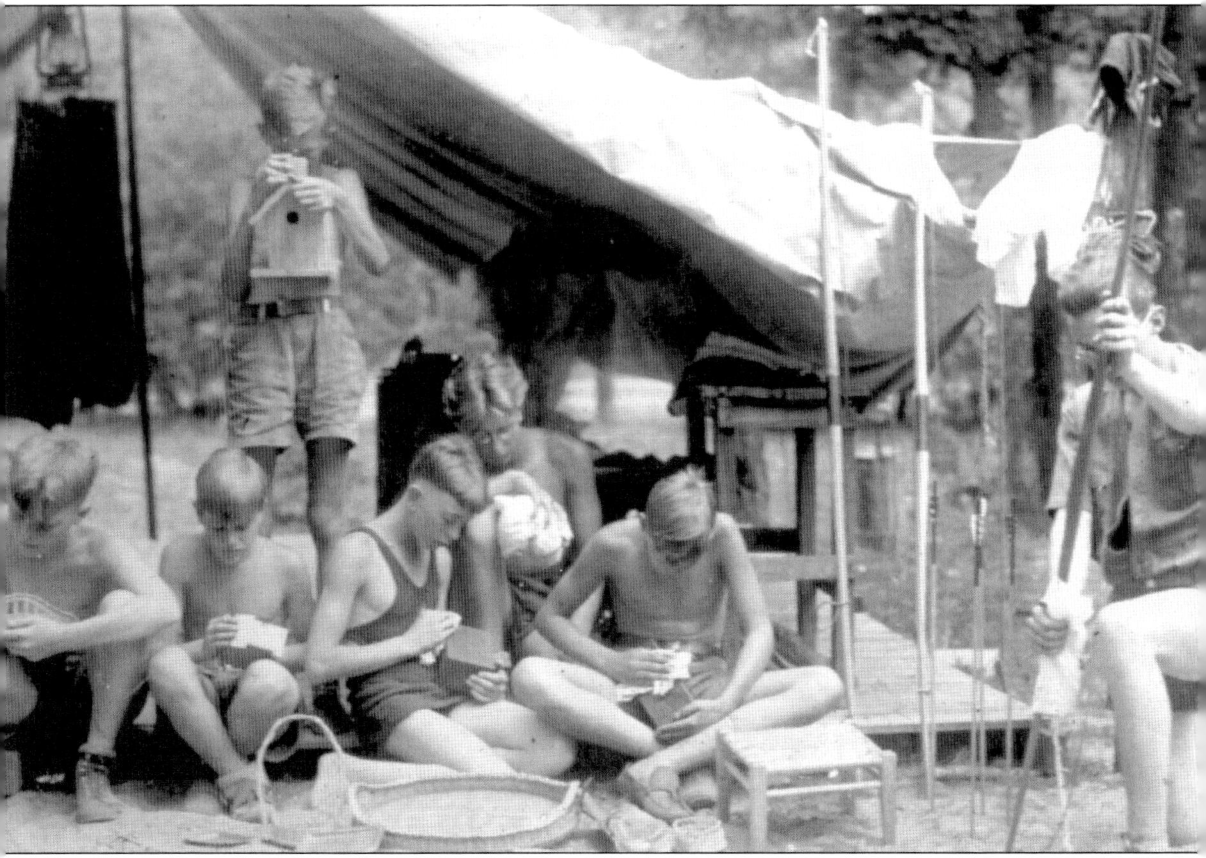

In 1919 and 1920, the Lowell Council organized Camp Maguncug on Keyes Pond in Westford, Massachusetts, as seen in this camp promotion photograph. It would be the first camp the council actively promoted with advertisement. Read Ripley, one of the first full-time professional Scout executives of the Lowell Council, would serve as camp director. The Scout executive serving as the camp director was a common responsibility. To the present day, camp promotions target parents. Boys are much more easily sold on the adventure and fun of summer camp. Scout camps would promote the benefits of their programs on campers' health. Parental fears and uncertainty were not trivial. In 1918 through 1919, Spanish Flu would kill 500,000 people in the United States. Infectious disease and accidents were sources of real concern.

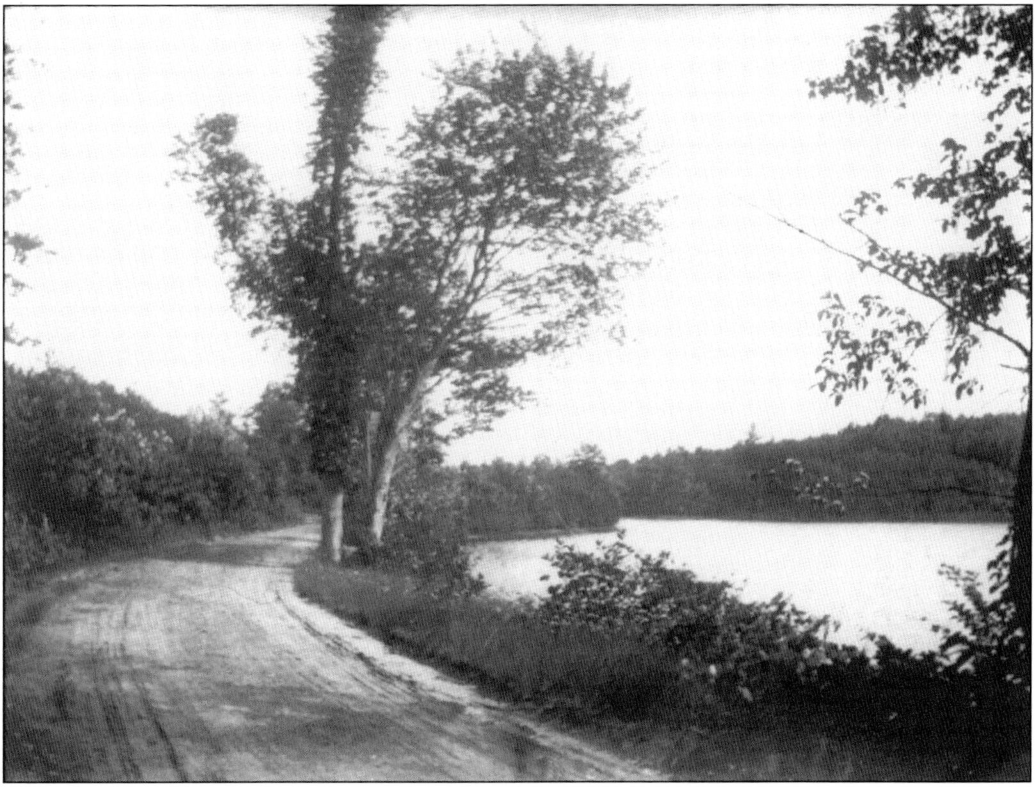

This picture of Keyes Pond in the early 20th century would look much like it did when Scouts camped there in the summers of 1919 and 1920. The name Maguncug was Native American in origin and was taken from one of the "Praying Indian Towns" from the 17th century. John Eliot, a missionary, set up these towns for local Native Americans who had converted to Christianity.

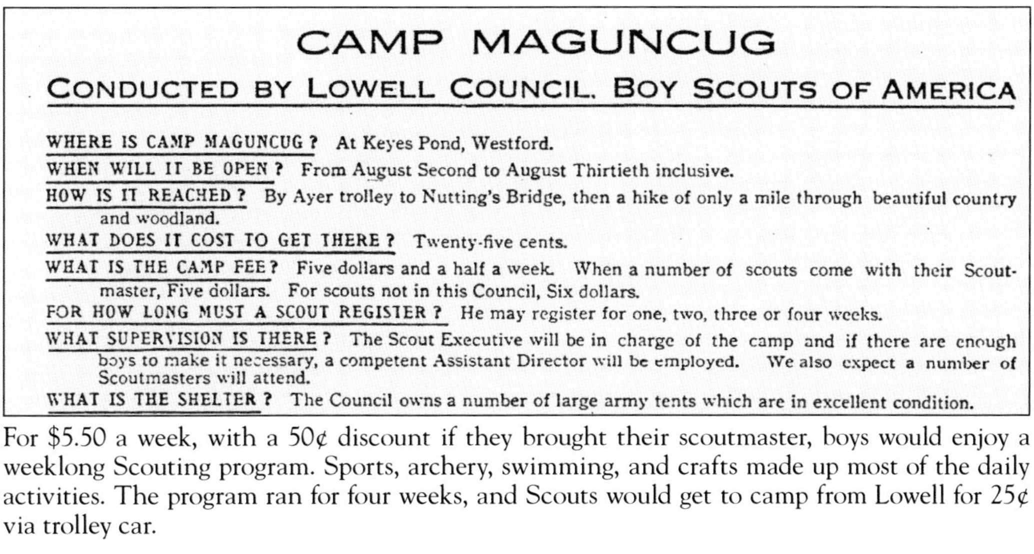

CAMP MAGUNCUG

CONDUCTED BY LOWELL COUNCIL, BOY SCOUTS OF AMERICA

WHERE IS CAMP MAGUNCUG? At Keyes Pond, Westford.

WHEN WILL IT BE OPEN? From August Second to August Thirtieth inclusive.

HOW IS IT REACHED? By Ayer trolley to Nutting's Bridge, then a hike of only a mile through beautiful country and woodland.

WHAT DOES IT COST TO GET THERE? Twenty-five cents.

WHAT IS THE CAMP FEE? Five dollars and a half a week. When a number of scouts come with their Scoutmaster, Five dollars. For scouts not in this Council, Six dollars.

FOR HOW LONG MUST A SCOUT REGISTER? He may register for one, two, three or four weeks.

WHAT SUPERVISION IS THERE? The Scout Executive will be in charge of the camp and if there are enough boys to make it necessary, a competent Assistant Director will be employed. We also expect a number of Scoutmasters will attend.

WHAT IS THE SHELTER? The Council owns a number of large army tents which are in excellent condition.

For \$5.50 a week, with a 50¢ discount if they brought their scoutmaster, boys would enjoy a weeklong Scouting program. Sports, archery, swimming, and crafts made up most of the daily activities. The program ran for four weeks, and Scouts would get to camp from Lowell for 25¢ via trolley car.

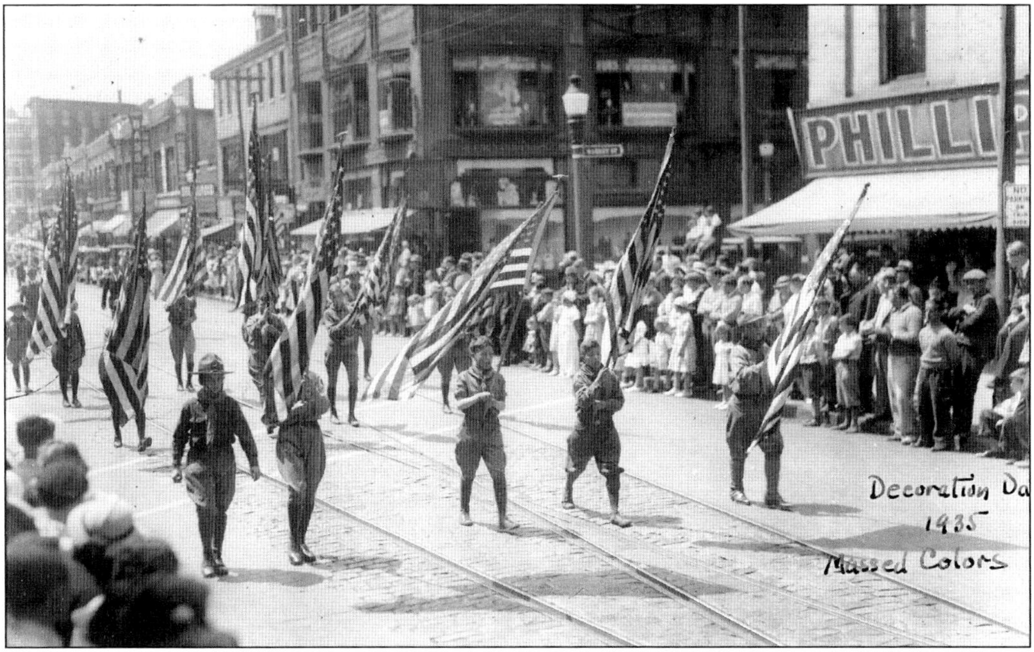

There would be three Lowell councils. Chartered by the National Council of the BSA, each council is essentially a franchise to run the Boy Scout program in a given territory. The first Lowell Council started in 1910 and lasted only a few years. The second ended abruptly in 1921. With the rise and fall of Scout councils, so would go Scout camps. At the end of the second Lowell Council, only three troops and 80 Scouts were left. To build a sustainable Scouting program would require strong community leadership united under a common vision. In 1922, a new council would be formed. The third Greater Lowell Council, BSA, would be organized by men of vision.

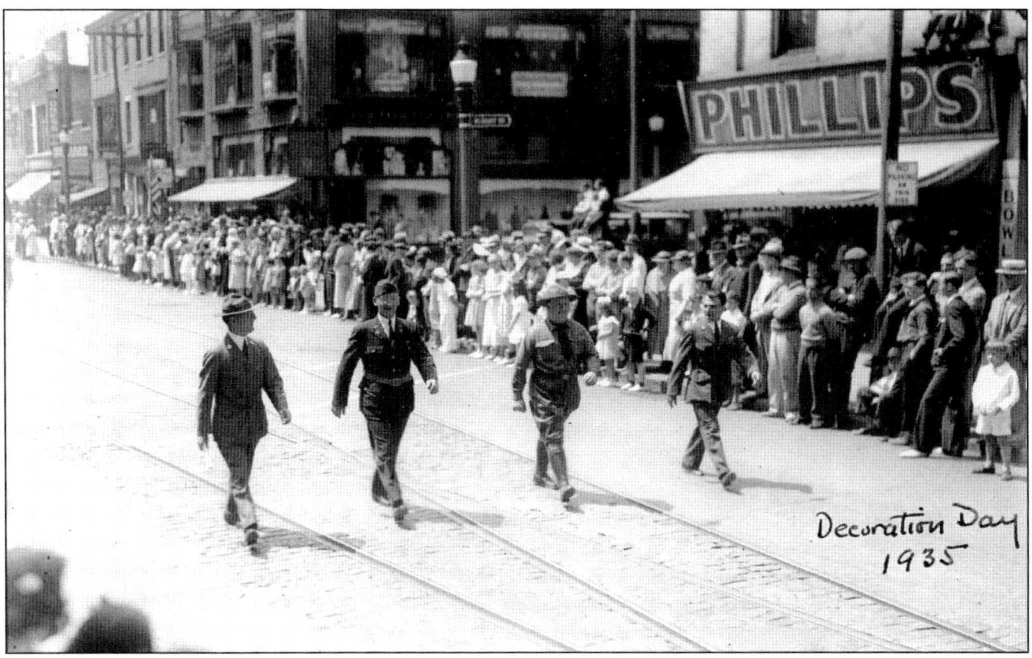

Frank G. W. McKittrick was a community leader and supporter of the reconstituted Greater Lowell Council. He created the McKittrick Industrial Supply Company, a business that provided equipment and hardware to Lowell's textile mills. McKittrick would remain active in Greater Lowell Scouting as a member of the council's executive board and a progressive member of the council's camping committee.

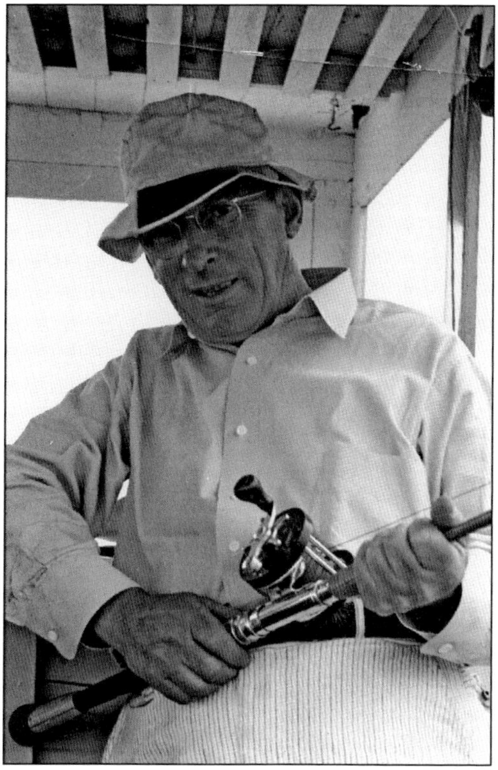

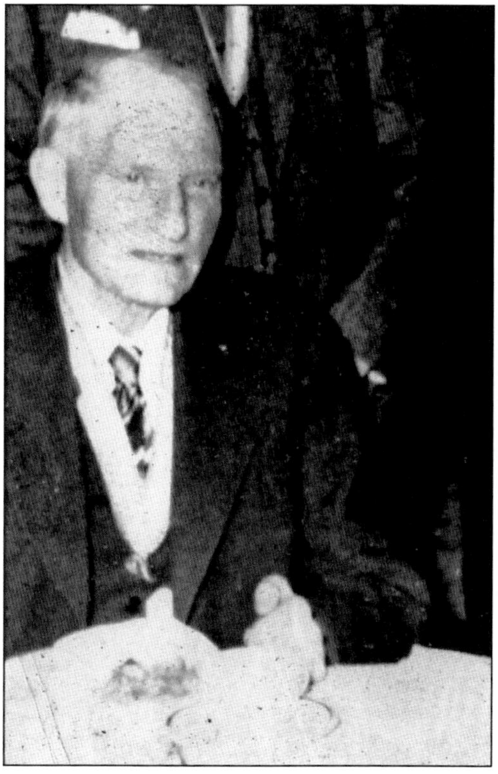

Dr. John H. Lambert was a highly respected physician and surgeon. In 1922, he assembled and chaired the committee that reorganized the Greater Lowell Council. He was passionate about the development of Scout summer camps. He would serve on the council's camp committee as health and safety chairman. During his years at Wah-Tut-Ca he would set very strict guidelines that assured the land would be used properly and respected.

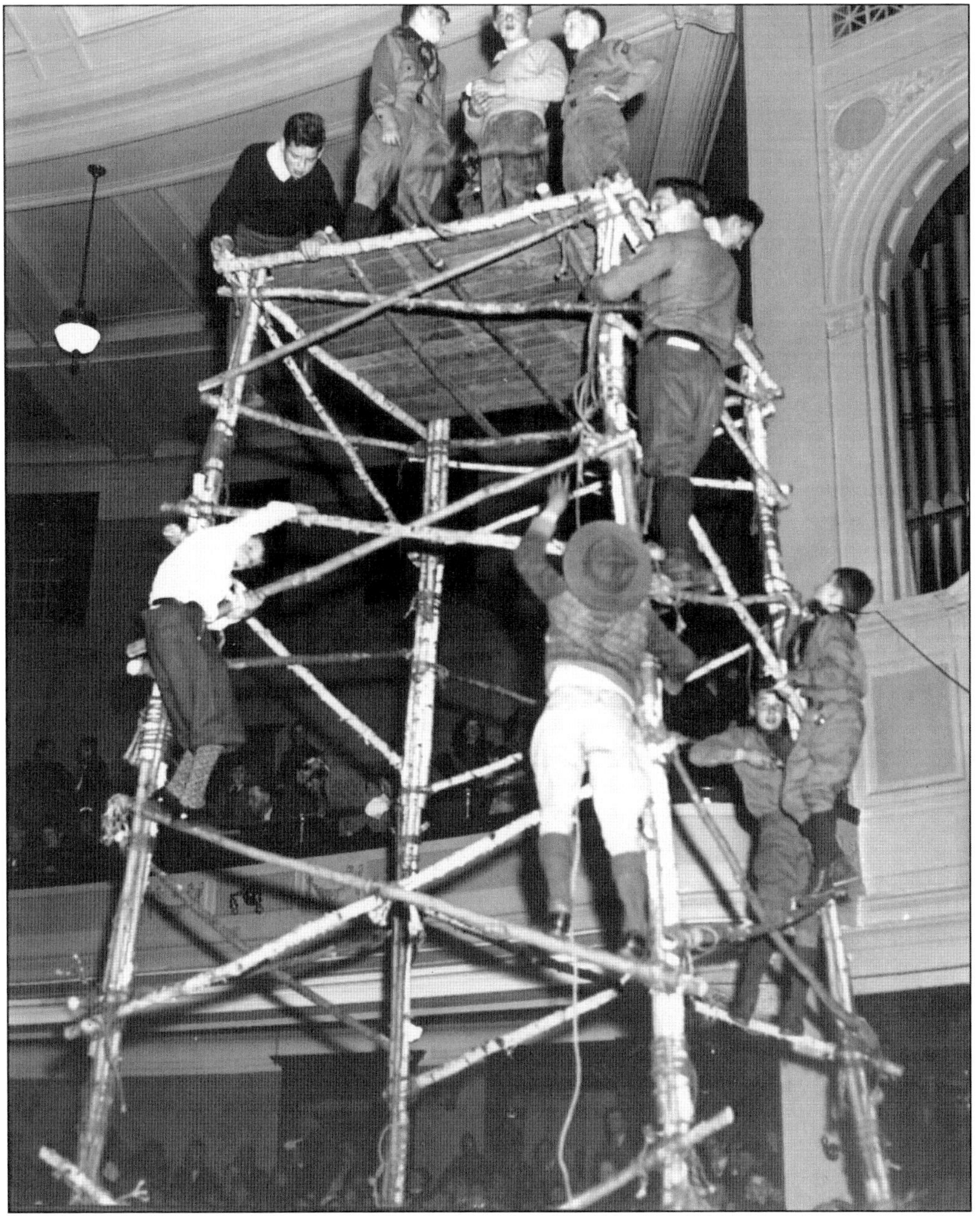

The new Greater Lowell Council would hold annual Scout shows at the Lowell Memorial Auditorium each spring. Hundreds of Scouts and their families would attend. The tower pictured here is over two stories high. The council was now being led by people who knew they were creating something that was meant to last. Many of the original council leaders such as Luther W. Faulkner and James Kiberd Sr. would remain active leaders in the new council. They would be joined in their quest to provide Scouting to boys by men like Dr. John H. Lambert and Frank G. W. McKittrick. The combination of business and professional leaders with talented program-orientated Scouters was key. This partnership was fundamental to building a sustainable Scout program. With new and determined leadership, the Greater Lowell Council was ready for a higher vision.

Three

Camp Chadwick

After two failed attempts to form a permanent Greater Lowell Council, the third would endure. Gordon R. Williams became the council executive in 1925. He was an important reason for its success. A newly formed camping and activities committee was charged with creating a summer camp opportunity. The camping committee created Camp Chadwick, named after Oliver Moulton Chadwick. Chadwick was born in Lowell in 1888 and graduated from Harvard University in 1911. Even before the United States entered World War I, he joined the Lafayette Escadrille in early 1917 and was killed in August of that year.

With Gordon R. Williams as camp director, Camp Chadwick operated for six to eight weeks each summer. For the most part, Scouts attended as individuals, not with their Scout troops. The boys were divided into age groups: juniors, for boys age 8–11, middlers for boys age 12–15, and seniors for boys ages 15 and up. The junior camp was called So-Kee-Tay and was led by James "Uncle Jim" Kiberd Sr. So-Kee-Tay came with controversy, however, since boys under the age of 12 were not allowed to enroll in Boy Scouting in the 1920s, and Cub Scouting did not begin until 1930. The junior division of Camp Chadwick therefore operated outside of the BSA.

At Chadwick, Gordon R. Williams founded an honor camper society called the Chadwick Braves, a local version of the Order of the Arrow (OA), which today is Scouting's national honor society. The OA did not become an official part of the BSA until 1948. Before that many troops and councils formed their own honor camper groups.

Although they rented the land, the Greater Lowell Council owned the Camp Chadwick buildings, including several purchased from the City of Lowell through the Girl Scouts. Gordon Williams's wife, Lydia, was a prominent leader in the development of Camp Runels, the Girl Scout camp in Pelham, New Hampshire. She served as Runels's first camp director. Built by the same people, the buildings of Wah-Tut-Ca and Camp Runels are understandably quite similar.

With the success at Camp Chadwick and the founding of Camp Runels, the Greater Lowell Council began to seek a higher vision. They were ready for a place of their own.

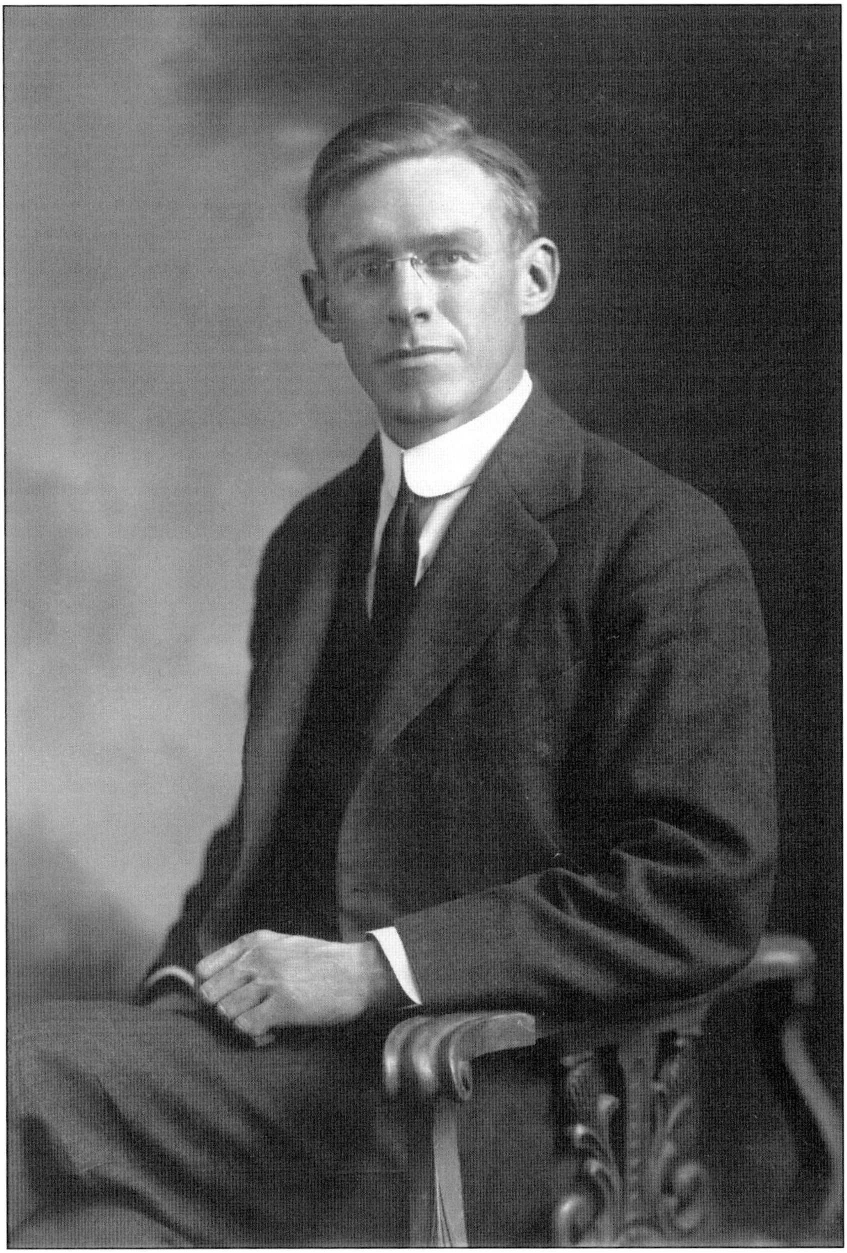

Camp Chadwick was named after Oliver Moulton Chadwick, who was born on September 23, 1888, in Lowell. He was the son of a prominent family. His father, Arthur K. Chadwick, was the president of the Lowell Five Cents Savings Bank. Oliver was educated in Lowell schools and attended Phillips Exeter Academy. Although a poor student, he was accepted into Harvard University. At Harvard his academic success did not improve. In spite of his difficulty with the schoolwork, he did have a keen interest in sports. At Phillips Exeter he was awarded the Yale Cup for excellence in athletics. At Harvard he played several sports. He was most noteworthy as the goalie for the Harvard hockey team. Chadwick managed to graduate from Harvard in 1911. He immediately entered the Harvard Law School and earned a degree in 1914. He then joined the law firm of Stone and Webster.

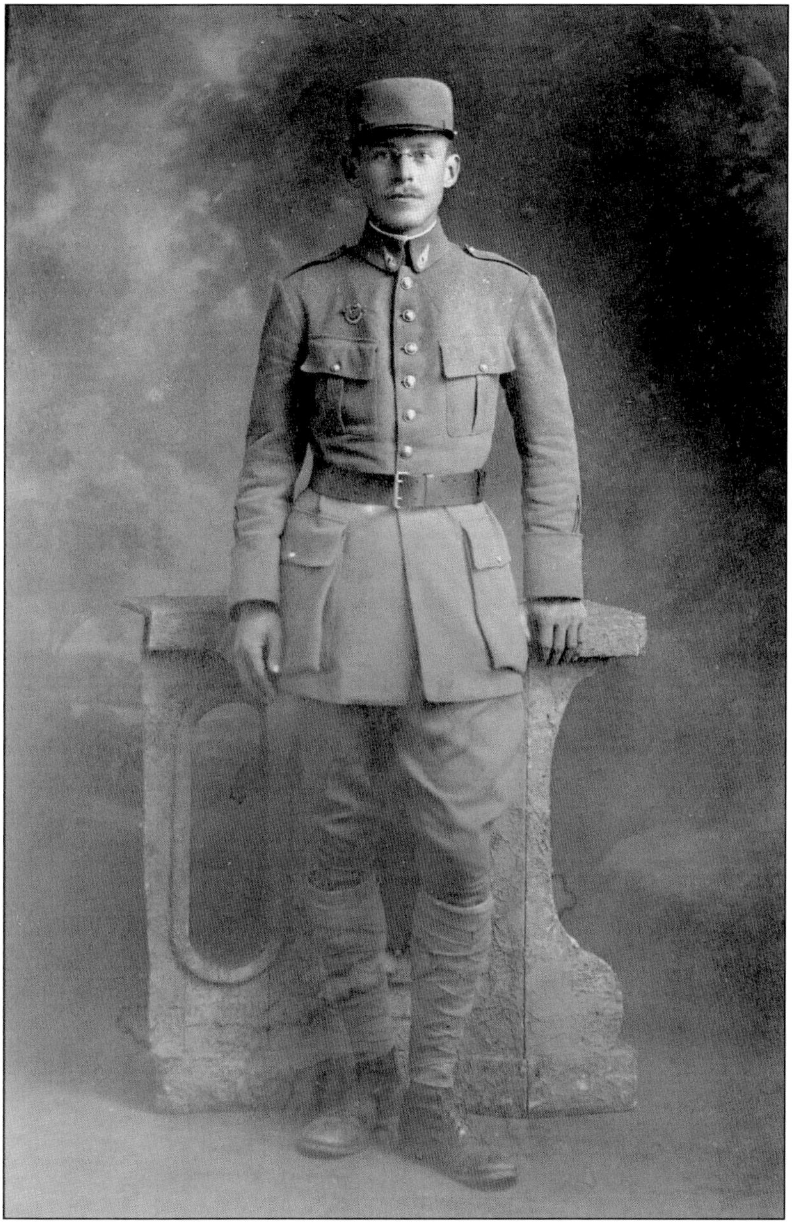

From the beginning of World War I, Chadwick dreamed of fighting for the Allies. In 1916, he enlisted in the army to gain military training. At this time, the United States was neutral in the "War in Europe." He made several unsuccessful attempts to join the French Foreign Legion. While in the U.S. Army, he was sent for four months to the Mexican border to fight in the conflict with Pancho Villa. Upon his return home, he entered the Curtiss Flying School in Newport News, Virginia. After gaining proficiency as a pilot, he sailed for France and joined the Lafayette Escadrille. On August 14, 1917, he was killed in combat, north of Bixschoote, Belgium. He had flown to help a British pilot that was being attacked by a German fighter. While in pursuit, he was attacked from the rear by two other Germans. The Allies found his crashed plane and, noting little damage to the aircraft, they concluded that Chadwick died from aerial machine gun fire. He is believed to be the first resident of Lowell to die in World War I.

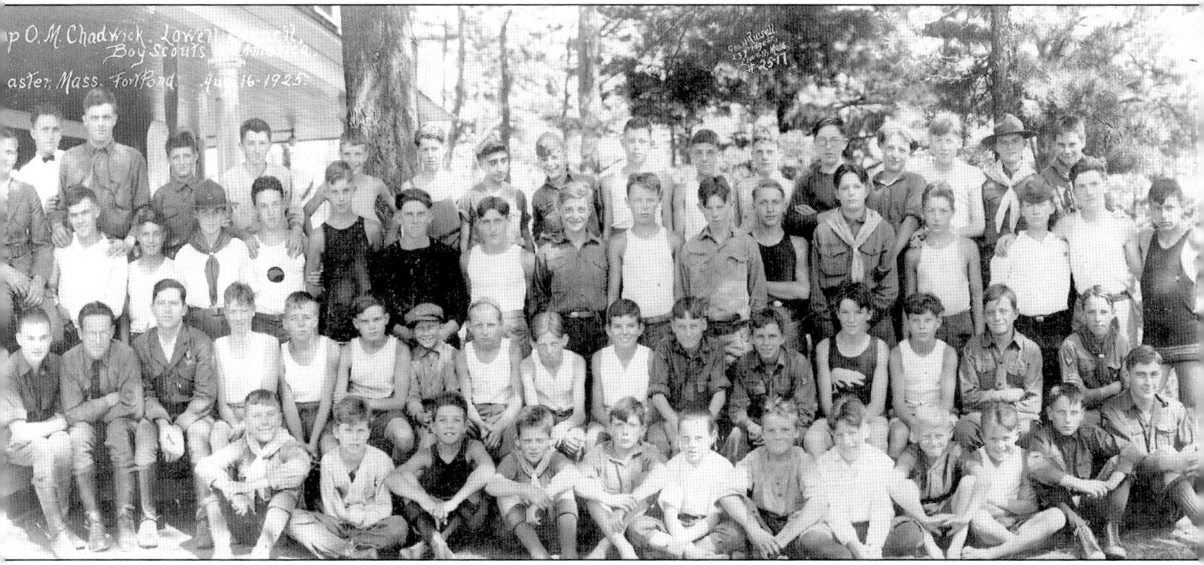

Camp Chadwick began in 1925 at Fort Pond in Lancaster, Massachusetts. The land was owned by the Leominster Country Club and was used for only one season. The council had placed a $200 deposit to purchase this land against the $6,000 asking price. The deal never went through, partially because the distance of 24 miles was considered too difficult for the boys of Lowell. Distance to camp would be a recurring theme in the 1930s and 1940s. Even if one's family owned a car, the drive on back roads that were poorly paved would take hours to travel 24 miles. Most people in the 1930s traveled by public transportation. There was great difficulty getting from the nearest train stop to the camp.

Gordon R. Williams became the full-time professional Scout executive of the Greater Lowell Council in 1925. He served as Scout executive and camp director from 1926 until 1938. The youth of the council thought of him as a Native American sachem and referred to him as "Chief." It is said that his smile would make one feel 10 feet tall and his scowl would turn one to stone.

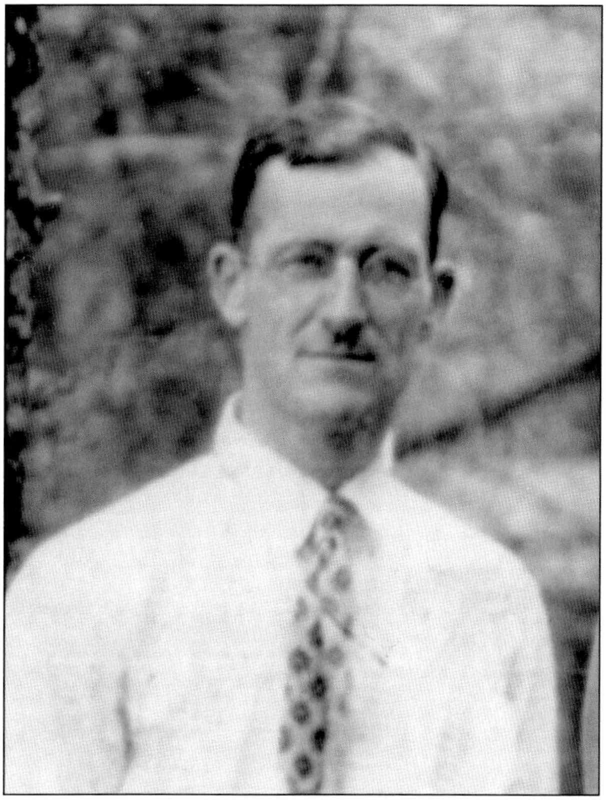

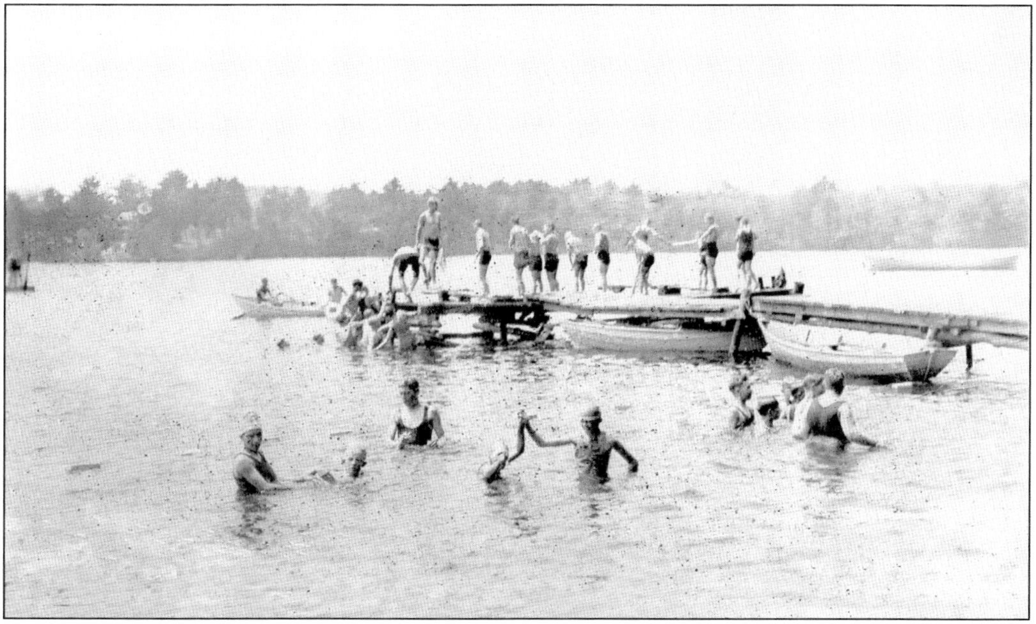

In 1926, Camp Chadwick was moved to Lake Massapoug in Dunstable, Massachusetts. A small site of just under 11 acres, the camp was on rented land owned by Herbert E. Kendall. The wooded areas were sparse and had the feel of a city park. The main attraction of the camp was the waterfront.

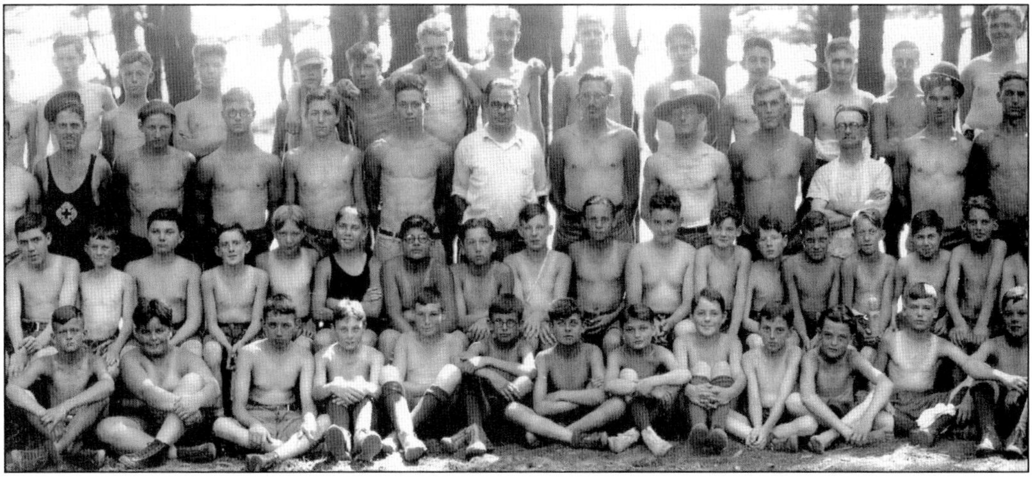

Campers of Chadwick pose for a picture in July 1928. Gordon R. Williams is in the second row from the back wearing the 10-gallon cowboy hat. Prior to the Dunstable site being used for Camp Chadwick, it was used by the Girl Scouts as their summer camp. When the Girl Scouts left the site they sold the buildings to the Boy Scouts. Many of these buildings would end up at Wah-Tut-Ca.

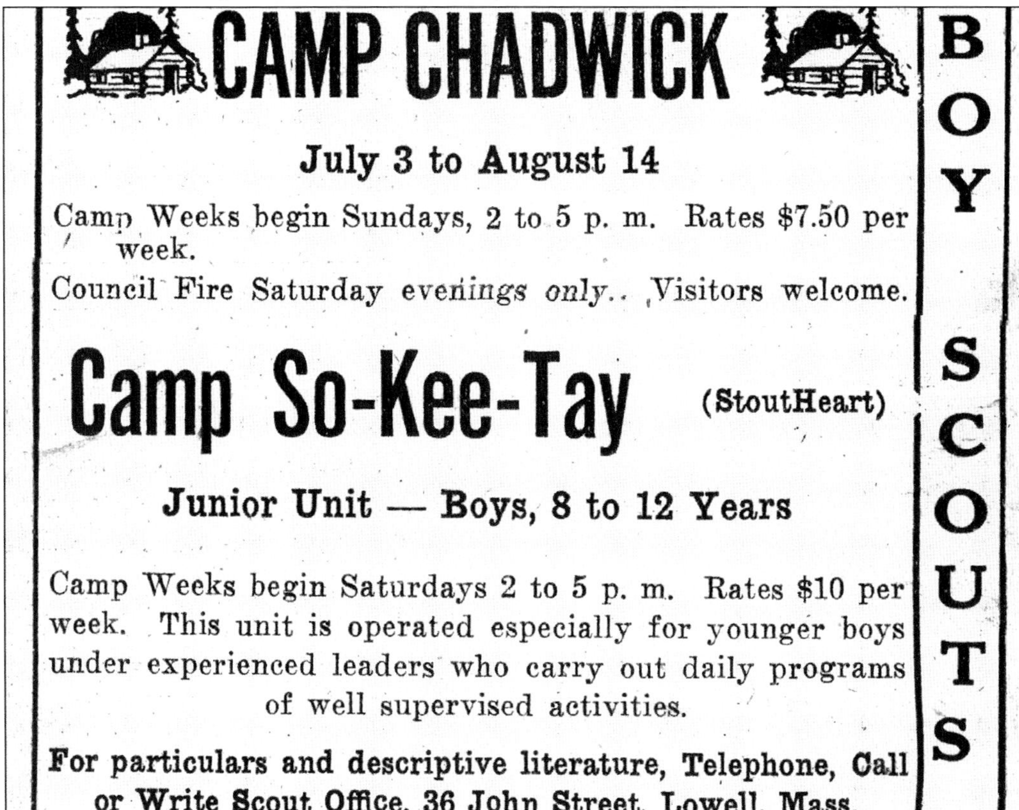

Camp Chadwick was not a camp limited to only Boy Scouts. Although it was operated by the Greater Lowell Council, it was open to all boys in the community. The council would actively promote the program to both Scouts and non-Scouts as is seen in this advertisement. All who attended the junior camp So-Kee-Tay were too young to be Boy Scouts.

Very few Scouts would attend camp with their Scout troop. They would attend as individuals. At camp, the boys would be divided by age groups into subcamps. Passaconaway and Kemosabee would be the subcamps for boys age 12 to 14. There would also be a subcamp for senior Scouts aged 15 and over. So-Kee-Tay was for boys 8–11 and was directed by James Kiberd Sr. So-Kee-Tay provided most of the campers.

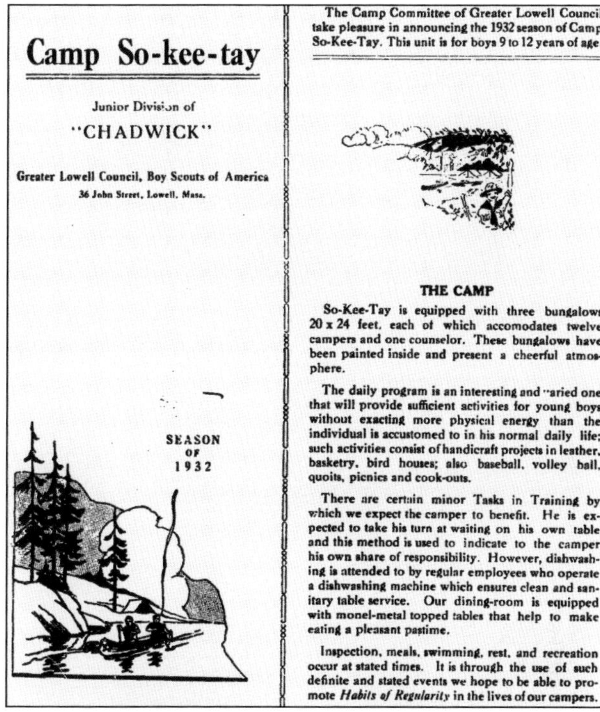

Camp So-kee-tay

Junior Division of

"CHADWICK"

Greater Lowell Council, Boy Scouts of America

36 John Street, Lowell, Mass.

SEASON OF 1932

The Camp Committee of Greater Lowell Council take pleasure in announcing the 1932 season of Camp So-Kee-Tay. This unit is for boys 9 to 12 years of age.

THE CAMP

So-Kee-Tay is equipped with three bungalows 20 x 24 feet, each of which accomodates twelve campers and one counselor. These bungalows have been painted inside and present a cheerful atmosphere.

The daily program is an interesting and varied one that will provide sufficient activities for young boys without exacting more physical energy than the individual is accustomed to in his normal daily life; such activities consist of handicraft projects in leather, basketry, bird houses; also baseball, volley ball, quoits, picnics and cook-outs.

There are certain minor Tasks in Training by which we expect the camper to benefit. He is expected to take his turn at waiting on his own table and this method is used to indicate to the camper his own share of responsibility. However, dishwashing is attended to by regular employees who operate a dishwashing machine which ensures clean and sanitary table service. Our dining-room is equipped with monel-metal topped tables that help to make eating a pleasant pastime.

Inspection, meals, swimming, rest, and recreation occur at stated times. It is through the use of such definite and stated events we hope to be able to promote *Habits of Regularity* in the lives of our campers.

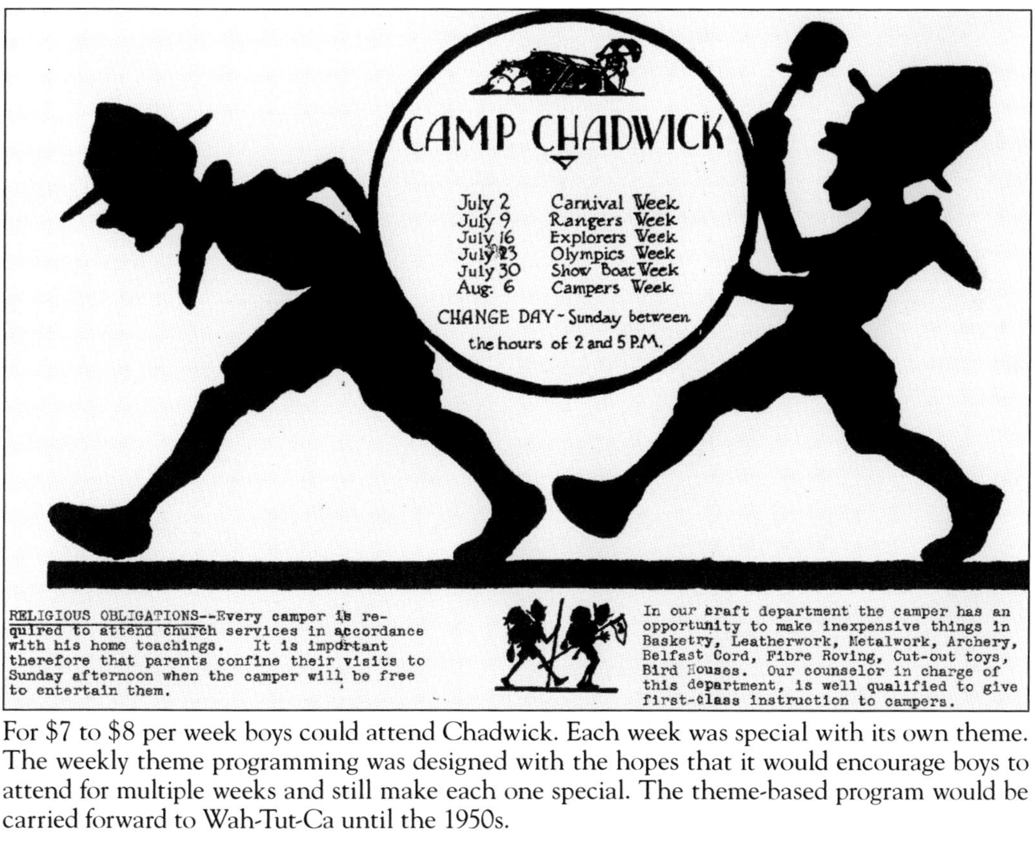

CAMP CHADWICK

July 2	Carnival Week
July 9	Rangers Week
July 16	Explorers Week
July 23	Olympics Week
July 30	Show Boat Week
Aug. 6	Campers Week

CHANGE DAY - Sunday between the hours of 2 and 5 P.M.

RELIGIOUS OBLIGATIONS--Every camper is required to attend church services in accordance with his home teachings. It is important therefore that parents confine their visits to Sunday afternoon when the camper will be free to entertain them.

In our craft department the camper has an opportunity to make inexpensive things in Basketry, Leatherwork, Metalwork, Archery, Belfast Cord, Fibre Roving, Cut-out toys, Bird Houses. Our counselor in charge of this department, is well qualified to give first-class instruction to campers.

For $7 to $8 per week boys could attend Chadwick. Each week was special with its own theme. The weekly theme programming was designed with the hopes that it would encourage boys to attend for multiple weeks and still make each one special. The theme-based program would be carried forward to Wah-Tut-Ca until the 1950s.

PARENTS AND CAMP

The camp committee and the camp staff have a real interest in every boy who attends "So-Kee-Tay"; we believe, also, that parents have an interest in the camp and desire to be considerate of our standards of morale and discipline.

Meals are well planned, the food wholesome and nourishing, and there is enough for all. Food, candy, and fruit, brought in from the outside not only may, but does, cause "stomach upset". It is not quite fair to hold the camp authorities responsible for the health of your boy when you bring him things to eat "between meals". If you want to bring him some token of your affection a few cookies are sufficient. It is important that we have your co-operation in this matter, otherwise there is little we can do for your son while he camps with us.

JAMES KIBERD, SR.
Camp Master

GORDON R. WILLIAMS
Camp Director

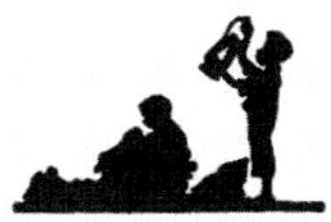

REQUIRED EQUIPMENT

Brown Shorts	3 Blankets or equivalent
Brown cotton shirts	Handkerchiefs
Woolen shirt	2 or 3 Towels
Two pairs stockings	Pajamas (flannel)
Sturdy shoes	Soap
Pillow	Comb
Change of underwear	Brush
Sweater or equivalent	Tooth Paste
Raincoat or Poncho	Tooth Brush
Bathing suit	Flashlight

Tennis shoes or moccasins

We have listed only the real necessities for camping. Each article should be marked with the owner's name or initials.

The distance to Chadwick clearly had its advantages. One disadvantage, though, was the fact that family members would often turn up during the week unannounced. Mothers and other family members would bring both food for the campers and advice to the staff. This resulted in a policy that limited visitor access to camp.

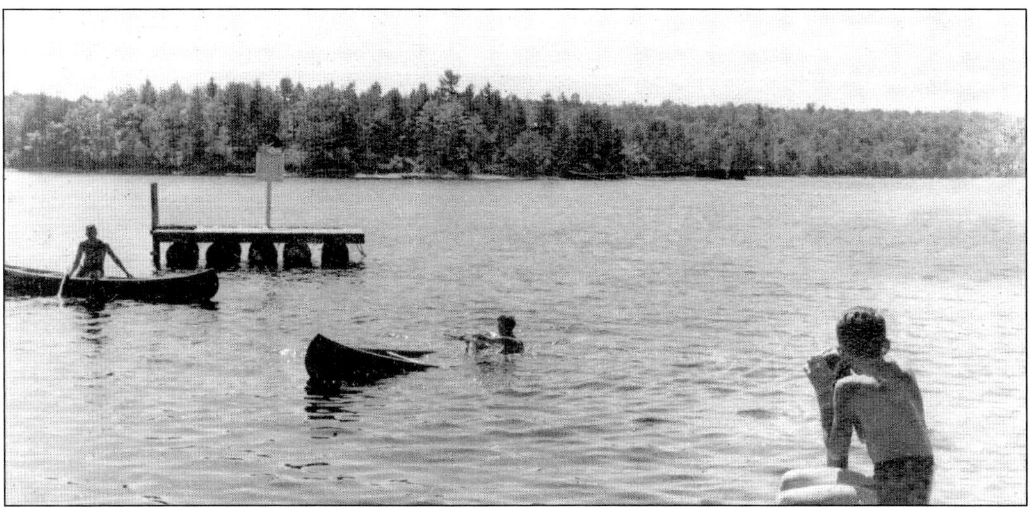

One of the lessons still taught today is how to handle a swamped boat. There is always a boyish enthusiasm for this procedure. As it is not the way the boat is supposed to float, it gives the young person permission to break the rules. It becomes an experience of summer freedom and leaves the boy with the confidence to handle the canoe under any condition.

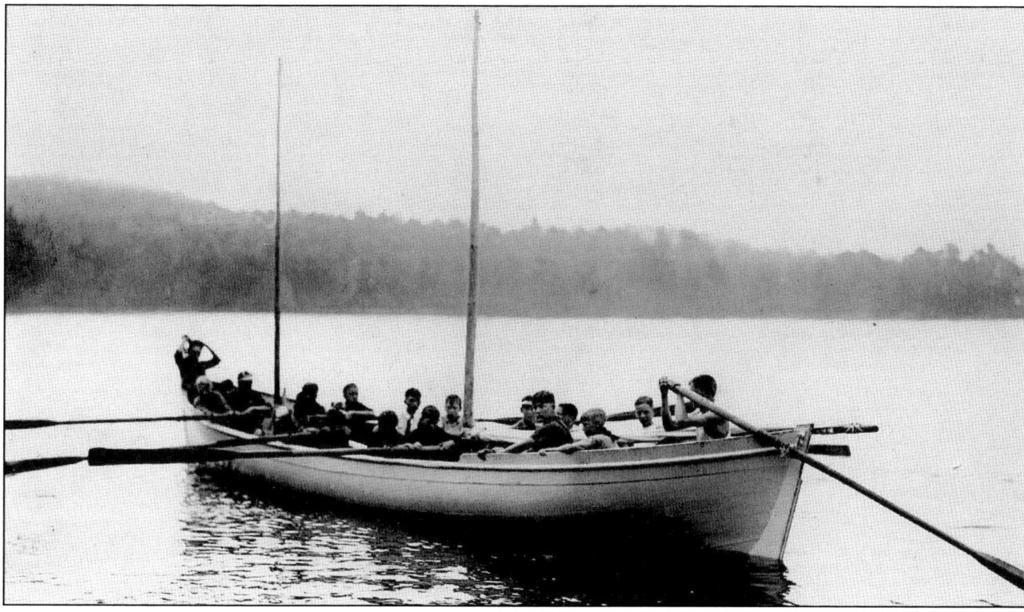

A great adventure of both Camp Chadwick and Wah-Tut-Ca Scout Reservation was going out on the lake in the whaleboats. The whaleboats were actually surplus Coast Guard rescue craft the camp used in its aquatics area. They would be used for a variety of program adventures and games and were one of the biggest attractions at the waterfront. Teams of Scouts would man the oars. It took coordination from the coxswain to keep the boat on course. Not always successful, the boat could spin in a circle or crash into the docks. Oars would be broken and knuckles bruised. In spite of the risks, boys lined up for their chance to climb aboard and sail out upon the lake.

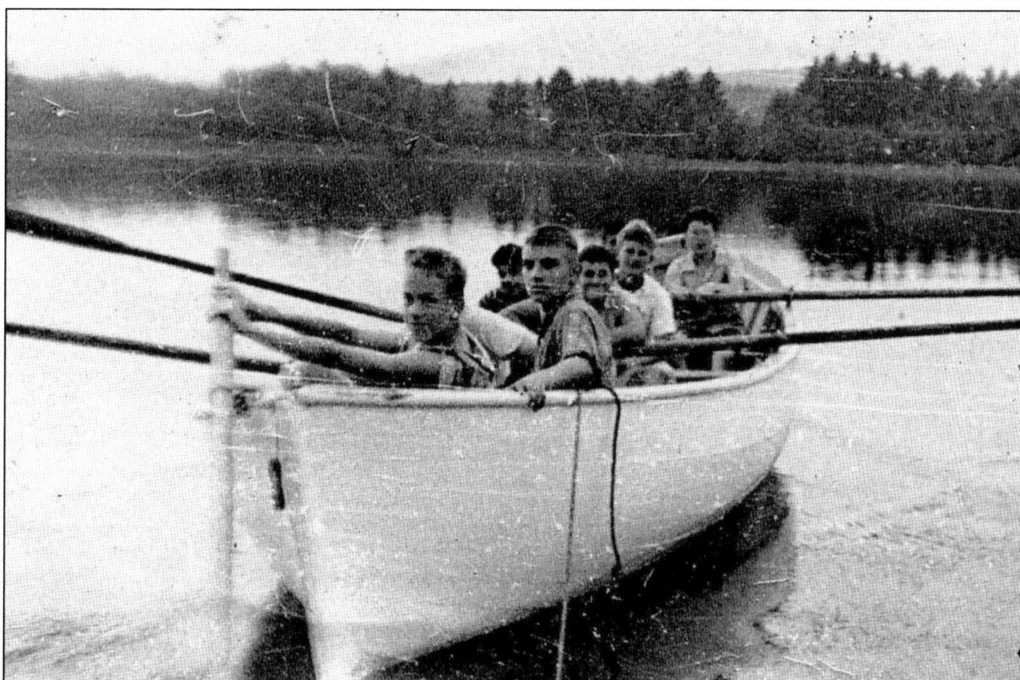

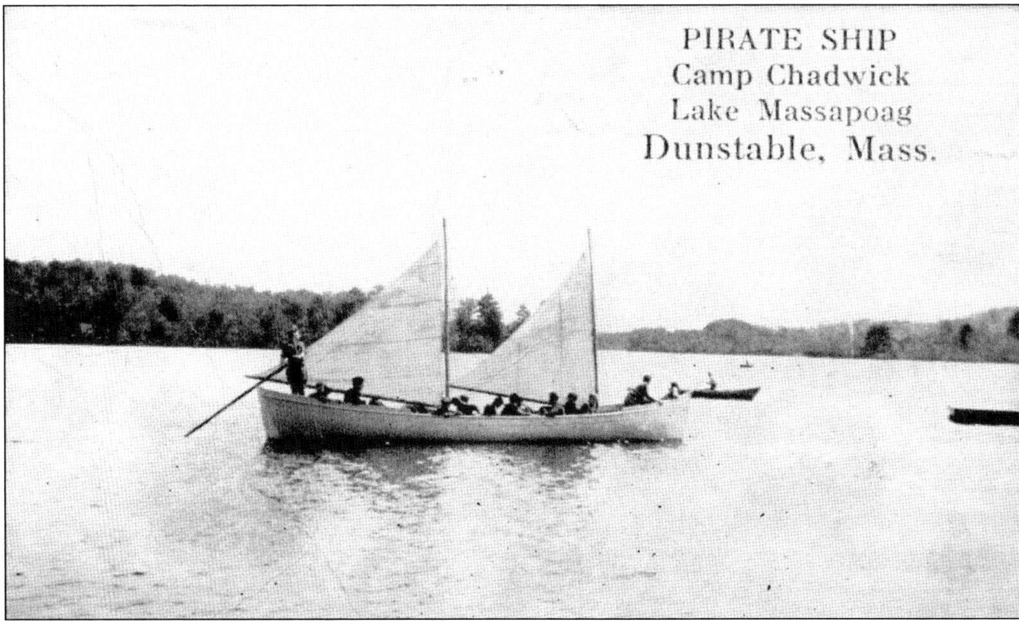

The whaleboats were often rigged with sails. It took a strong gust of wind to move the craft. By flying a Jolly Roger, the whaleboats became pirate ships. With the use of their imaginations, the boys were suddenly back in the time of Blackbeard, out on the lake searching for buried treasure.

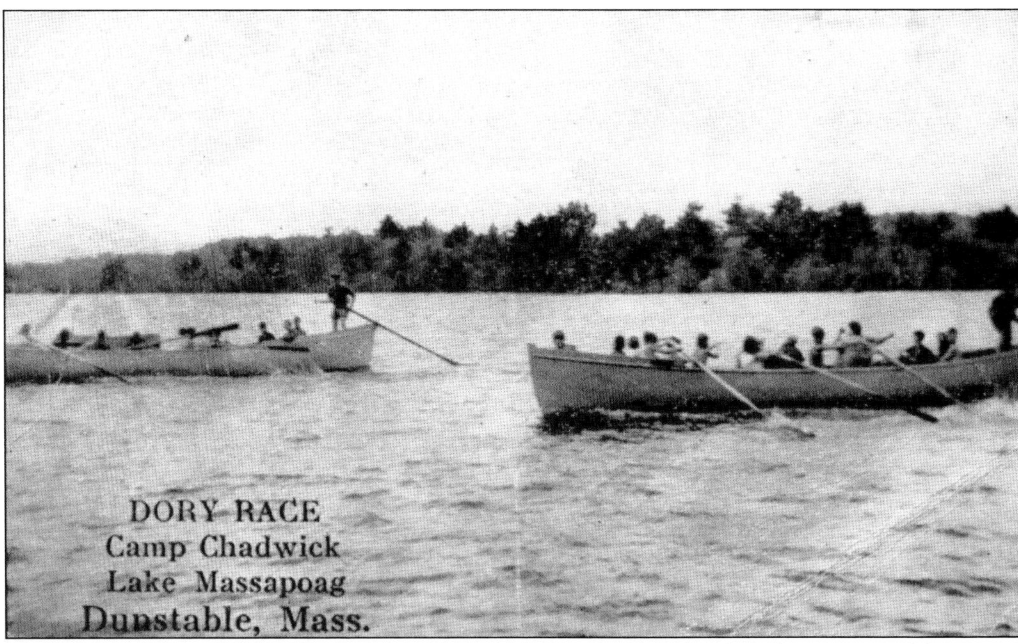

The water carnival was a highlight of each week at Camp Chadwick. Subcamps would compete with each other in an event that closed each week. Whaleboat (dory) races were one of the carnival activities. Not only did the boys have to coordinate their own boats, they needed to avoid the others.

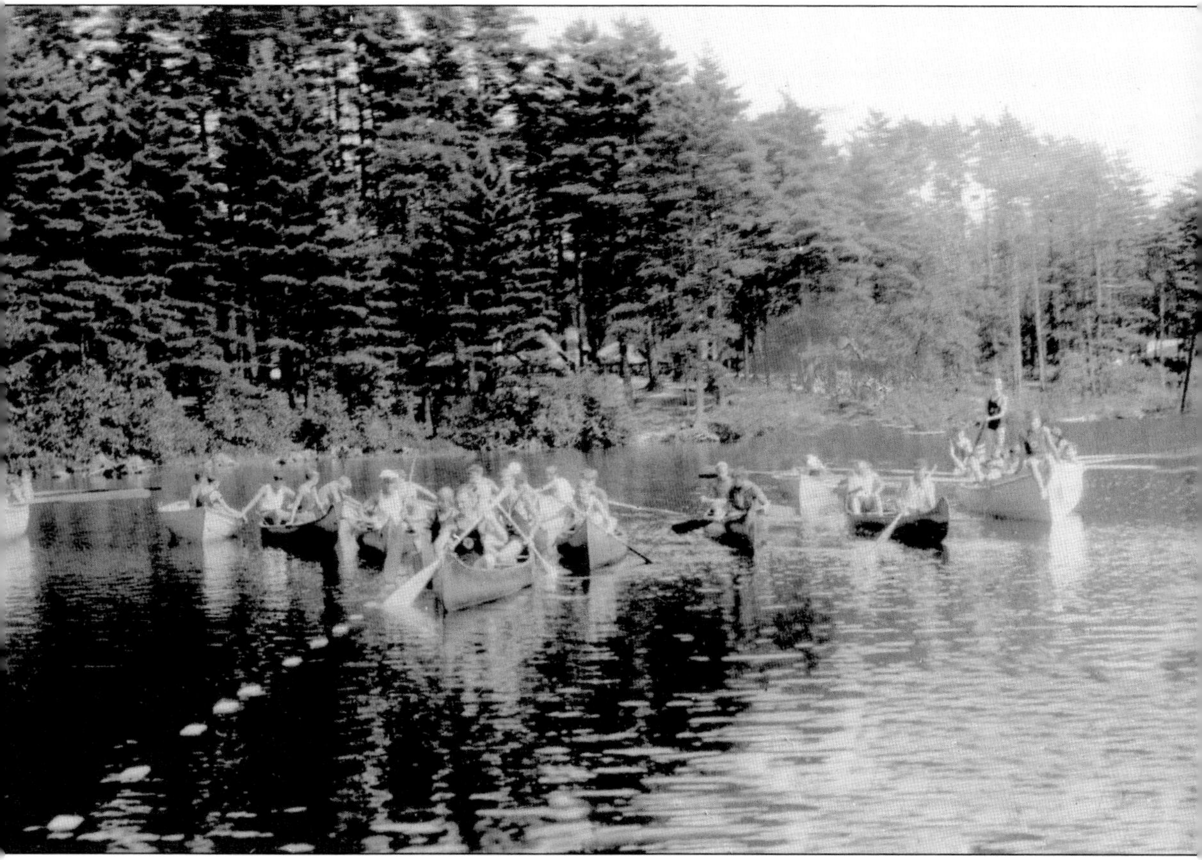

One aspect of the water carnival was to get everything that could float out on the lake. This included the boats, and although not always intended, the boys themselves. One of the best summer activities at camp is to be in or on the water. The carnival provided an opportunity for both. The boat race, and the chaos that it created, is one of the experiences that a boy would not easily forget. The excitement generated by participating in this end-of-week activity was remembered throughout the coming year. Boys returned to their troops and talked about the carnival, the winners, and any inequities that may have occurred.

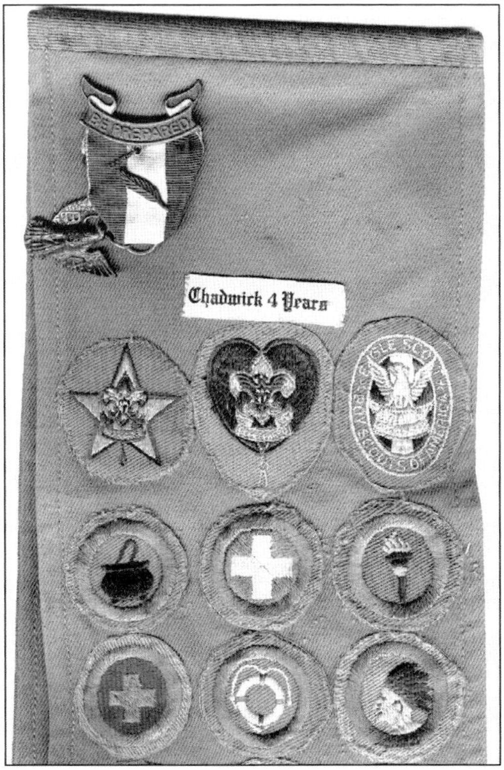

Although not a camp exclusively for Scouts, most of the boys outside of the So-Kee-Tay subcamp were. Camp has always been a place for Scouts to advance in rank. The availability of counselors and equipment combined with the advantages of weather and time proved to be ideal. Many Scouts attended camp to take advantage of these resources. Pictured here is camper Ulmner B. Robinson, who attended Camp Chadwick in the 1930s. When the required number of badges and years of service were finally gained, an Eagle Scout Court of Honor would be held to mark the achievement. Often held in church halls and public meeting rooms, many Eagles decided to hold their court of honor at camp. Such was the case with Robinson, who was awarded his Eagle at Camp Chadwick on August 17, 1935.

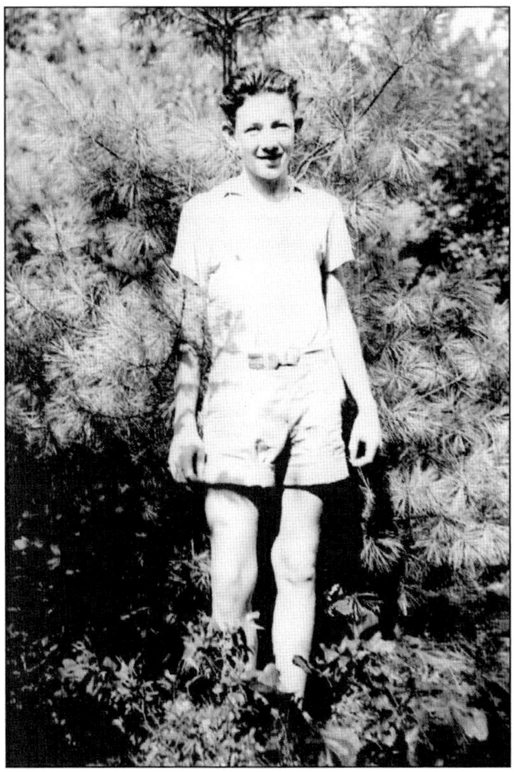

Warren E. Bryant was another of Camp Chadwick's Eagle Scouts and a camp staff member. He joined Scouting as a member of Troop 2B, from Billerica, Massachusetts, in 1928. Just two years later, in 1930, at the age of 15, he was presented his Eagle badge at Camp Chadwick. This was an unusual achievement for a boy so young.

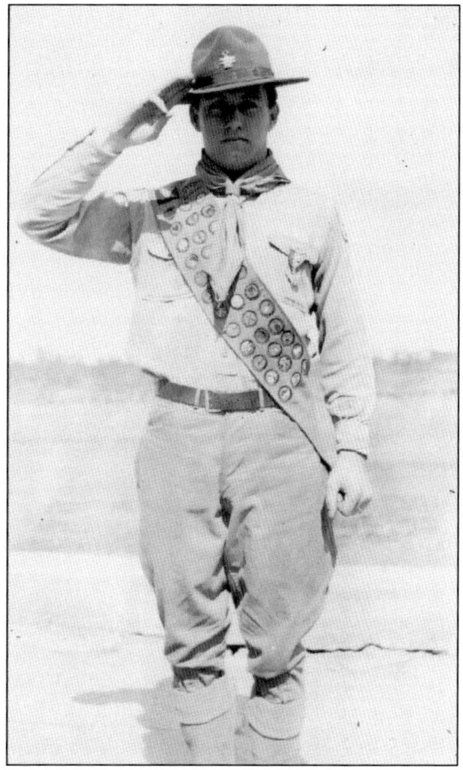

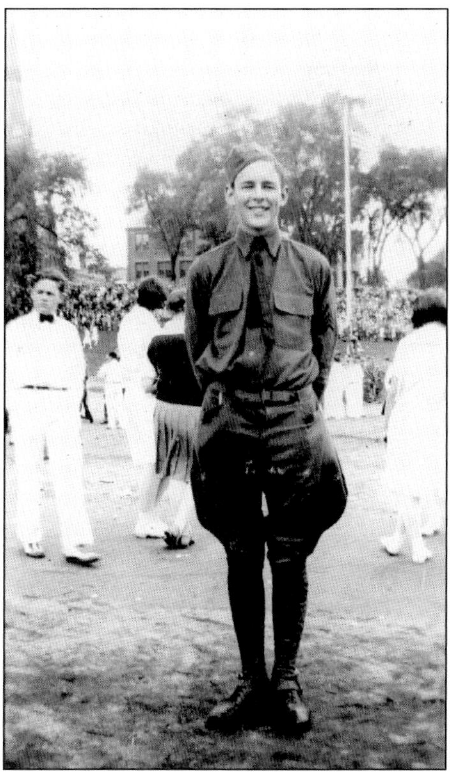

J. Bradley Varnum worked on staff at both Camp Chadwick and Wah-Tut-Ca. Like many of the Chadwick staff, he was awarded his Eagle badge at Camp Chadwick. Varnum served as Wah-Tut-Ca's first aquatic director. He later attended medical school and was a member of the Greater Lowell Council's executive board.

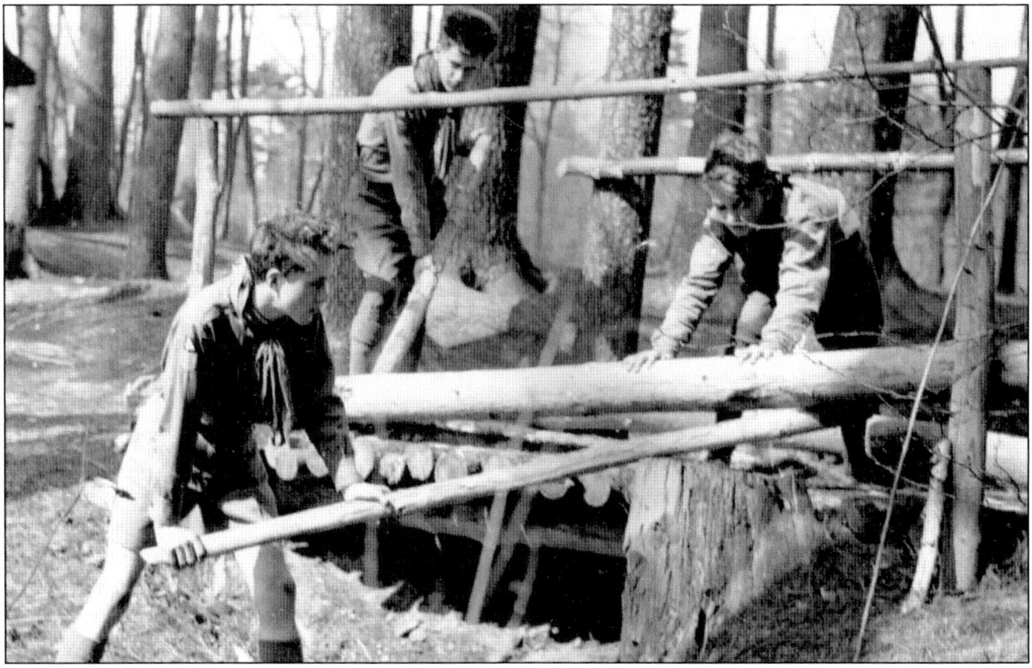

Chadwick Scouts shown here are building a bridge at the Passaconaway subcamp. Intrigued by building things with their own hands, the boys were required to work as a team on this activity. With a lack of timber, pioneering projects were limited. Timbers often would have to be brought in from other sites for Scouts to use in these projects.

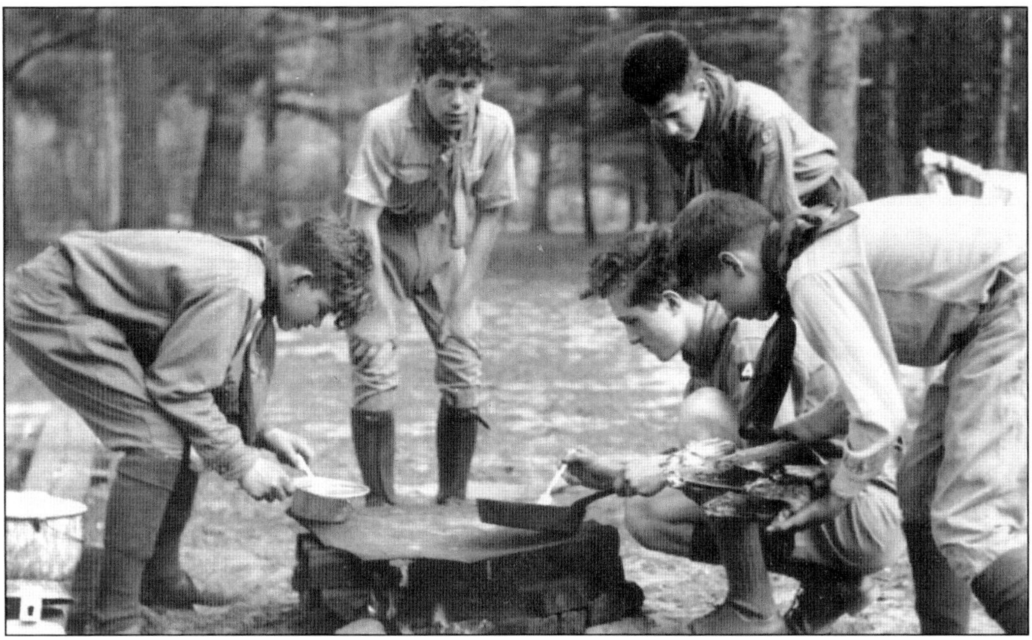

Chadwick Scouts with a makeshift grill cook in their campsite. Scout cooking should never be confused with Scout eating. Cooking is actually a game that practices organizational dynamics. No matter the quality of the food, to prepare it requires leadership, coordination, resource assessment, and timing. If they failed, there was always food in the dining hall.

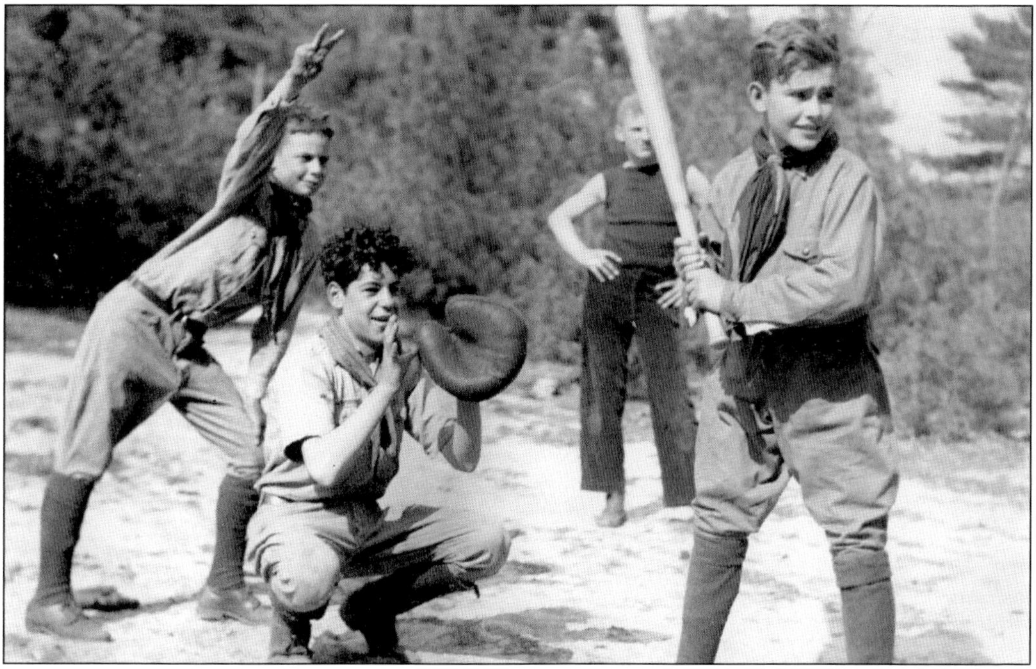

Sports were always a major activity at camp. As seen here by these Chadwick Scouts, baseball and other athletic sports were enthusiastically played. It was the second most popular activity next to the waterfront. Today these activities have almost disappeared from Scout camp, replaced by other programs that focus on the individual.

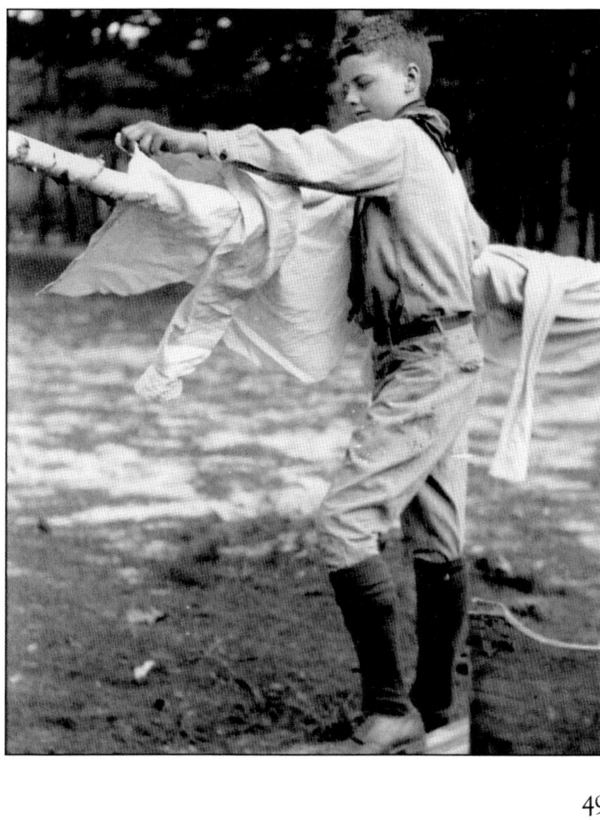

Being on one's own at Scout camp, without one's mom, brings with it certain challenges. One such challenge is laundry. Although Scouts would avoid it as long as possible, eventually clean clothes would be desired. One of the unadvertised skills learned at camp was how to do laundry. Running them on a pole and heating them over a fire is a risky but sometimes effective means to dry them.

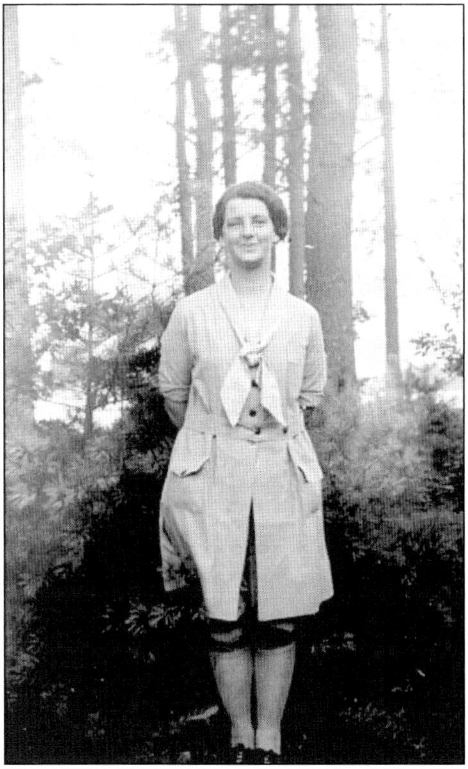

In 1929, both the Boy Scouts and the Girl Scouts bid on 300 acres of land that was made available for a youth camp. Gordon R. Williams led the cause for the Boy Scouts, and he was opposed by Lydia Williams, his wife, who represented the Girl Scouts. The Girl Scouts' bid was accepted, and Camp Runels would open in 1930 for the girls of Greater Lowell.

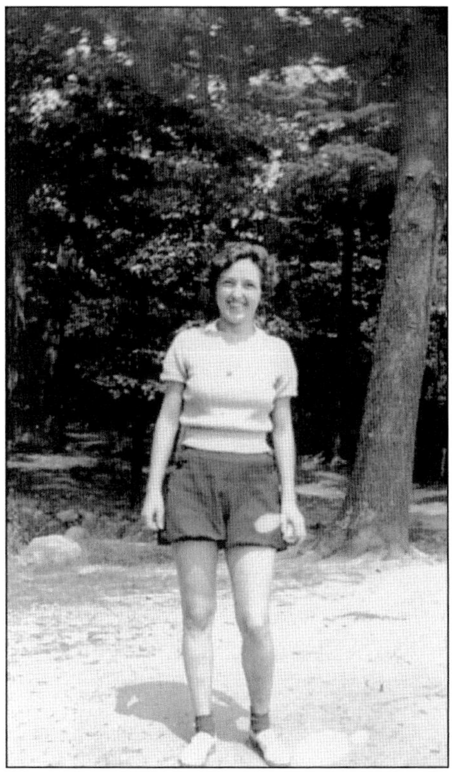

Many of the spouses of the Greater Lowell Council leadership were leaders in the Girls Scouts. Jennie M. Robinson, another of Camp Runels's staff, was the wife of Charles A. Robinson. Robinson was a leader in building both camps. Since Runels and Wah-Tut-Ca were built by the same people, Runels can appropriately be called Wah-Tut-Ca's older sister.

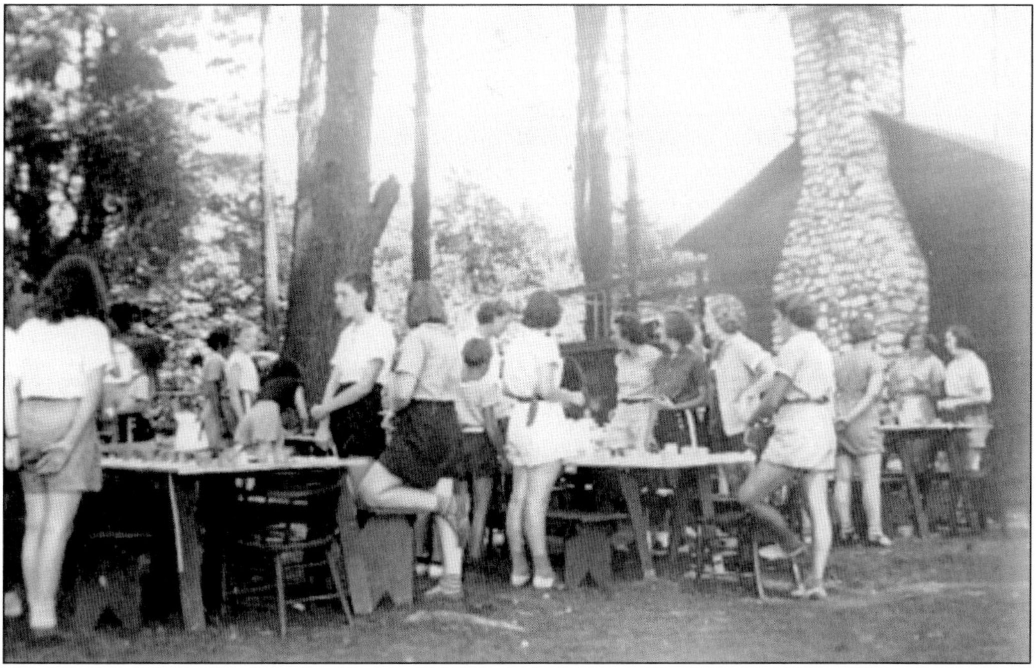

The dining hall at Camp Runels bears more than a passing resemblance to the dining hall at Wah-Tut-Ca Scout Reservation. The same people constructed both buildings. This is just one example that shows the close relationship between the camps and the people that helped to create and build them. The dining halls of both Runels and Wah-Tut-Ca are dedicated to the memory of Charles A. Robinson.

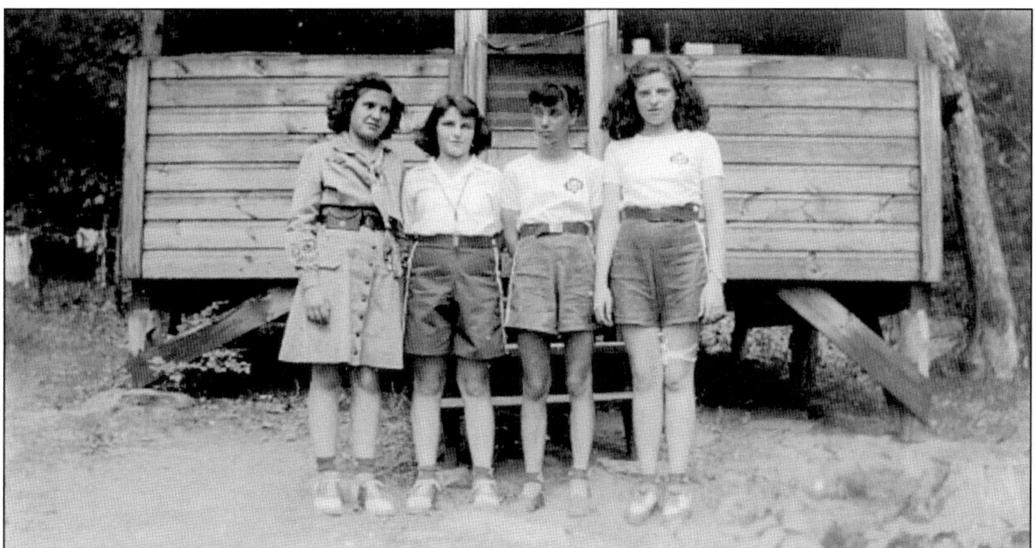

Other buildings shared designs as well. These small dormitory cabins would house campers at both Camp Runels and Camp Chadwick. Sometimes the open screening would be boarded up. They would house six to eight people including a counselor. Many of these buildings are still in use, three of which stand today in Northwood.

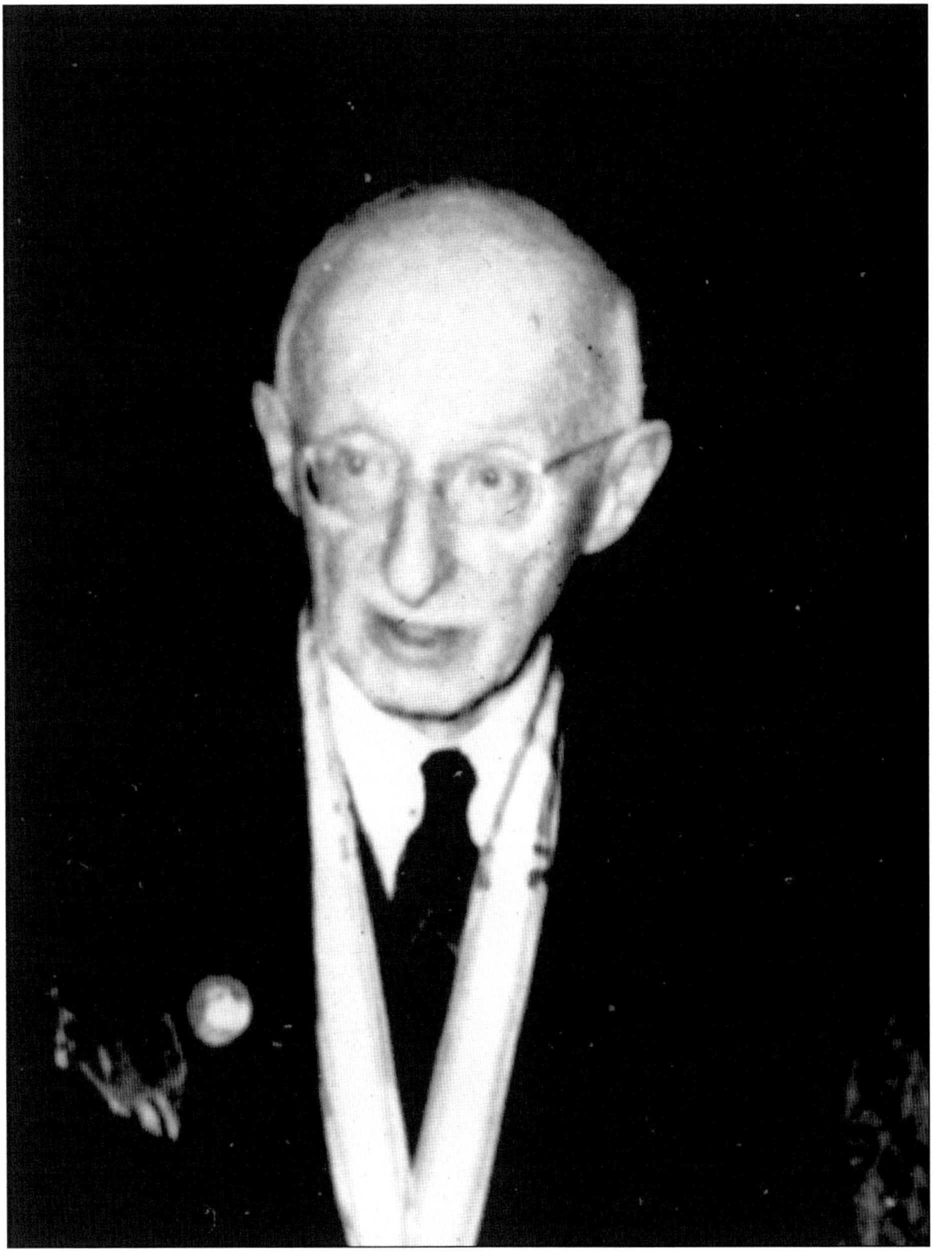

Charles A. Hosmer was the chairman of the Greater Lowell camping committee. Camp Chadwick was his major responsibility and focus. He organized promotion, facility support, and programs. Each year in his annual report on the summer camp program of the previous season he wrote of the limitations of Chadwick. He was completely dissatisfied with this camp, and each year he became more critical. He felt strongly that the rented land was not suitable for a proper Scout camp. Hosmer would constantly advocate that the Greater Lowell Council needed "a place of our own." Hosmer's vision became tangible in 1935. The lease on Chadwick was to expire in 1936, and the owner would not consider a long-term lease. Hosmer used this as an opportunity to pursue his dream. In the fall of 1935, he and members of the camping committee visited an old farm in Northwood. He put all his efforts into acquiring this new site.

Four

THE NEW SITE

Emboldened by the success of Camp Chadwick and its sister Camp Runels, the Greater Lowell Council began to think big. Charles A. Hosmer, camping committee chair, wrote in 1934, "It may be visionary, utopian, but if Scouting in its truest sense is really worthwhile, I feel we should have a camp that will bring our boys closer to nature as it really is."

In the fall of 1935, Hosmer and the camping committee found what they thought would be the perfect place for a camp. In the 1935 annual report, Hosmer wrote,

> One thing that stands out particularly this season is the preponderance of interest in waterfront activities. Such interest is healthy and normal, but it occurs to me that the reason lies in the fact that, outside of the waterfront and athletics, the Massapoug site has little else to offer. There are no opportunities for "voyages of discovery," no chance for that eager search for what is "over there," to discover different plant life; to trace out lava and quartz protruding through moss and pine needles. Our present camp is sadly lacking in facilities and scope for the study of nature and practice in forestry, pioneering, path finding and camping. The Camping Committee has such a new site under consideration and if ways and means can be found to procure and equip this site, no stone will be left unturned to accomplish it.

The issue was brought to a vote on February 16, 1936. After an "animated debate," the Greater Lowell Council boldly voted, with an 80 percent majority, to purchase an initial 180 acres of land in Northwood. The opposition noted that the location, 60 miles from the center of Lowell, made the new site impractical.

For the next 18 months, the New Site Committee would dismantle Chadwick and rebuild it in Northwood. Wah-Tut-Ca opened on July 4, 1937, and volunteers and families that had helped to build the camp held a great celebration. At the end of the opening ceremonies, they congratulated Robinson for his efforts in completing the camp. His reply was simple yet prophetic. Robinson smiled and said, "Wah-Tut-Ca will never be completed."

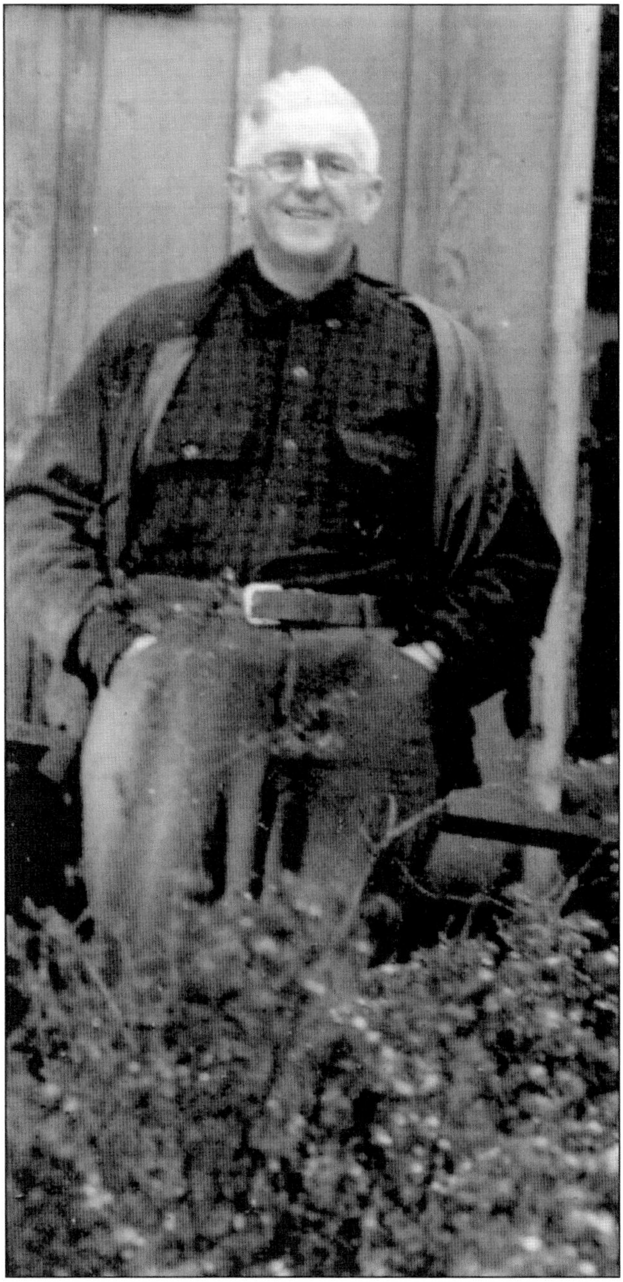

Charles A. Robinson was a foreman at the Merrimack Manufacturing Company in Lowell and chairman of the New Site Committee. It was he, more than anyone else, who made the transition to Northwood possible. He was skilled in mechanics and construction, but more importantly, he was a natural leader and director and had a spirit and enthusiasm that motivated people. There were at least 18 troops and more than 500 people who assisted with the construction in Northwood. Many local businesses donated supplies and the use of their trucks to move equipment from Camp Chadwick to Northwood. It was Robinson who organized and directed the efforts of all of the volunteers. Over a period of 17 months, he found resources and solved a great number of problems associated with a project of this size and scope.

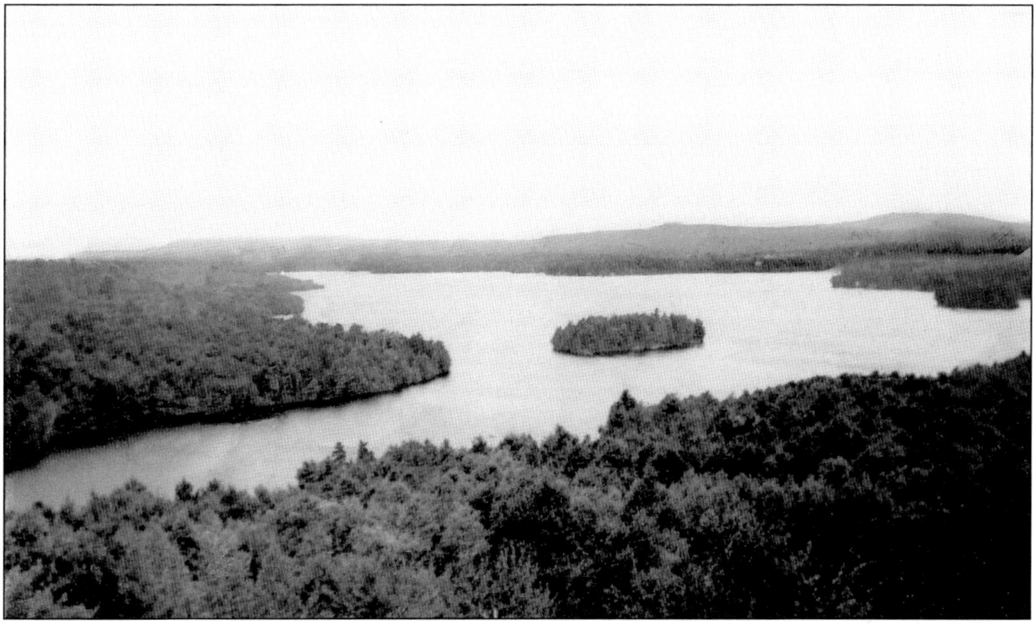

Norman P. Mason, future commissioner and camp committee member, had a summer home in Northwood. Mason was aware of two adjoining pieces of property that were available on Northwood Lake that would be suitable for a summer camp. Papers were signed on the property early in 1936.

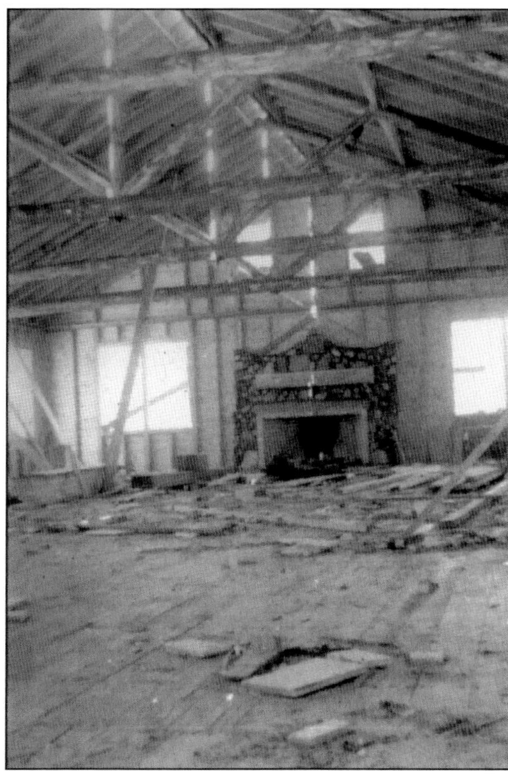

Raising the estimated $13,000 to purchase and equip the property was a daunting task. Gordon R. Williams led a community campaign to acquire the funding necessary to build the camp. Some money was raised by local troops. A total of $5,800 was borrowed to make up the difference. The biggest single undertaking and expense was the dining hall, known as "the New Building." The completion of this building was necessary to open the camp in 1937.

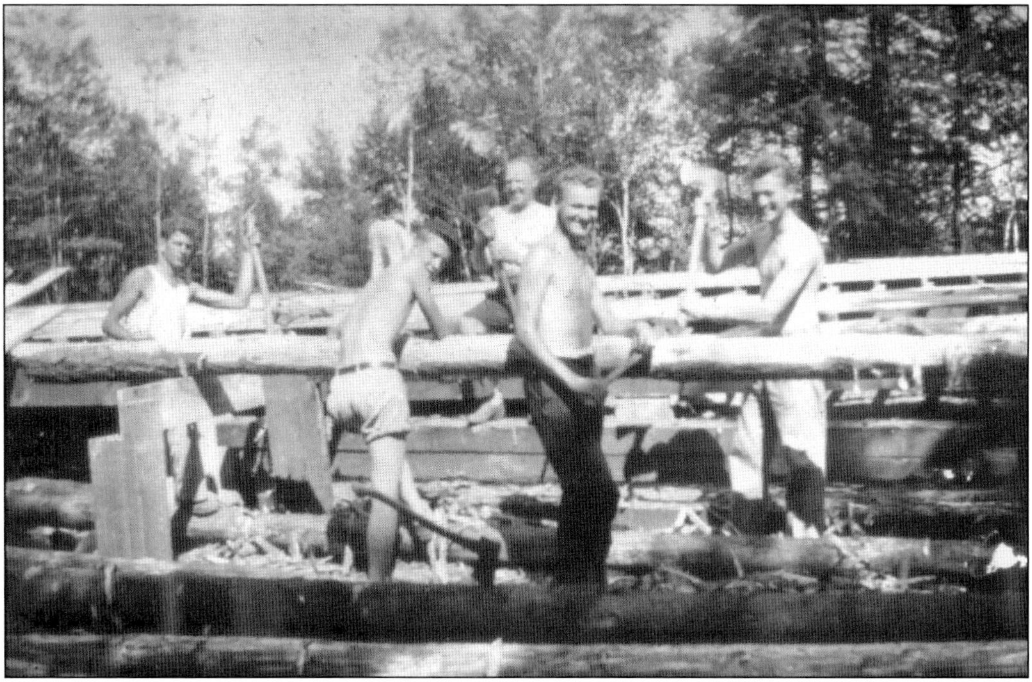

The new dining hall was designed by Harrison Byam. Byam was an architect from Lowell and a Troop 1 committee member. The dining hall uses a truss structure, a relatively new technique at the time, which eliminates the need for supports in the middle of the room. These trusses were fashioned from red pines that stood on the site.

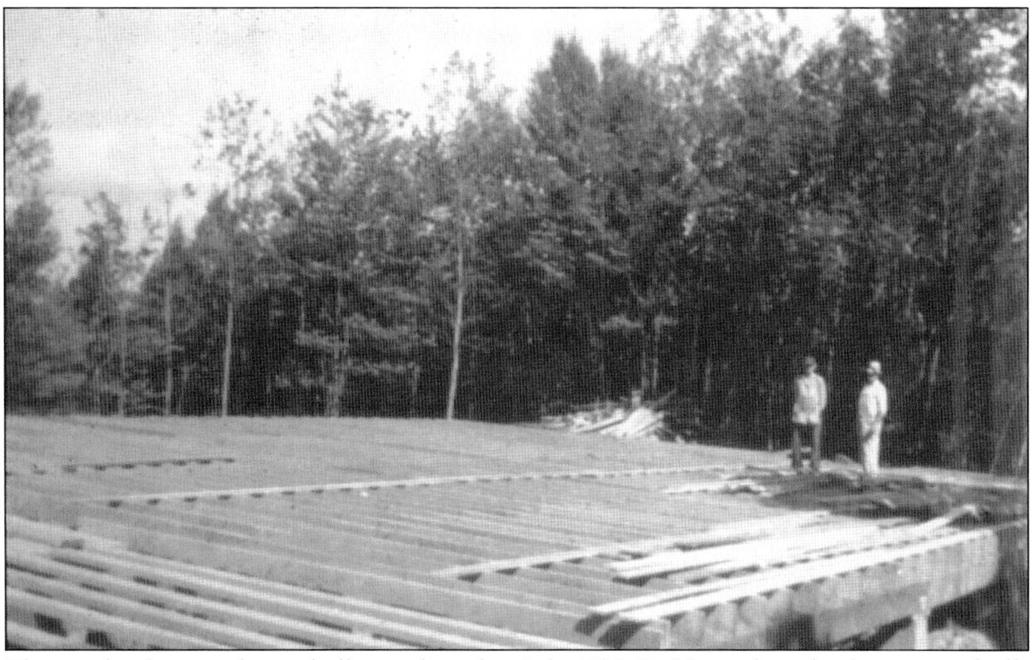

The site for the new dining hall was cleared in July 1936. By November, the footings and sills were in place, the framing and sheathing were done, and the building was closed to the weather. The fireplace is built from local rocks, and the siding is rough-cut white pine.

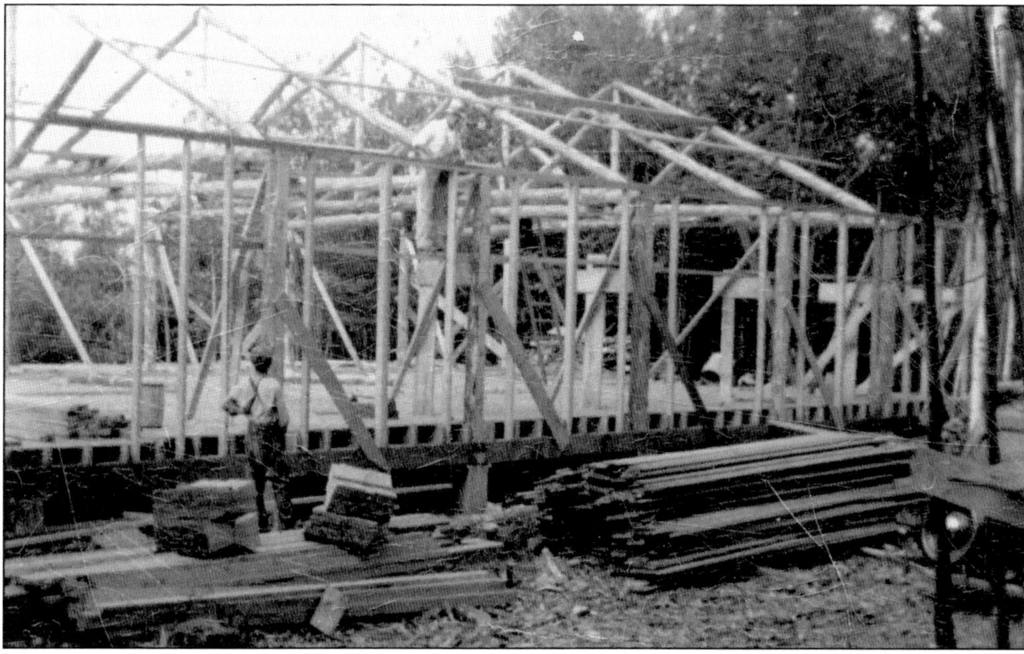

The craftsmanship of the new dining hall was outstanding. In 1936, carpenters would cut the lumber, drill holes for bolts, and plane boards without the use of power tools. Even the cement used for the footings and the stairs would need to be mixed by hand. Attention to detail is always the sign of a great craftsman, and the dining hall would show many.

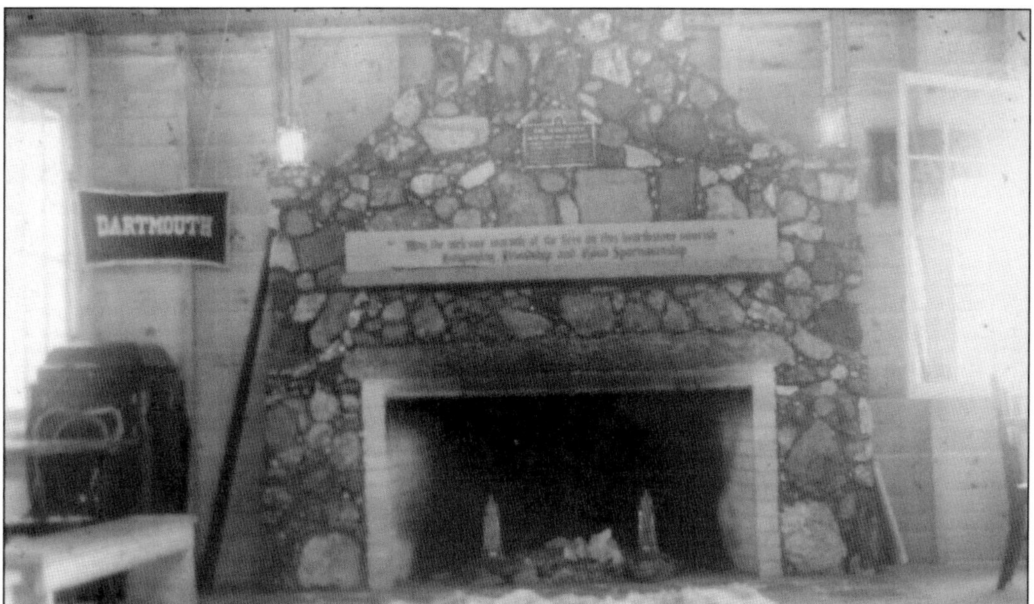

Attendance at Camp Chadwick was down during the summer of 1936 because many troops decided to spend their time working on the new site. During the final Chadwick campfire in August 1936, a metal box was passed around into which each Scout placed a coin. Later the ashes from that campfire were added and the box was placed in the foundation of the fireplace of the new dining hall.

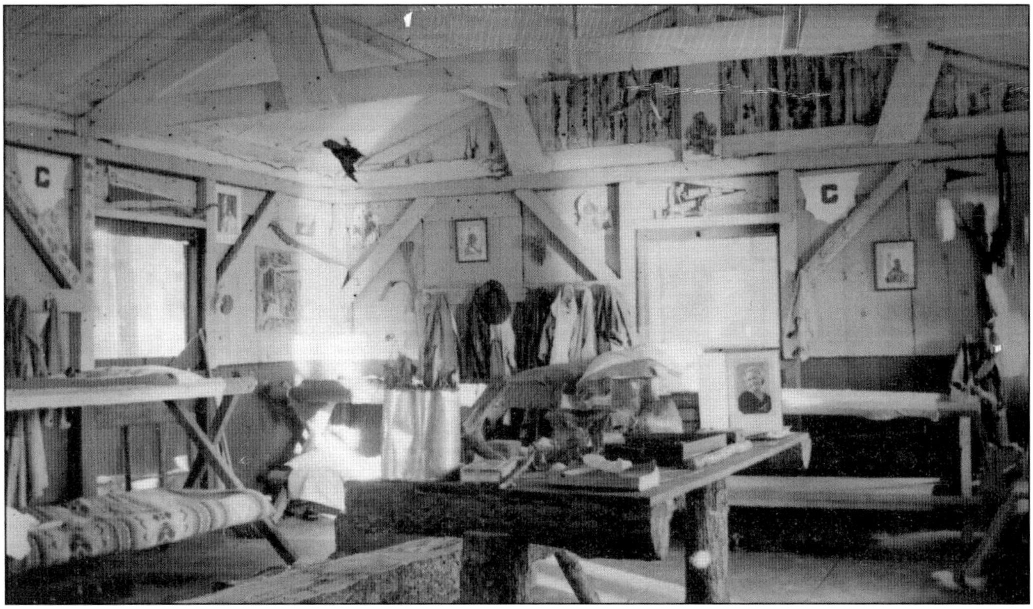

Northbrook Lodge was the first building to be assembled at the new site. It was dismantled at Camp Chadwick and reassembled in Northwood. Work crews that built the dining hall would stay in Northbrook. Inside there was an old cast-iron coal-fueled stove that was used to cook food for the workers.

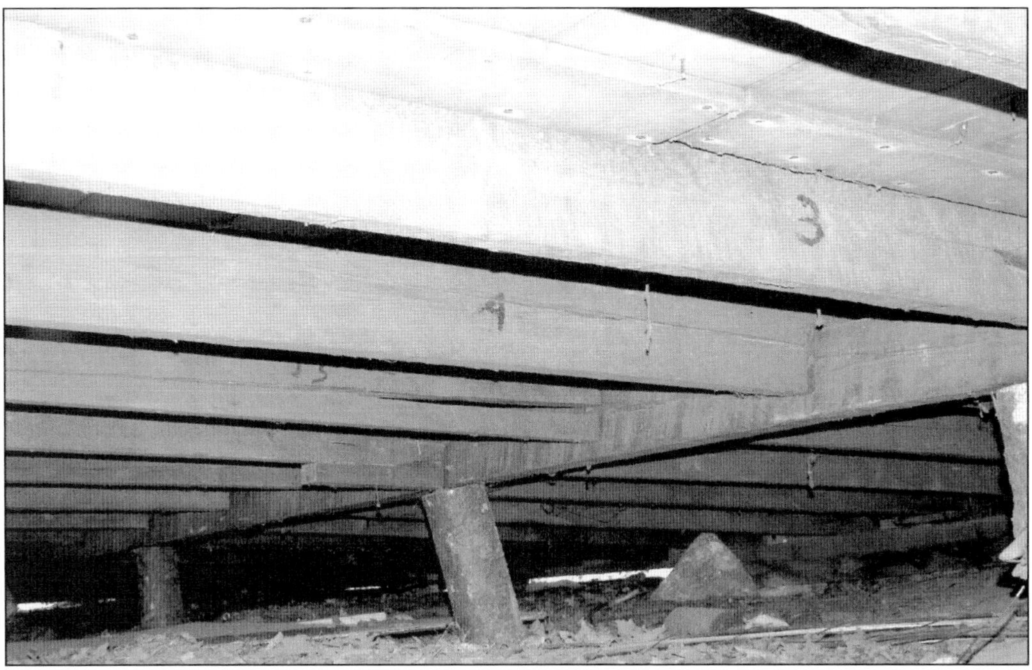

Before being moved from Camp Chadwick to Northwood, each piece of every building was dismantled and carefully labeled for transport on one of the many trucks loaned by local businesses. A total of 16 buildings would be brought to the new site in this way. Even now, after 70 years, the marks used to reassemble the buildings in their new locations are still clearly visible on the floor joists.

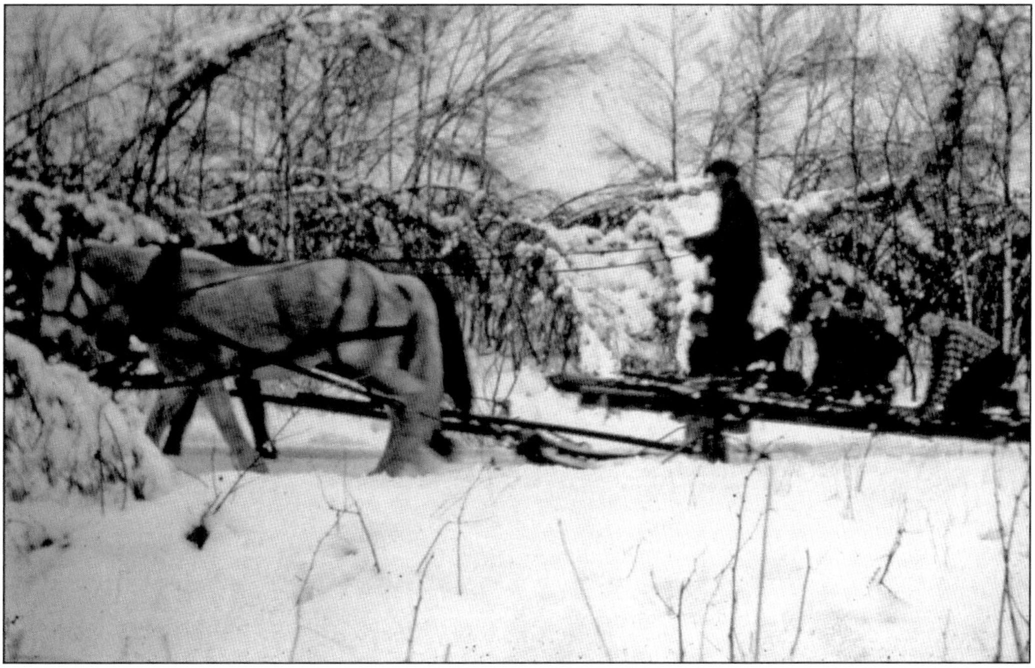

The New Site Committee was well aware that in order to have the camp ready they would need to work through the winter of 1936–1937. In fact, they picked up the pace. Often the road that leads into the camp was impassable by the trucks of the day. These trucks travelled the 60 miles from Dunstable to Northwood only to be stopped at the camp gate. Horse-drawn sleds were used to keep the material and buildings moving into camp. Workers braved the cold, and on snow-covered work sites they continued with multiple construction projects. Only two weekends brought weather so inclement that work was not able to continue.

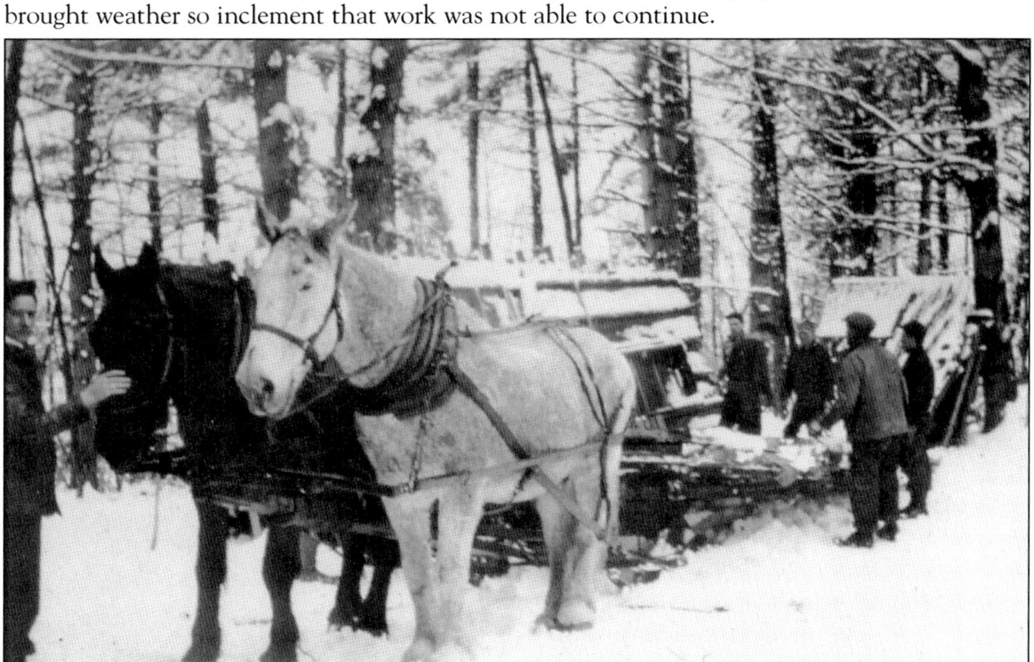

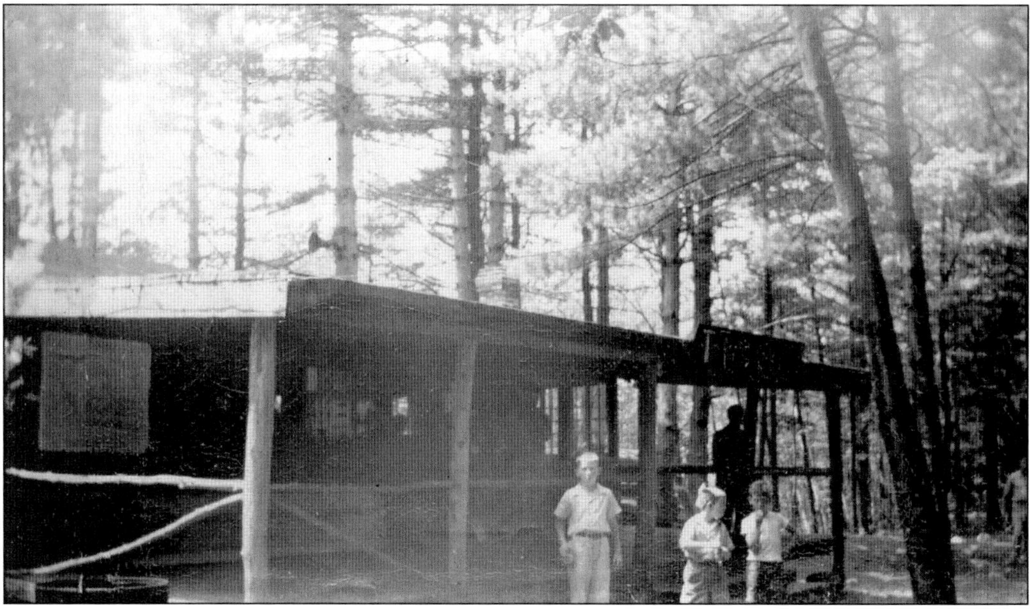

The trading post and the So-Kee-Tay cabins were moved from Camp Chadwick to Northwood. The trading post also served as the camp office. It was officially named Williams Lodge in 1939 in honor of Wah-Tut-Ca's first camp director of the first two seasons, Gordon R. Williams. In 1969, Williams Lodge was replaced with a new administration building on the same site and the name Williams Lodge was kept for the new building. The So-Kee-Tay cabins were located in the So-Kee-Tay campsite, now known as Wannalancit campsite. These buildings housed the youngest boys who attended the new camp. Two of these cabins are still standing today as they did in 1937: one in its original So-Kee-Tay location and one that was moved to Shanawanda campsite. Two more were combined to build the Cobbler Shop that stands today at the camp entrance.

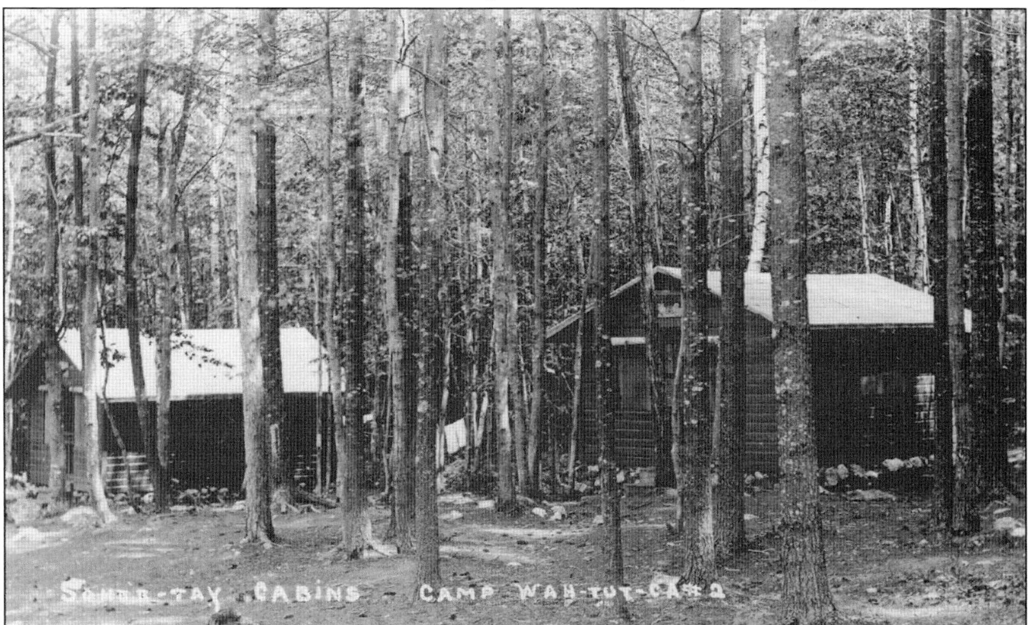

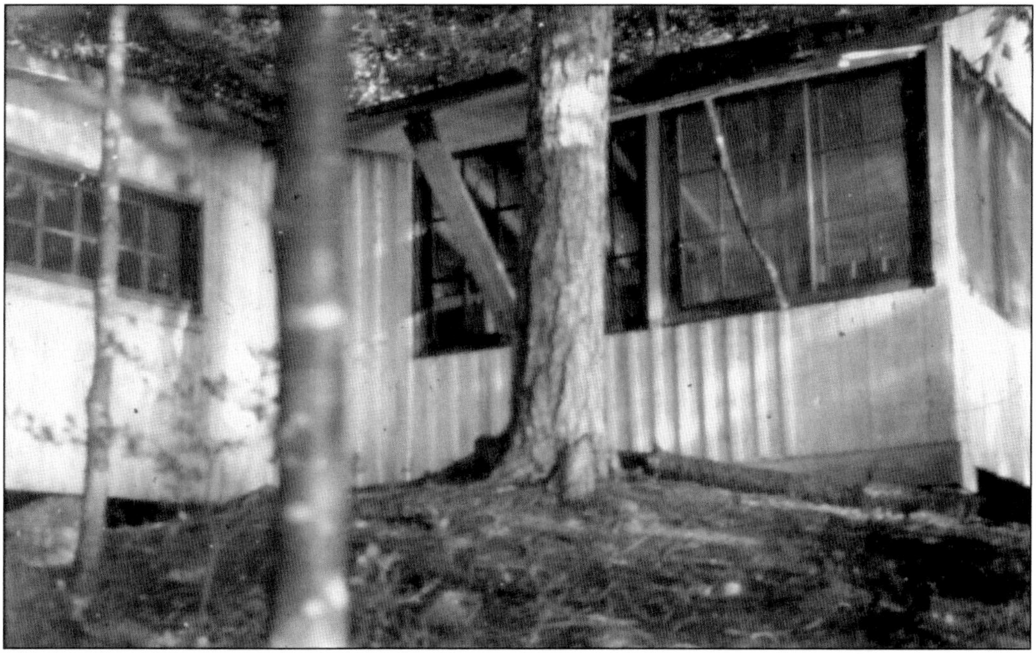

Another Chadwick building assembled at the new site was the camp hospital. The camp hospital had a large solarium that overlooked Northwood Lake. It was painted white so that it would stand out from the other camp buildings. It was replaced as the camp hospital in the 1940s. It was torn down in 1974.

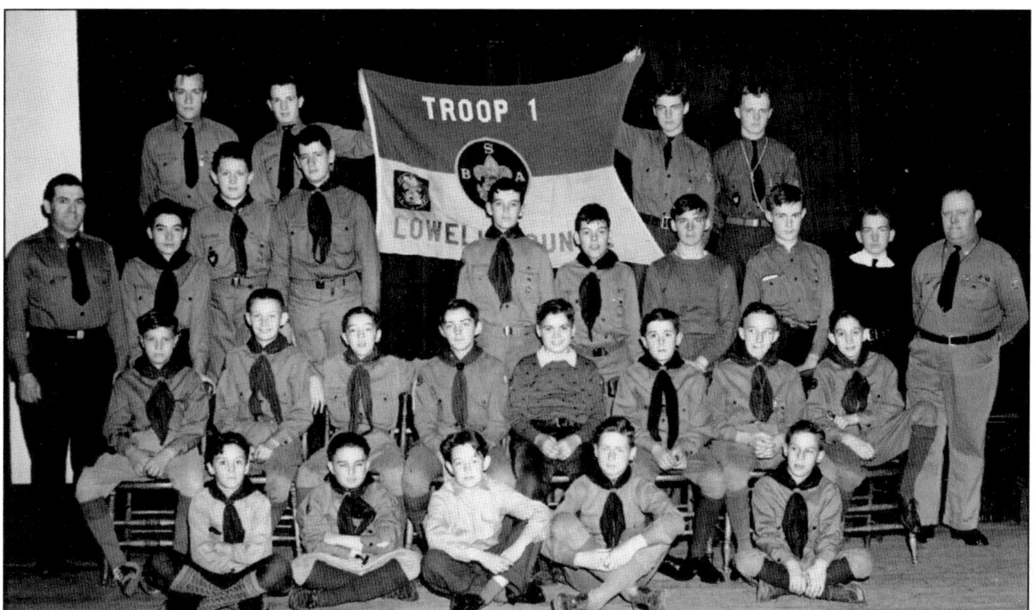

The New Site Committee held a contest to name the new camp. The winning entry, Wa-Tut-Ca, was submitted by Robert W. Foisey of Troop 1 who was awarded two weeks at camp. The new name was announced at the council's annual camp reunion and was received enthusiastically. The *h* was added soon after to aid in pronunciation. The name *Wa-Tut-Ca* means "For Friends and Brothers."

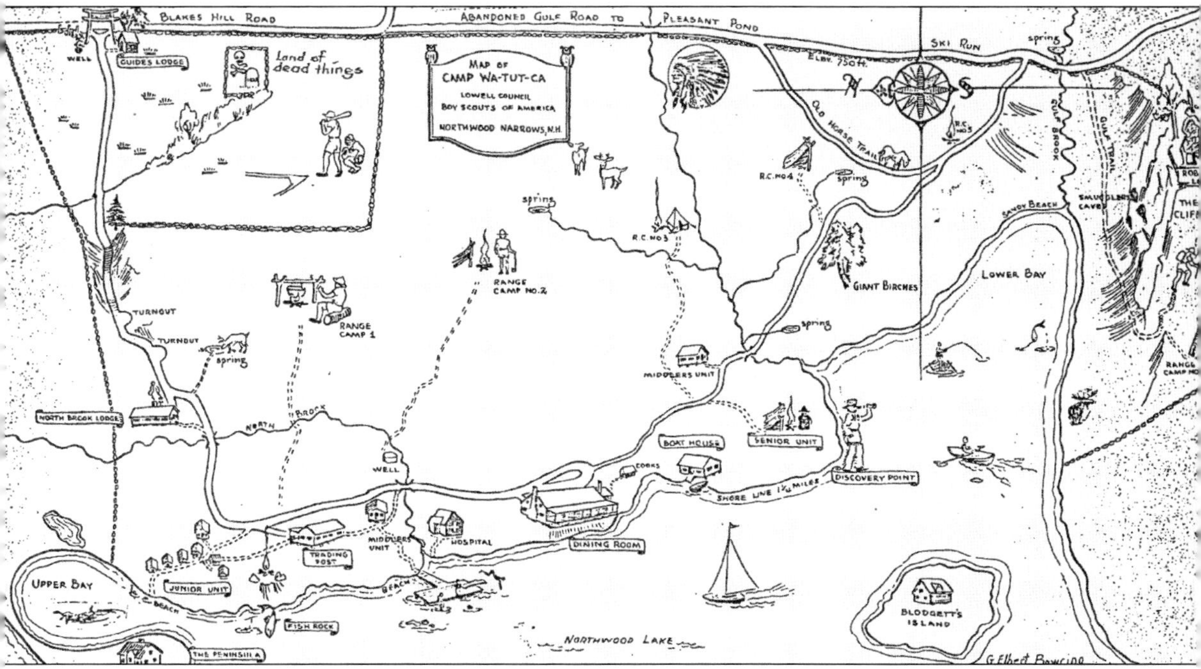

The first map of Wah-Tut-Ca was drawn by G. Elbert Bowring. Bowring was a Camp Chadwick and Wah-Tut-Ca staff member. The map was included in the 1937 camp folder and for the first time Scouts and Scouters were able to see the layout of the camp. Site names from Camp Chadwick were taken to the new site: So-Kee-Tay for the junior unit, Kemosabee for the first-middlers, and Passaconaway for the second-middlers. The senior camp was more often referred to by its geographic location, Discovery Point. In addition to the layout of the camp, the map shows many of the natural elements that attracted the New Site Committee to this location. The sandy beaches, the springs and streams, the cliffs, the caves, and even a stand of large birch trees were viewed as something worth exploring. Compared to Camp Chadwick, Wah-Tut-Ca was seen as a massive wilderness.

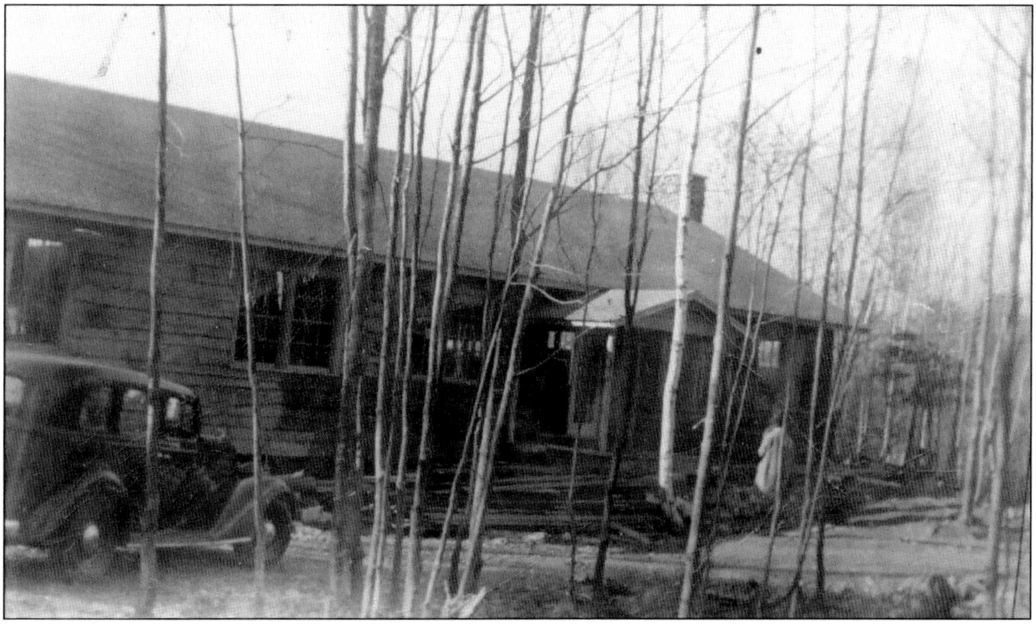

It is a testament to the determination of the New Site Committee and the leadership of Charles A. Robinson that the camp would be built in a little more than a year's time. Robinson would not live to see the opening of the second camp season. In 1939, Wah-Tut-Ca's dining hall was officially named Robinson Lodge in honor of the one man who, more than anyone else, was responsible for building Wah-Tut-Ca.

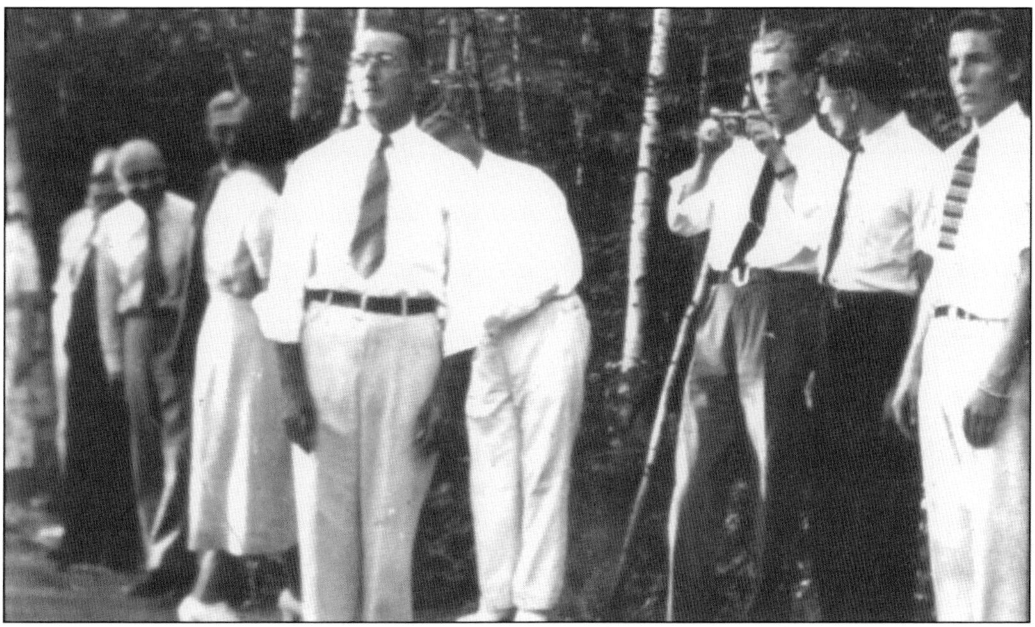

On July 4, 1937, Wah-Tut-Ca was ready to open for its first season. Gordon R. Williams, Scout executive and camp director, is seen here at the opening day festivities. In the evening, a fireworks display was put on by Lowell's Pollards department store. During the festivities, one of the dignitaries in attendance congratulated Robinson on the completion of the camp. Robinson responded, "Wah-Tut-Ca will never be completed."

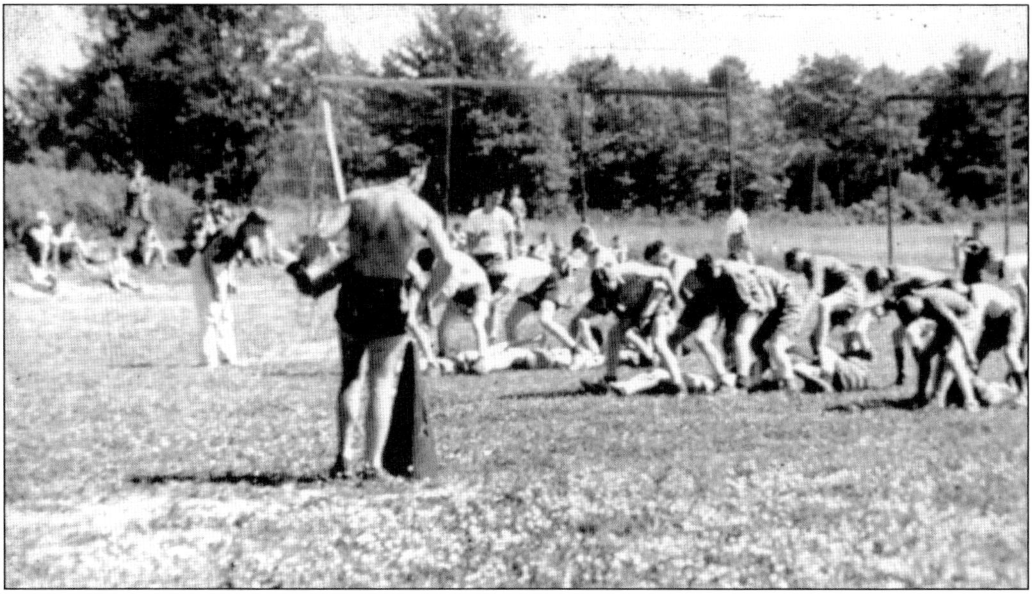

The program at Wah-Tut-Ca during the first summer was a continuation of the program that was in place at Camp Chadwick. Athletics continued to play a large role in the daily activities. Boys are seen here playing on a field that for generations had been used by the residents of Blake's Hill as farmland.

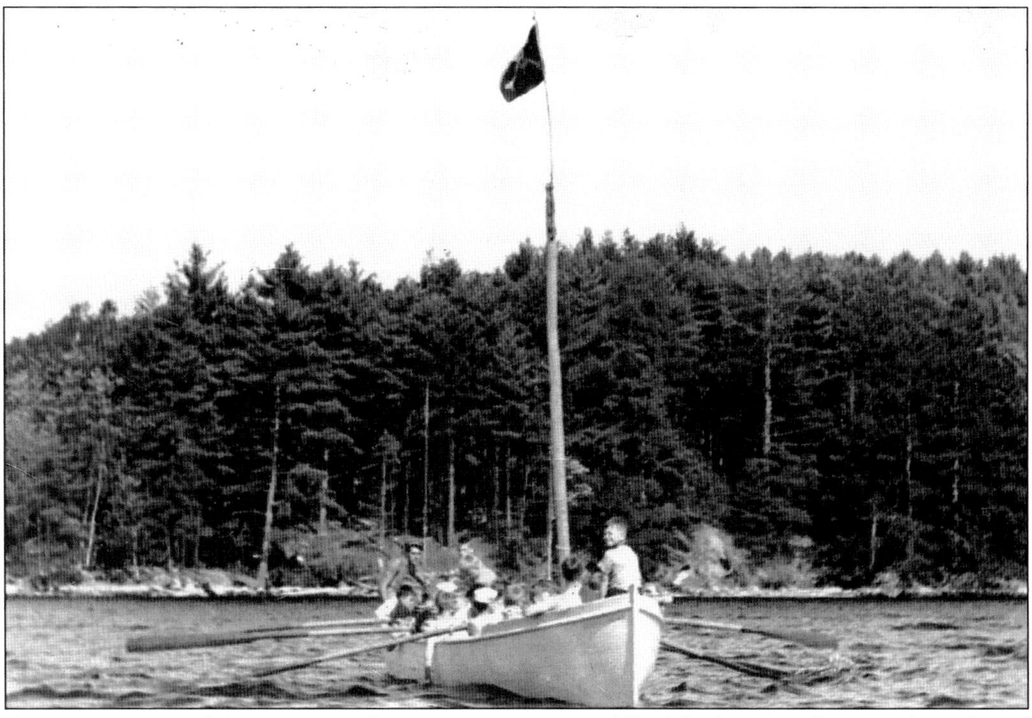

Aquatics are one of the most popular activities in camp. All of the boats and canoes from Camp Chadwick were trucked to their new home in Northwood at the end of the 1936 season. The $90 cost of moving the whaleboats, "paid by a friend," was quite a large sum when compared to the $7 to $8 per boy it would cost for a week at Wah-Tut-Ca in 1937.

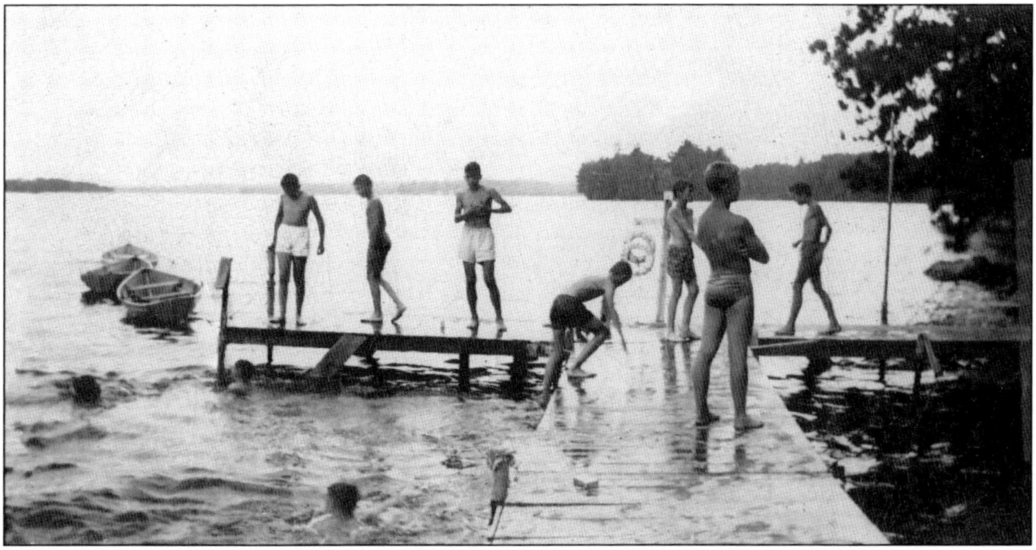

Three waterfronts were planned at Wah-Tut-Ca, but only two, located at So-Kee-Tay and Kemosabee, were completed in time for the summer of 1937. Dr. John H. Lambert was skilled in all the waterfront activities. He could often be found at one of the waterfronts, his favorite places in camp, teaching the staff and the campers. He was able to procure two sailboats prior to the 1940 season, and he personally educated and trained the staff in their use. The boats were a big hit, and the staff was always ready to delight the campers and themselves with an afternoon of sailing.

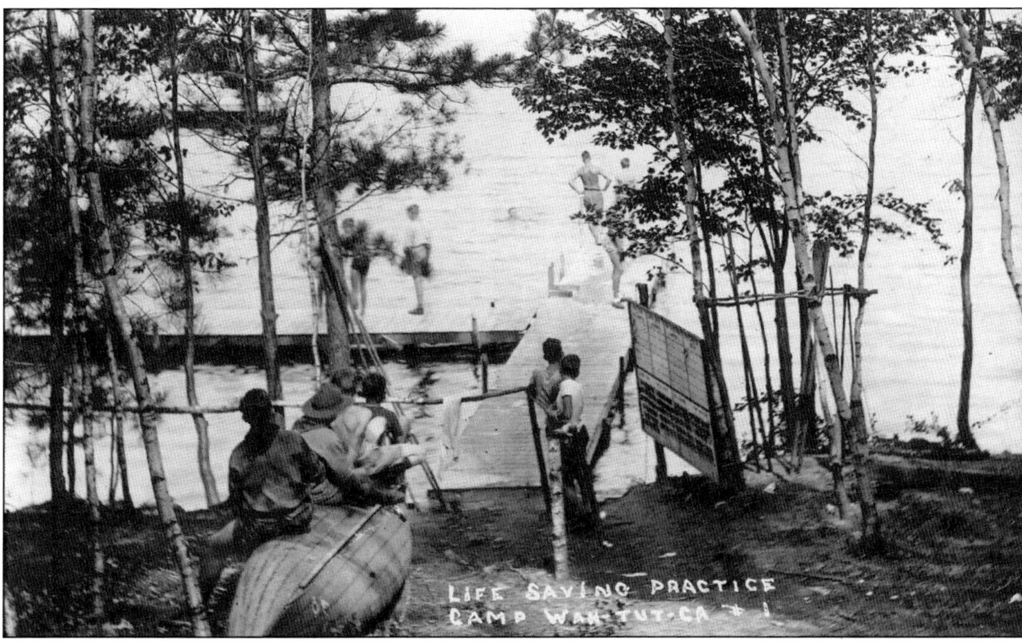

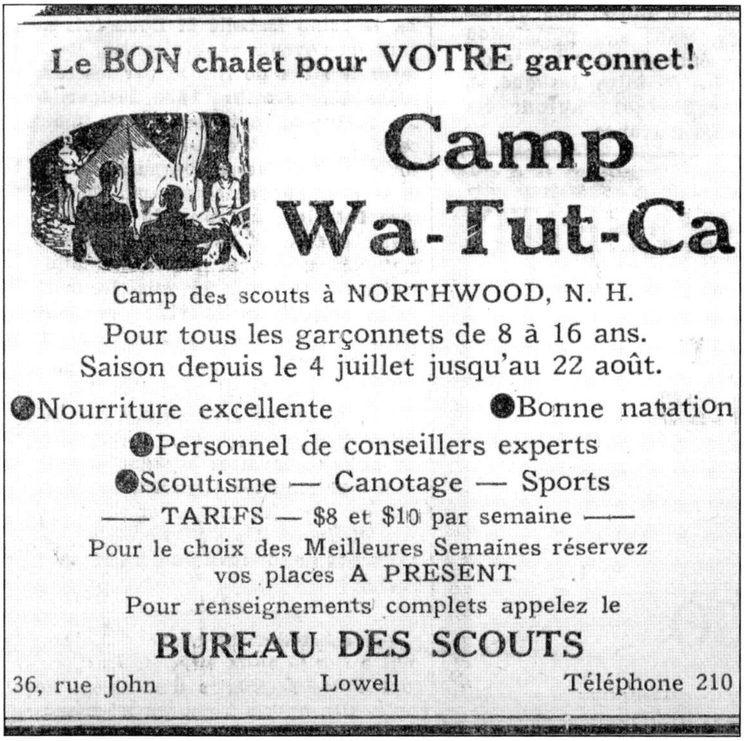

This advertisement from 1937 illustrates the council's promotion to the boys of Greater Lowell. Like Chadwick, Wah-Tut-Ca was not exclusively built for Boy Scouts. The advertisement appeals to the French-speaking population living in Lowell. Although the boys were likely to have spoken English, their parents often kept their native tongue.

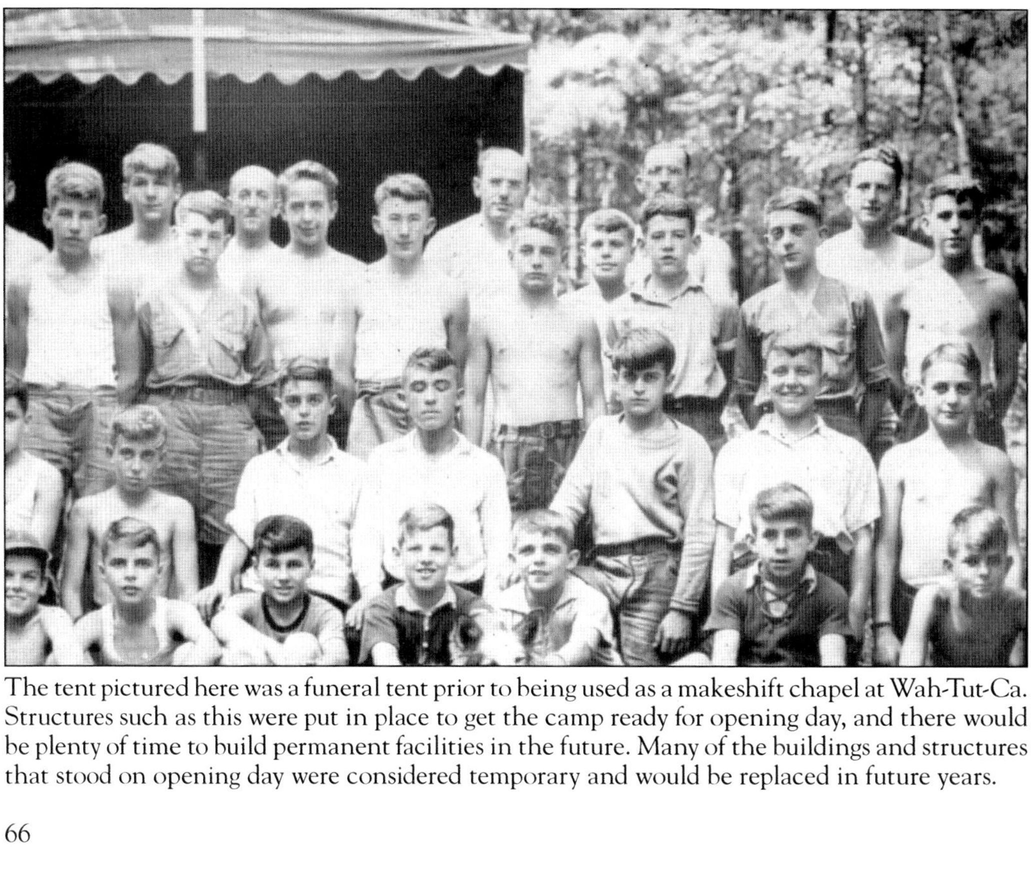

The tent pictured here was a funeral tent prior to being used as a makeshift chapel at Wah-Tut-Ca. Structures such as this were put in place to get the camp ready for opening day, and there would be plenty of time to build permanent facilities in the future. Many of the buildings and structures that stood on opening day were considered temporary and would be replaced in future years.

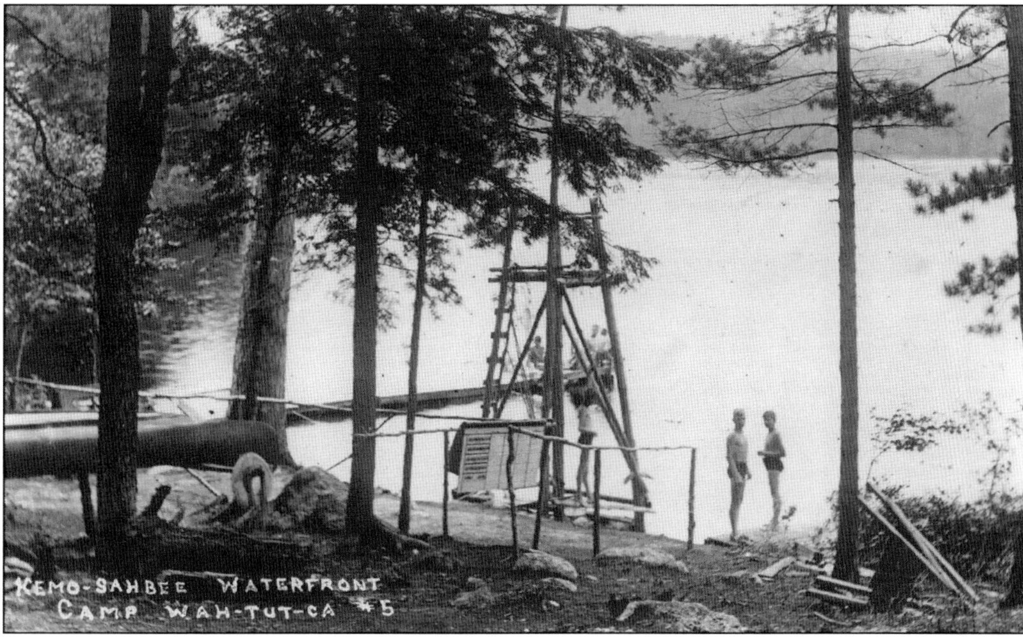

The Kemosabee waterfront was shared by the two middler camps. This waterfront area would be abandoned in the 1940s. In 1938, the Passaconaway waterfront opened and eventually became the main waterfront of the camp. Another waterfront was located at So-Kee-Tay, which was closed in 1952. In the 1990s, with the brief reactivation of Cub camping on the reservation, the So-Kee-Tay waterfront was reopened.

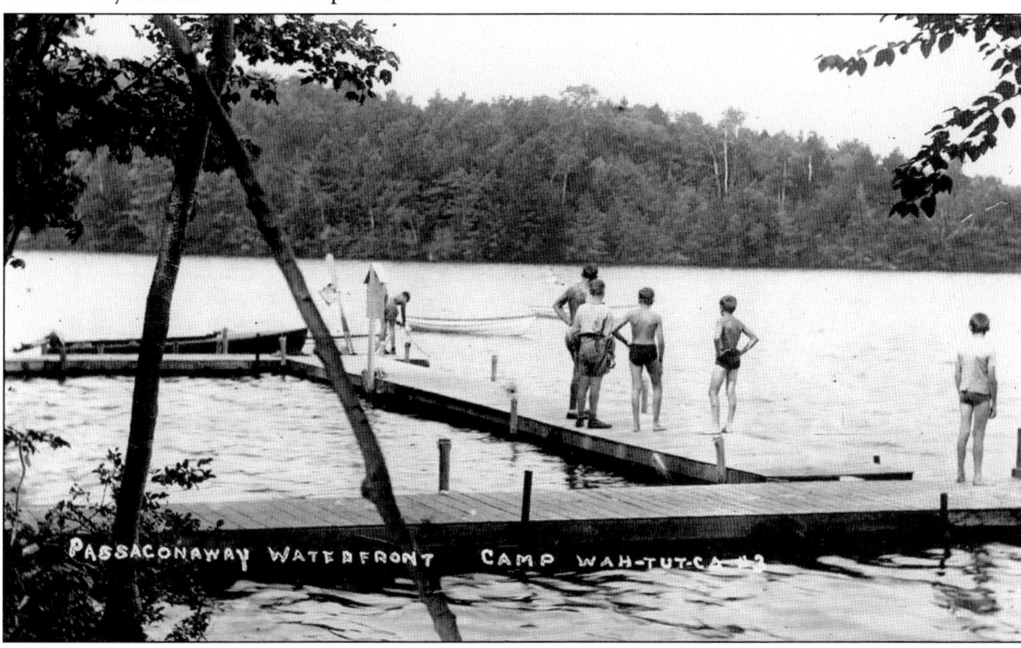

In comparison to Camp Chadwick, everything at Wah-Tut-Ca seemed massive. Even Chadwick's most popular activities on Lake Massapoug seemed to be dwarfed by what could be done on Northwood Lake. It was truly felt that the camp's grand scale was something spectacular. Although it always had its critics, no one could deny Wah-Tut-Ca's beauty and potential.

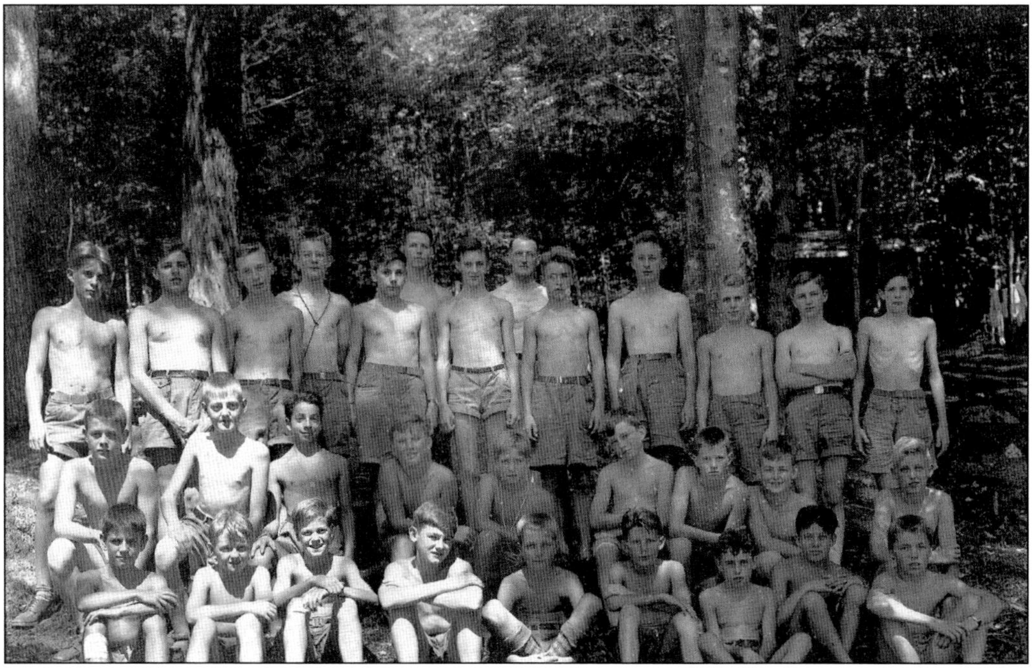

But for a few short weeks in the summer of 1937, when there were heavy rains washing out roads or damaged shelters that needed to be rebuilt, the New Site Committee and the boys who camped that first season at Wah-Tut-Ca enjoyed themselves. The work and planning that went into building the camp had paid off. Boys were camping in a place they could call their own.

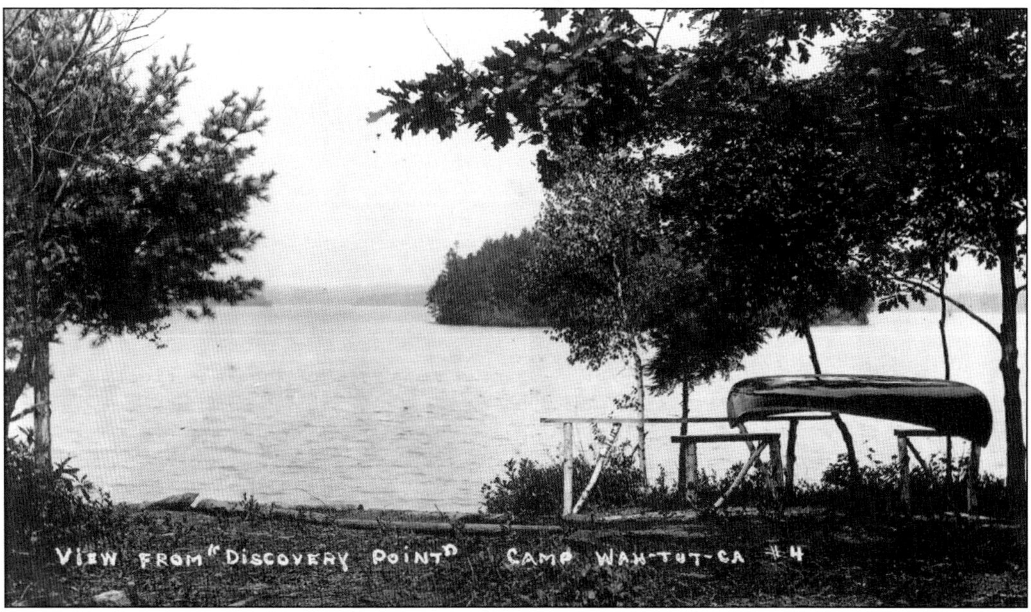

At Discovery Point, Scouts could look out onto Northwood Lake and see the island. Looking up in another direction they could see the cliffs and the gulf. Today it is known as Pawtucket. It has served as the senior camp, a campsite, a campfire circle, and a ceremonial ground. Scouts still gather here in moments of introspection, gazing at the sunsets and waiting for tomorrow's adventure to unfold.

Five

Symbols of America

The distance from the Greater Lowell area to Northwood seemed to grow when the United States entered World War II. Gas and other materials were heavily rationed, and attempts to gain exemptions for boys attending summer camp were denied.

Hal Kellogg was the Scout executive and camp director during most of World War II. His enthusiasm for summer camp was unsurpassed. In his wartime camp promotions, Kellogg said there were four great symbols of America: the Statue of Liberty, the Washington Monument, the Lincoln Memorial, and Wah-Tut-Ca Scout Reservation!

In 1950, a new council executive, John Adams, turned the council on its ear. Unlike his predecessors, he insisted the camp be run strictly under the national guidelines. Adams's tenure as Scout executive was but 15 months. His departure was the result of tensions with the council's executive board. However brief his service, the changes in direction he made were sustained and expanded by his replacement, Edward Butler.

Butler served for 17 years. His personal style was progressive yet measured. He kept a steady pace forward, but allowed the camp and council to keep up with him.

First at Chadwick and then at Wah-Tut-Ca, the Greater Lowell Council had its own honor camper society called the Braves. Started by Gordon R. Williams, the Chadwick and Wah-Tut-Ca Braves were mostly made up of camp staff members.

In 1951, Adams dissolved the Braves and replaced it with the National Order of the Arrow program. Alexander A. Vervaert, who had been a camper in 1937, returned from the war and was the first adviser to the new OA lodge, which he named Wannalancit Lodge No. 451.

One tradition that was continued from the Braves was its ties to camp staff. In its early years, Wannalancit Lodge membership was primarily made up of staff members. Although the OA program would later be expanded, the program of Wannalancit Lodge and Wah-Tut-Ca were always linked.

The postwar economy had relieved the challenges of the distance to Wah-Tut-Ca, but the social revolution of the 1960s had an impact on Scouting across the nation. Youth were developing different interests and needs.

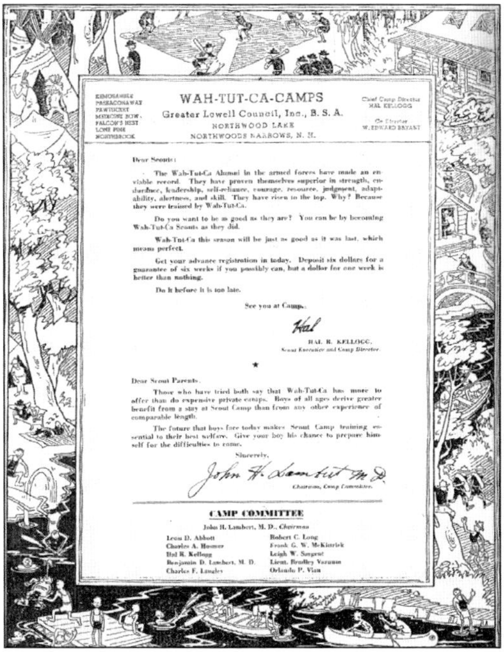

KEMOSABBEE
PASSACONAWAY
PAWTUCKET
MEDICINE BOW
FALCON'S NEST
LONE PINE
NORTHBROOK

WAH-TUT-CA-CAMPS
Greater Lowell Council, Inc., B. S. A.
NORTHWOOD LAKE
NORTHWOODS NARROWS, N. H.

Chief Camp Director
HAL KELLOGG

Co Director
W. EDWARD BRYANT

Dear Scouts:

The Wah-Tut-Ca Alumni in the armed forces have made an enviable record. They have proven themselves superior in strength, endurance, leadership, self-reliance, courage, resource, judgment, adaptability, alertness, and skill. They have risen to the top. Why? Because they were trained by Wah-Tut-Ca.

Do you want to be as good as they are? You can be by becoming Wah-Tut-Ca Scouts as they did.

Wah-Tut-Ca this season will be just as good as it was last, which means perfect.

Get your advance registration in today. Deposit six dollars for a guarantee of six weeks if you possibly can, but a dollar for one week is better than nothing.

Do it before it is too late.

See you at Camp.

Hal

HAL R. KELLOGG,
Scout Executive and Camp Director.

★

Dear Scout Parents.

Those who have tried both say that Wah-Tut-Ca has more to offer than do expensive private camps. Boys of all ages derive greater benefit from a stay at Scout Camp than from any other experience of comparable length.

The future that boys face today makes Scout Camp training essential to their best welfare. Give your boy his chance to prepare himself for the difficulties to come.

Sincerely,

John H. Lambert M.D.
Chairman, Camp Committee.

CAMP COMMITTEE

John H. Lambert, M. D., *Chairman*

Leon D. Abbott	Robert C. Long
Charles A. Hosmer	Frank G. W. McKitrick
Hal R. Kellogg	Leigh W. Sargent
Benjamin D. Lambert, M. D.	Lieut. Bradley Varnum
Charles F. Langley	Orlando P. Vian

Hal Kellogg became Scout executive shortly after the attack on Pearl Harbor. Kellogg, although impressed by the camp itself, was outraged by the poor attendance. In 1942, only about 10 percent of the council's Boy Scouts would attend Wah-Tut-Ca. During the war, many Scouters and college students would enlist and no longer be available for camp staff. Kellogg's fight to keep Wah-Tut-Ca open would be an uphill battle.

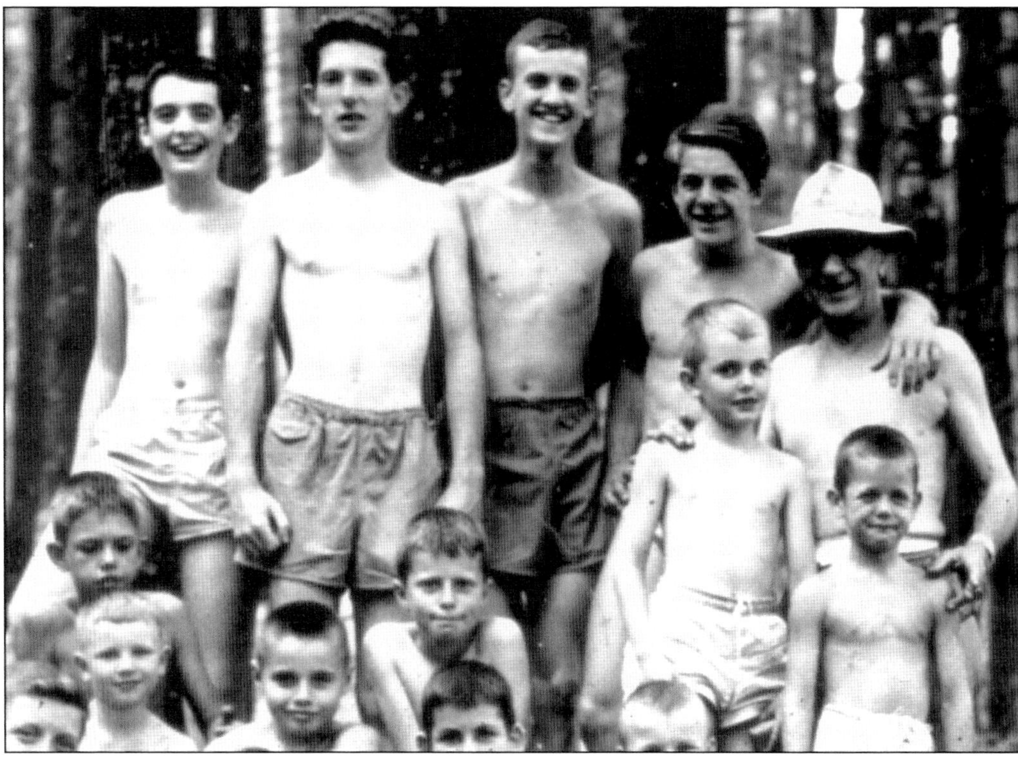

During World War II and throughout the 1940s, the junior non-Scout camp, So-Kee-Tay, would be important to the financial viability of Wah-Tut-Ca. So-Kee-Tay staff is pictured here with some campers. Arthur C. Dawes was So-Kee-Tay's Director seen here wearing a hat at the far right. The National Council would close this camp in the 1950s.

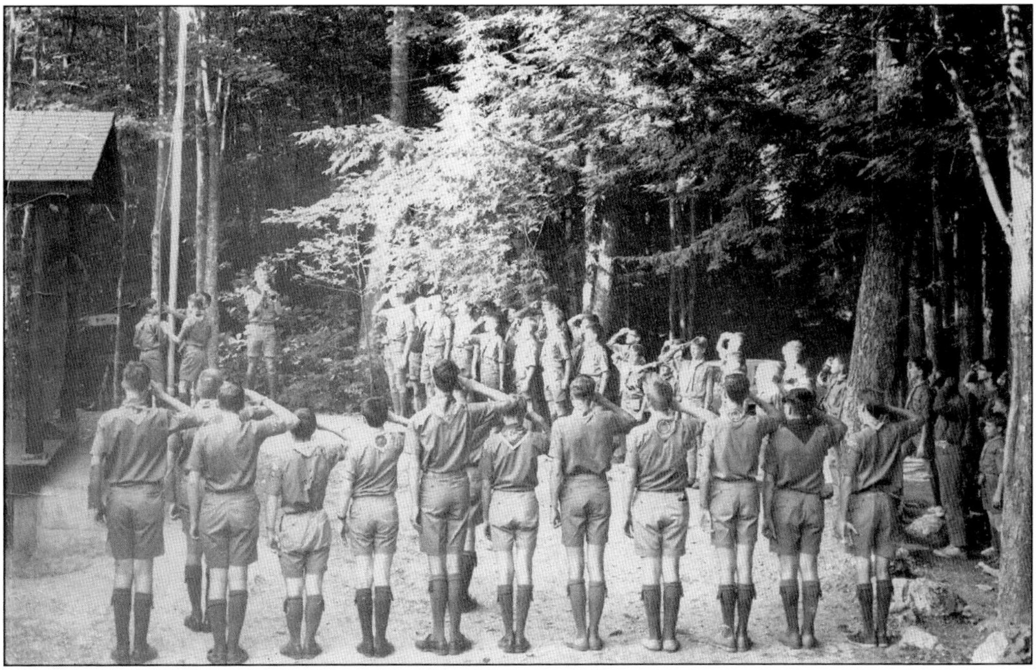

The war changed the camp's program. Appealing to boys who were waiting for their chance to enlist, Wah-Tut-Ca's wartime program included paramilitary features. From the 1944 camp promotion brochure would come "Wah-Tut-Ca will prepare you this season, better than ever before, [for War Service], because we're going to have pre-ranger training with a taste of everything soldiers, sailors and marines get."

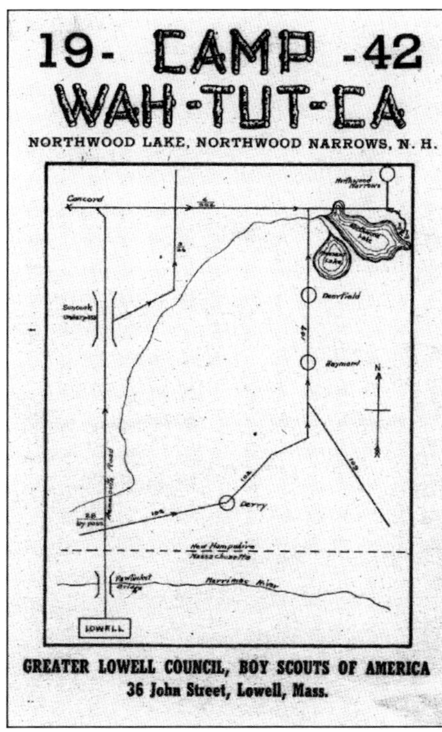

With gasoline rationed to three gallons per week, taking a car to camp was almost impossible. This nonproportional 1942 map showed how it was almost a straight line from Lowell to Wah-Tut-Ca. Most boys got to camp by taking a train from Lowell to Concord, then taking a bus to Northwood.

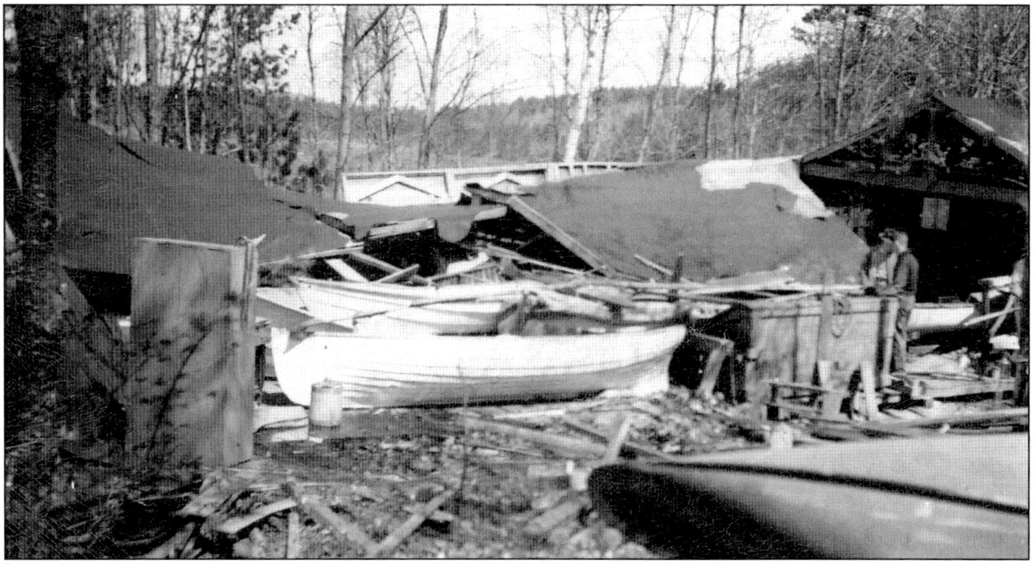

The war resulted in a shortage of manpower and materials. The boathouse was one of the last Chadwick buildings to be reassembled in 1937. In the rush to complete the camp for its opening, several of the buildings were never considered to be used for more than one or two seasons. The boathouse collapsed in the spring of 1945.

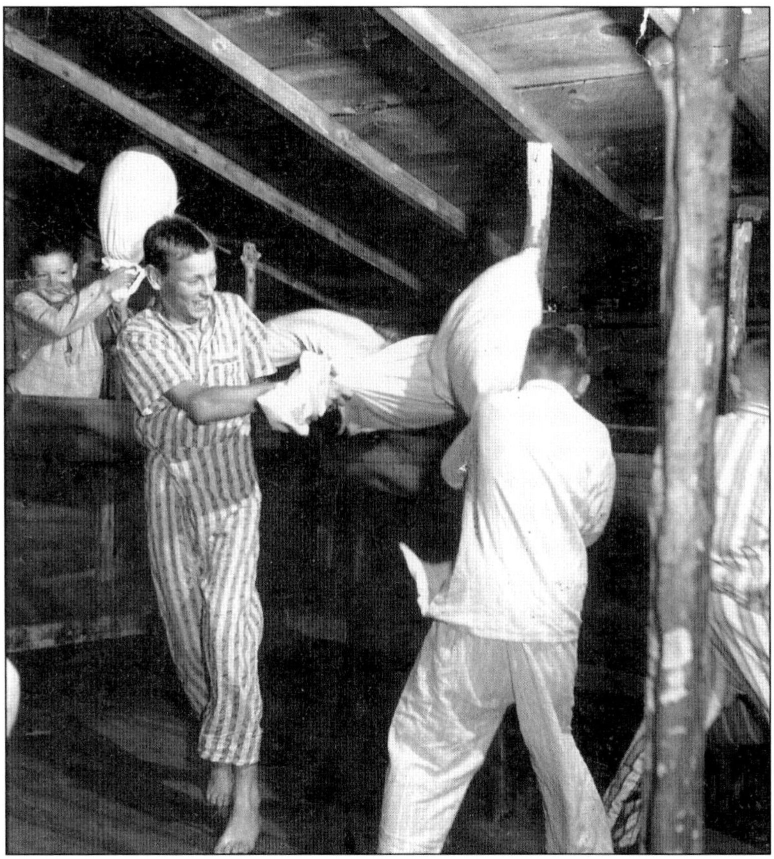

For many that would fight in World War II, Wah-Tut-Ca would be the last place they could just be a boy. A harmless pillow fight would be forgotten, but the memories of happiness and laughter would remain. Boys would leave these battles at Wah-Tut-Ca for the real thing in Europe and the Pacific.

The world at war was in stunning contrast to the peace of Northwood Lake. The sound of loons and paddles skimming the water was nothing like the sounds of battle. In every town in Greater Lowell, boys returned from Wah-Tut-Ca and exchanged their Boy Scout uniform for a military one. Those who served on the beaches of Normandy and Iwo Jima undoubtedly longed for the shoreline of Northwood Lake.

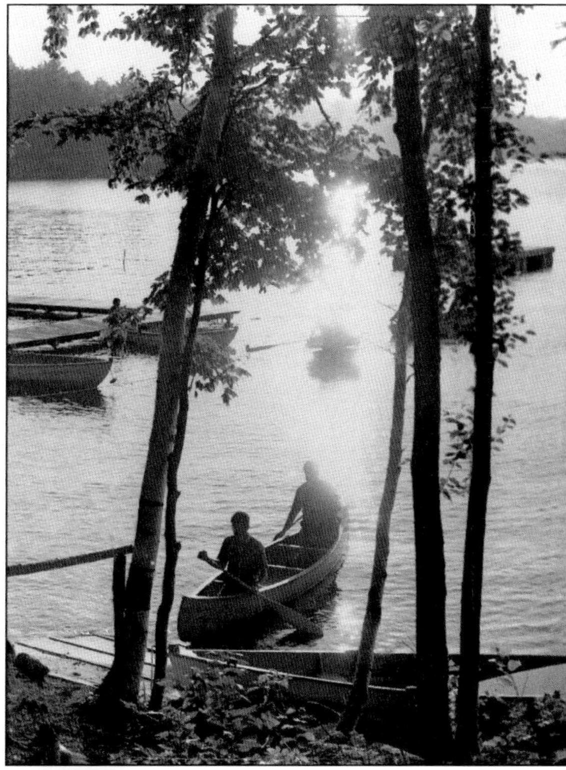

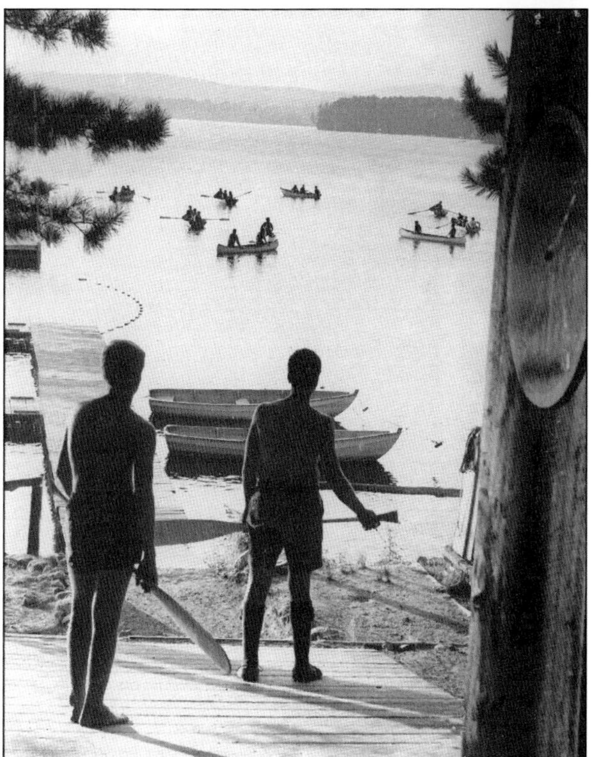

For the Scouts of Wah-Tut-Ca there were two worlds. The freedom to launch a boat and explore the lake is such a simple thing. In Europe and the Pacific, many of Wah-Tut-Ca's alumni gave their lives to preserve such simple pleasures.

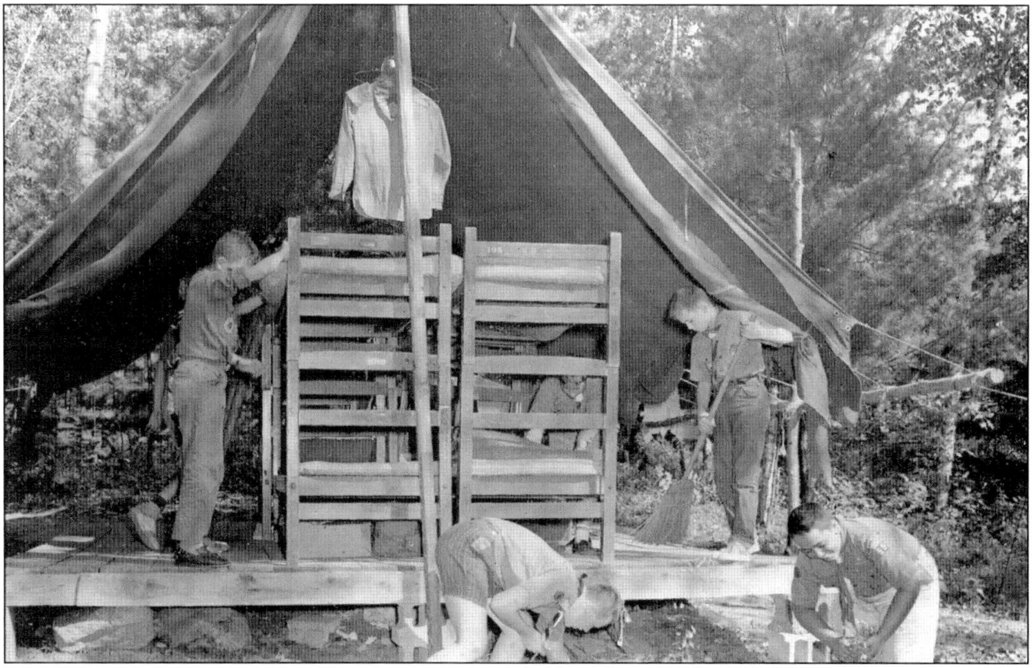

Most of the boys at camp lived in dwellings like these. From the 1940s to the 1960s, they slept in large tents on platforms. Each of these tents held 4 to 10 boys in bunk beds. The responsibility for keeping the area clean was shared by the group. In the 1960s, they would be replaced by two-man tents.

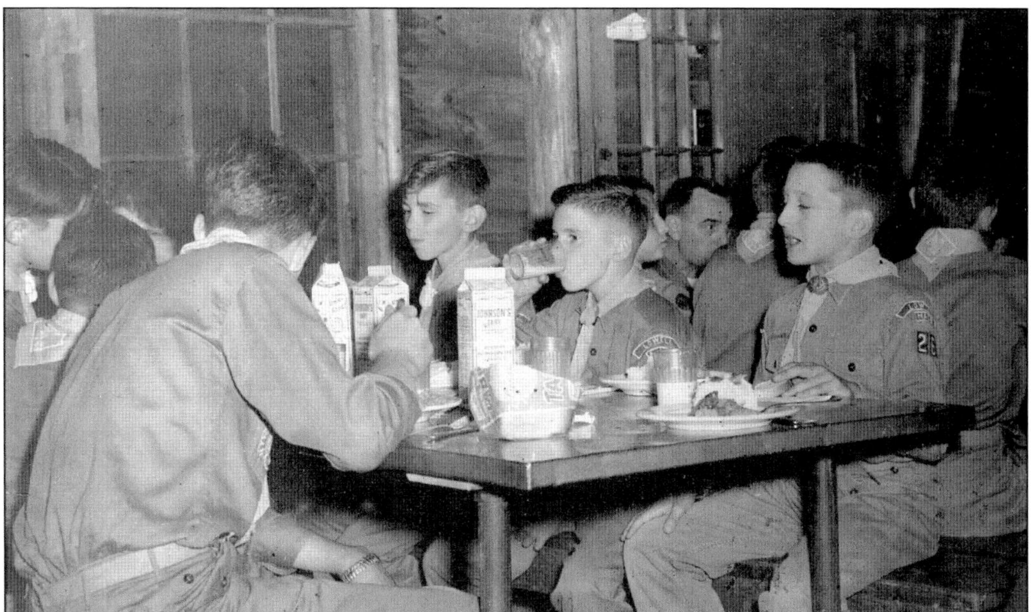

Hal Kellogg spent considerable time with war rationing boards asking for exemptions to operate the camp. Food was hard to come by. Scouts were required to bring their food ration book to camp. It was suggested that although a camper could bring his sugar ration book, the preferred option was to bring a half pound of sugar per week for the period of his stay.

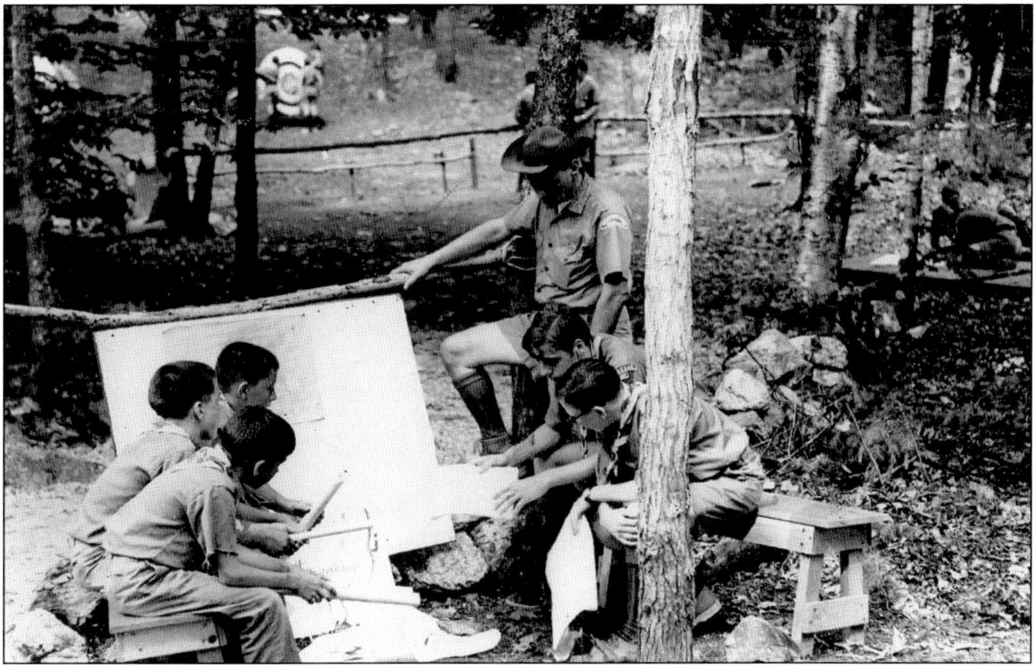

Other than the waterfront and the shooting ranges, few programs of camp had defined areas. The camp's program was activity based. A schedule of programs was made, and these activities were changed on a daily basis. Staff members were generalists. One day they ran a nature hike and the next day taught how to use a map and compass.

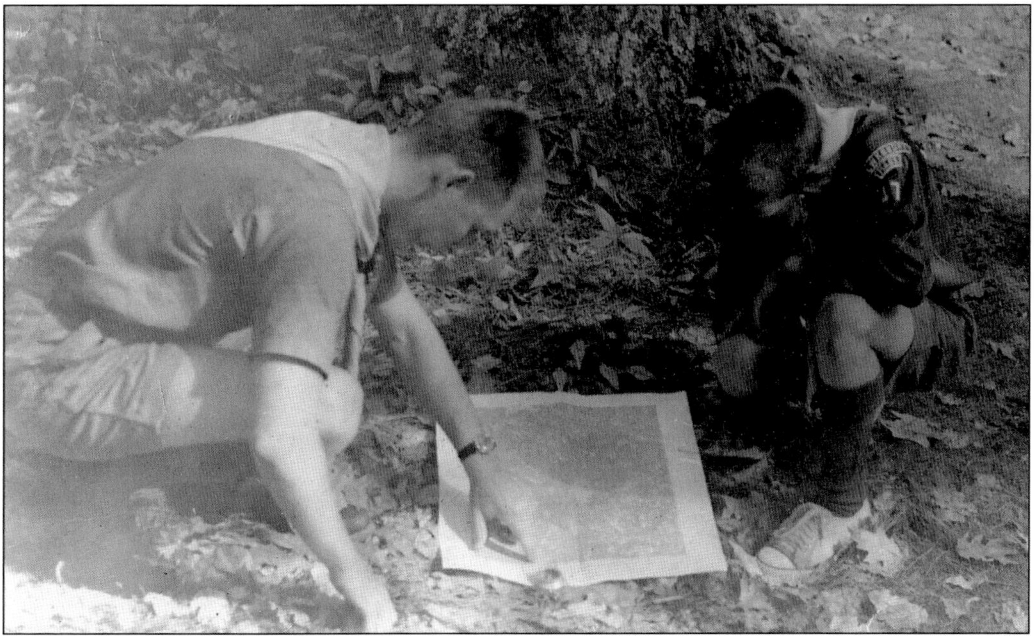

Learning to find one's way by map and compass is a skill that has been taught from the very beginning of Scouting. It is something that one boy could teach another. As a result, both boys are learning. One learned how to use the map, and the other, how to teach. At Wah-Tut-Ca there were, and still are, places to explore and opportunities to grow.

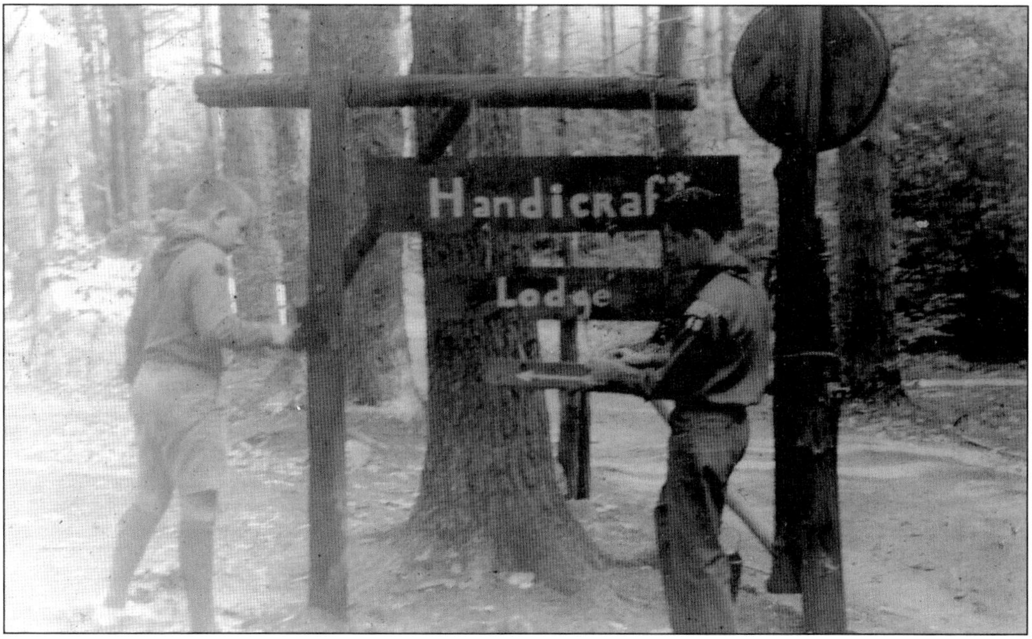

Handicrafts are another activity associated with summer camps. Woodcarving, leatherwork, and basketry were some of the options offered. Throughout its history, the craft area at Wah-Tut-Ca was located in several areas. In the 1940s, it was based at So-Kee-Tay Lodge (So-Kee-Tay Lodge would later be renamed Wannalancit). Since 1970 handicrafts have been located in Abbot Lodge.

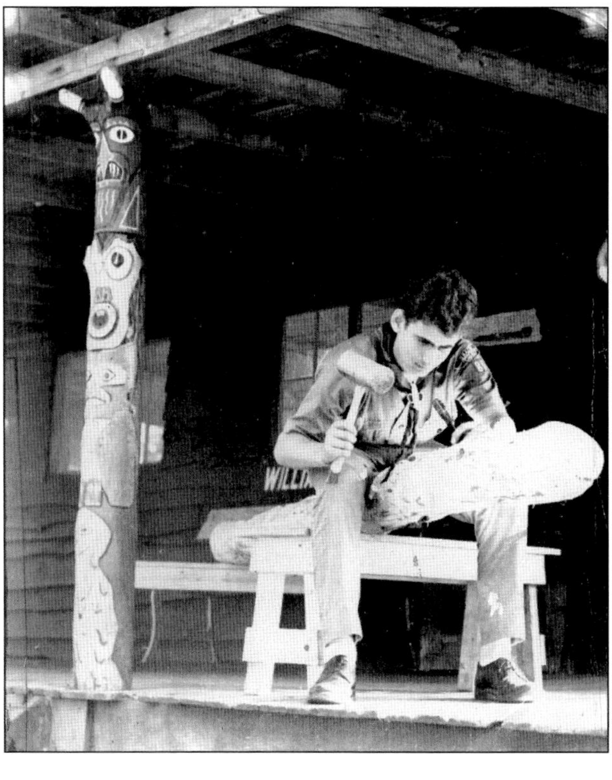

Crafts provide boys an opportunity for expression. Here a Scout is carving a totem pole. These poles would be used to embellish the front porch of Williams Lodge. Although the original building was torn down and rebuilt in 1968, these poles still exist. They have been used in multiple program areas, such as the Indian Village, Scoutcraft, and the Frontier.

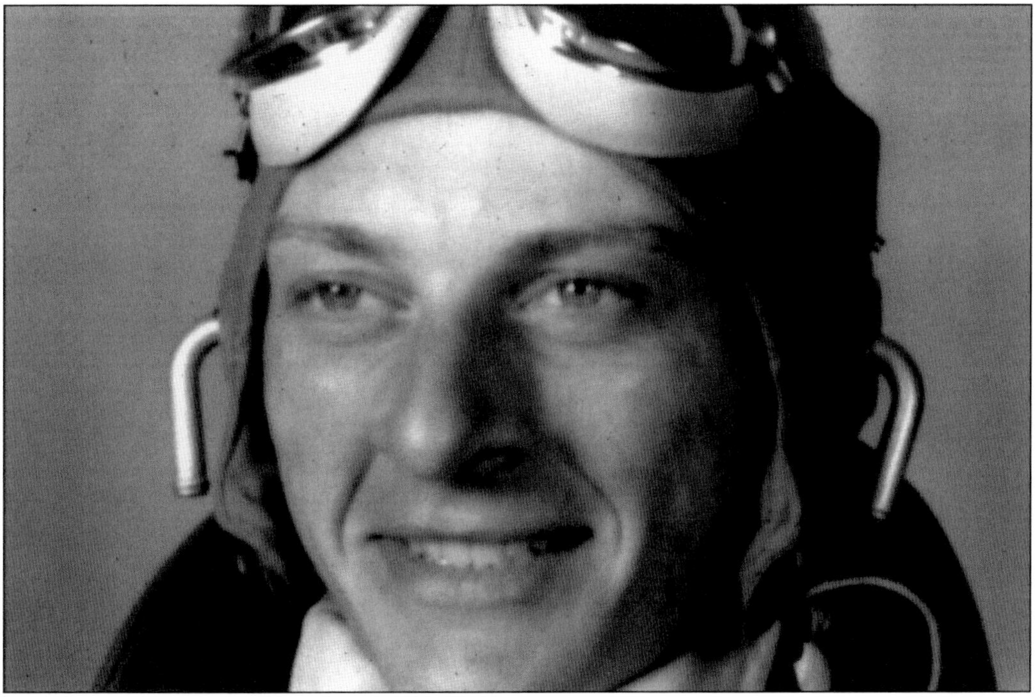

Alexander A. Vervaert was like many of Wah-Tut-Ca's campers who went to war. Upon his return he would become one of the most dedicated leaders of the Greater Lowell Council and Wah-Tut-Ca. His service spanned decades and inspired generations. He had a powerful theatrical voice and spoke with great eloquence. Although he served Scouting in a variety of positions, Wah-Tut-Ca would always be the center of his heart and spirit.

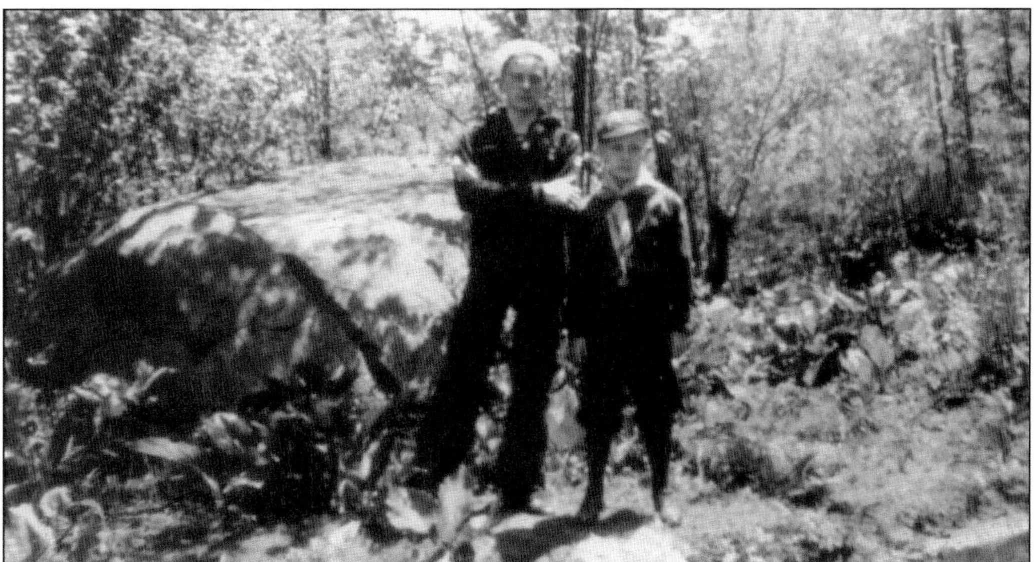

As a boy, Alexander was a Sea Scout and is pictured here with his brother John, who was a Cub Scout. Alexander grew up in the French American section of Lowell and was a camper at Wah-Tut-Ca during its opening season. After the war, he returned to Lowell and worked for the Lowell Electric Light Company, which later became Mass Electric.

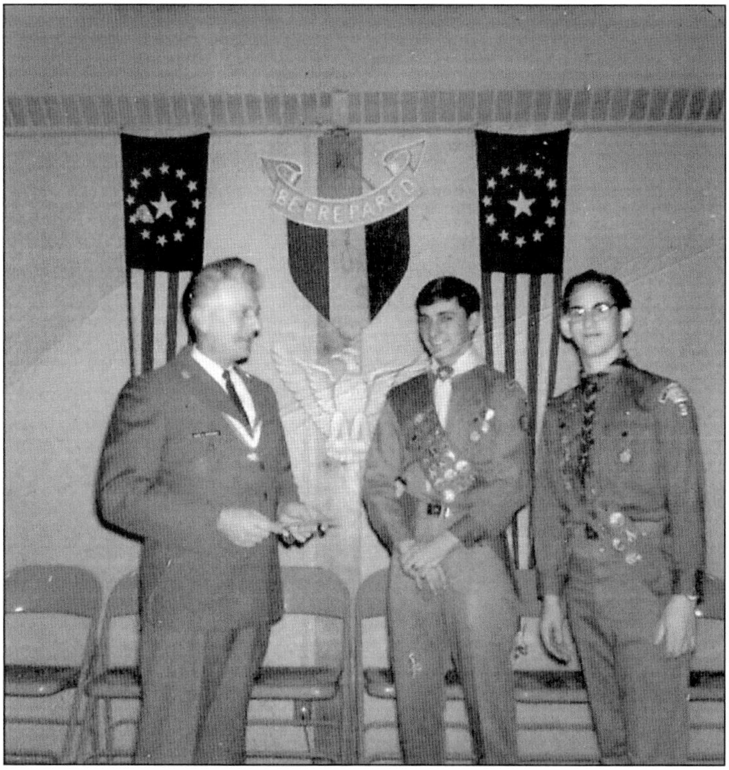

In the 1950s and 1960s, Alexander A. Vervaert served as the council's commissioner. His dramatic speaking style placed him in demand at any type of gathering such as this Eagle Scout Court of Honor. There was more to Vervaert than the powerful tone of his voice. He had an exceptional gift to use words in a way that expressed the values of Scouting and its importance to youth.

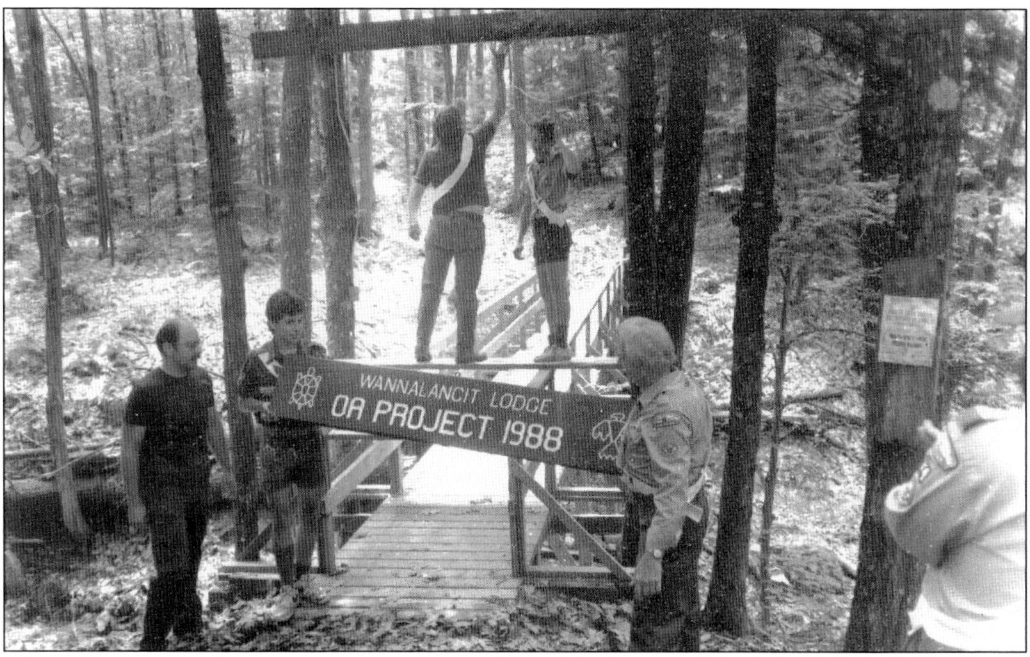

Most of Vervaert's weekends belonged to Wah-Tut-Ca. From the 1940s until his death in 1991, every building and project at Wah-Tut-Ca benefited from his handiwork. As a craftsman he insisted on quality, no detail was to be compromised. How it looked was just as important as how it stood the test of time.

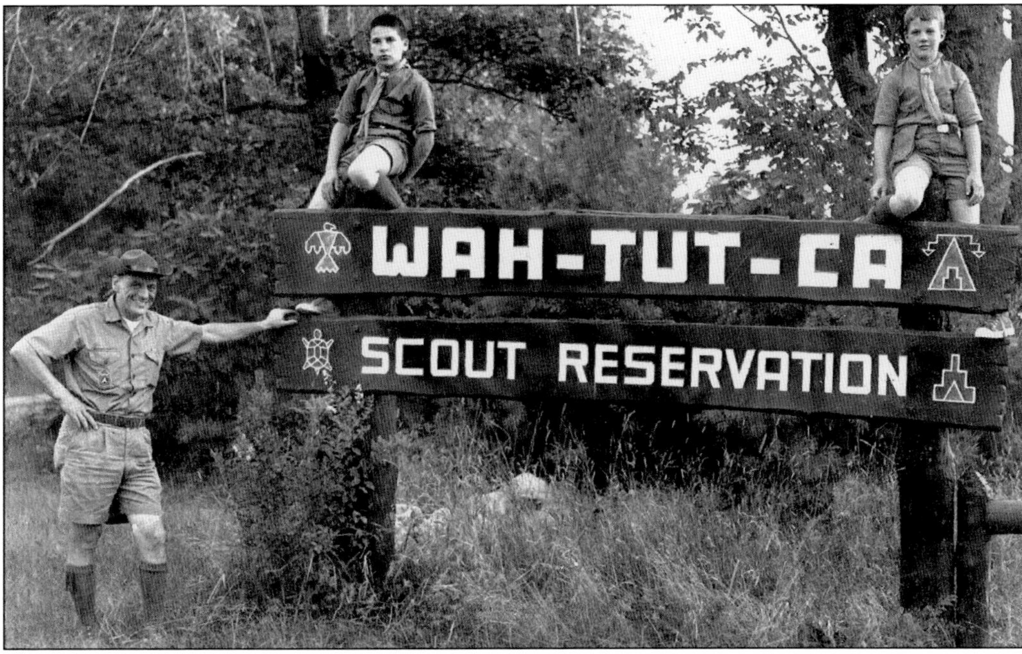

The camp gate was redesigned and rebuilt in the 1950s by Vervaert. Like all of Vervaert's camp projects, the artwork had small details that reflected a Native American theme. He treated Wah-Tut-Ca as a large stage for the great performances of youth development, and he dressed that stage appropriately.

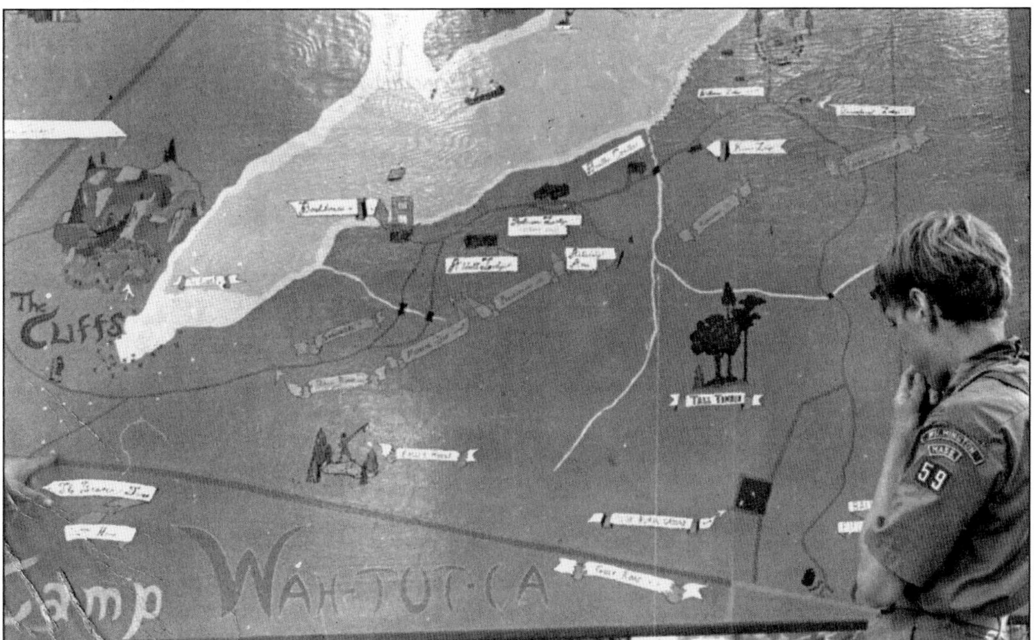

This map, produced by Vervaert, adds to the mystery, tradition, and folklore of the camp. It successfully takes a practical function and turns it into an adventure that showed Scouts more than how to get from one place to the other. The map is embellished with "crazy loons" and old logging roads that lead to nowhere that were labeled "trail to adventure."

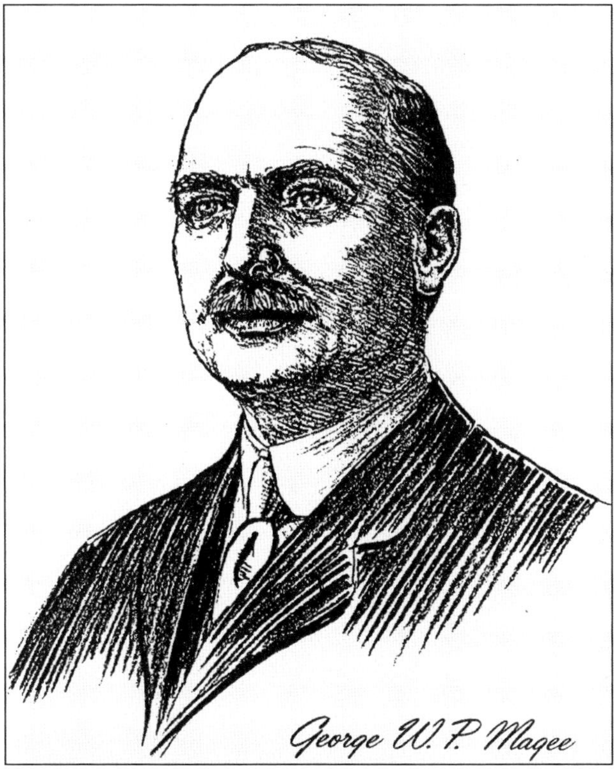

Beginning in 1947 and continuing to the present day, Wah-Tut-Ca's facilities would be expanded and improved by generous grants from the George W. Magee Memorial Trust Fund. Magee was a theatrical agent and philanthropist. In 1939, he established a trust that was directed to helping Massachusetts Scout councils with the purchase and maintenance of summer camps in New England.

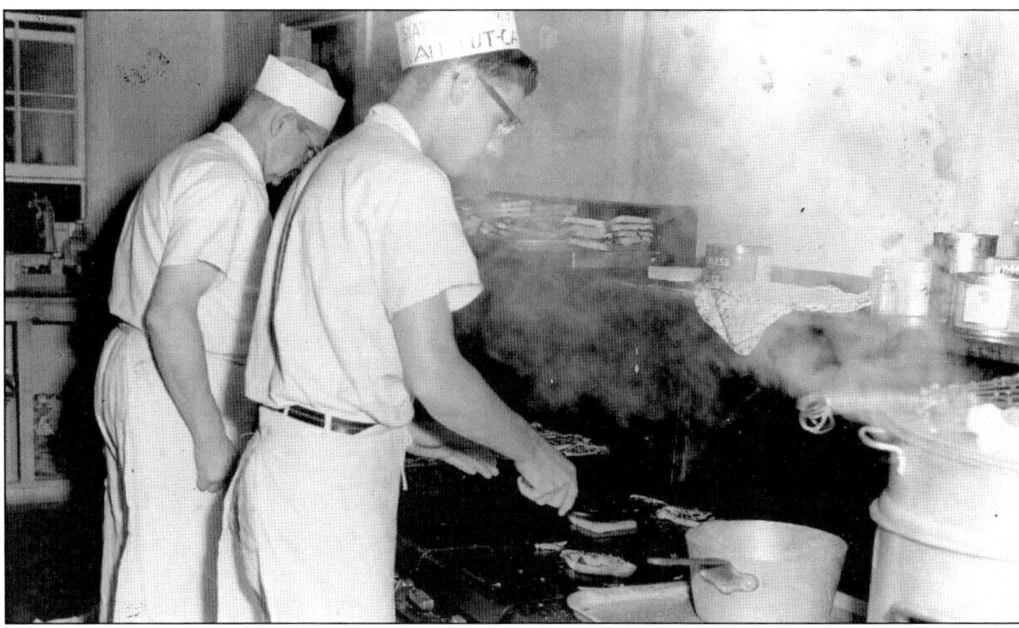

One of the most important Magee projects took three years to accomplish. With increased attendance at the camp, the dining hall needed to be expanded. From 1961 thru 1964, Alexander A. Vervaert monitored the project and insisted that the addition was to be made seamlessly in keeping with the character of the original design. Vervaert duplicated the details of the 1937 design, including the wagon wheel chandeliers and red pine truss.

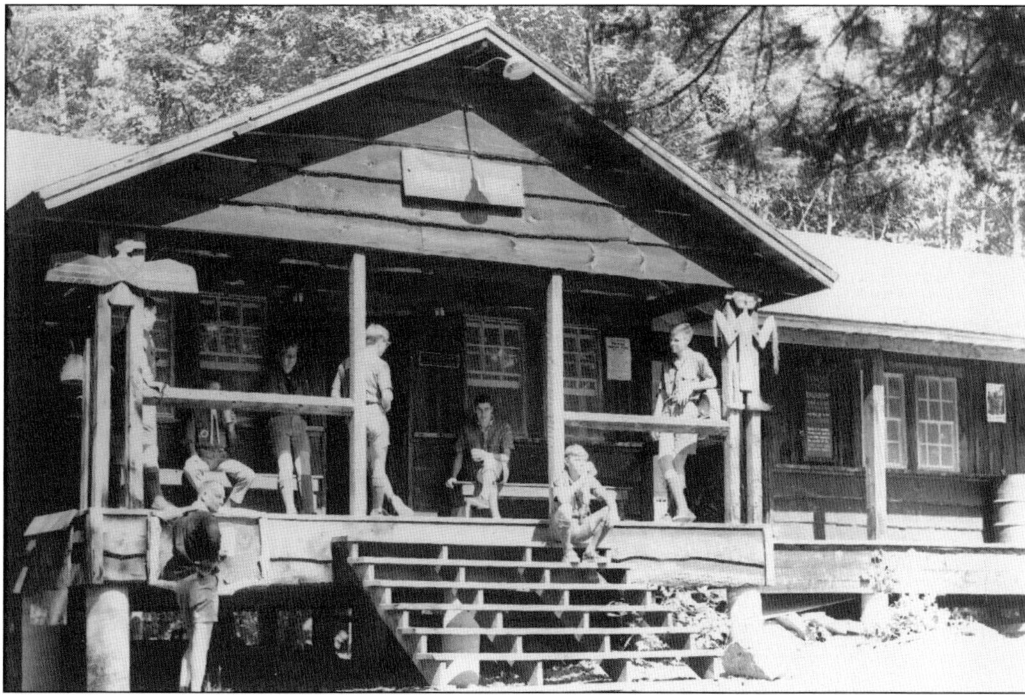

The Magee Trust also funded the building of Abbot Lodge. This building was built from timber harvested and milled at Wah-Tut-Ca. The location of the cut became an activity field. The building was originally designed to be the camp's trading post and administration building, and in the off-season, the building would be converted into a storage facility for the tents and mattresses.

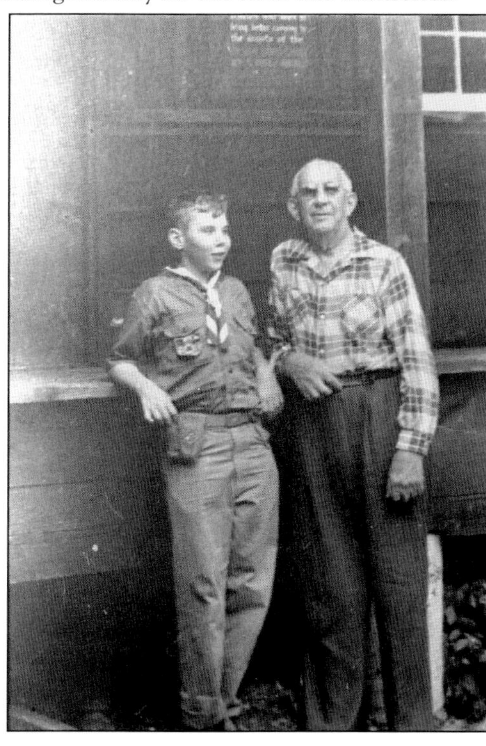

Abbot Lodge is named for Leon D. Abbot, pictured here with his grandson. He was one of the foremost weekend warriors of Wah-Tut-Ca. He was a modest, self-effacing man. One weekend, while working on the building, he noticed an unusually large gathering in front. He was shocked to find that the new camp building was being dedicated to him.

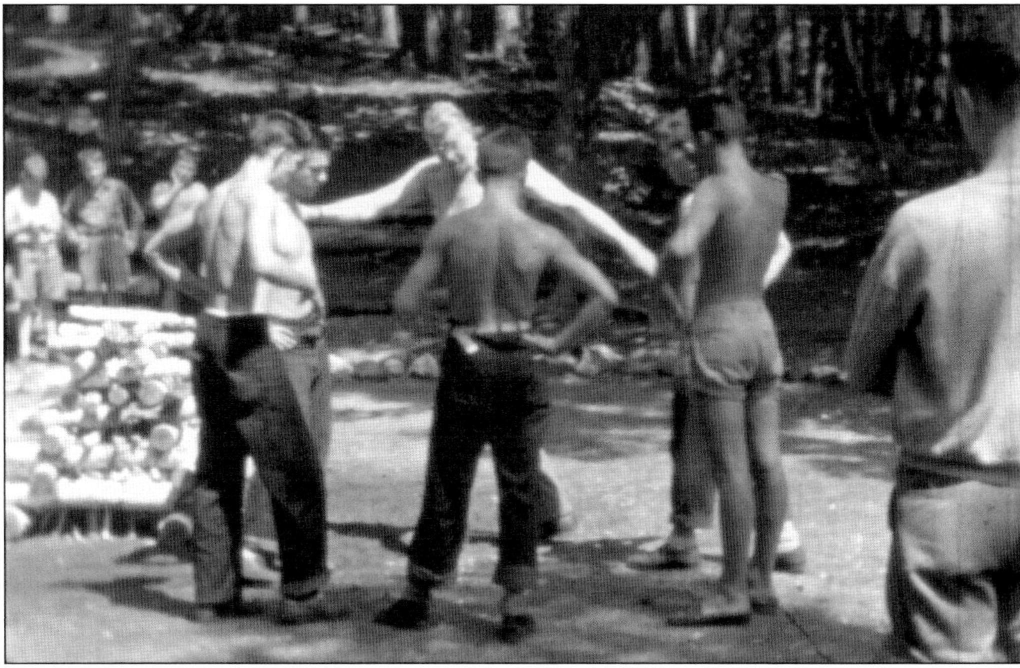

Hal Kellogg coaches the Wah-Tut-Ca Braves in preparation for a ceremony in the council ring. The Wah-Tut-Ca Braves were a local version of the National Order of the Arrow program. Started by Gordon R. Williams at Camp Chadwick, the Braves recognized Scouts and Scouters who showed leadership and dedication to the camp and its traditions.

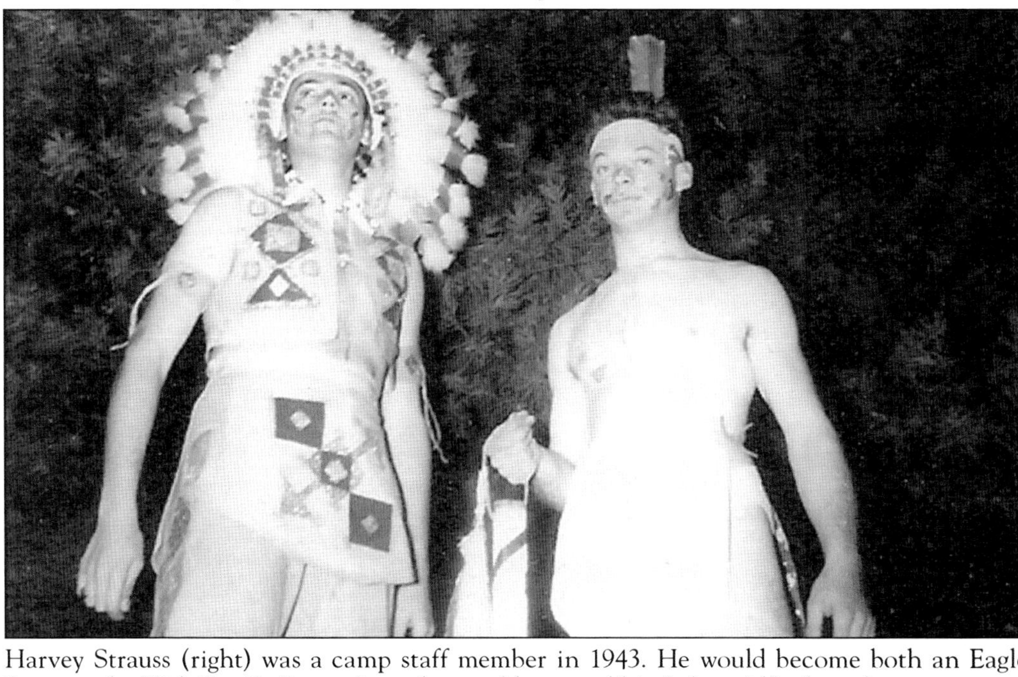

Harvey Strauss (right) was a camp staff member in 1943. He would become both an Eagle Scout and a Wah-Tut-Ca Brave. Later he would succeed his father, Alfred, as the scoutmaster of Troop 3 in Lowell's Highlands. Troop 3 established its own honor camper program called the Troop 3 Braves that continued long after the original Wah-Tut-Ca Braves ceased to exist.

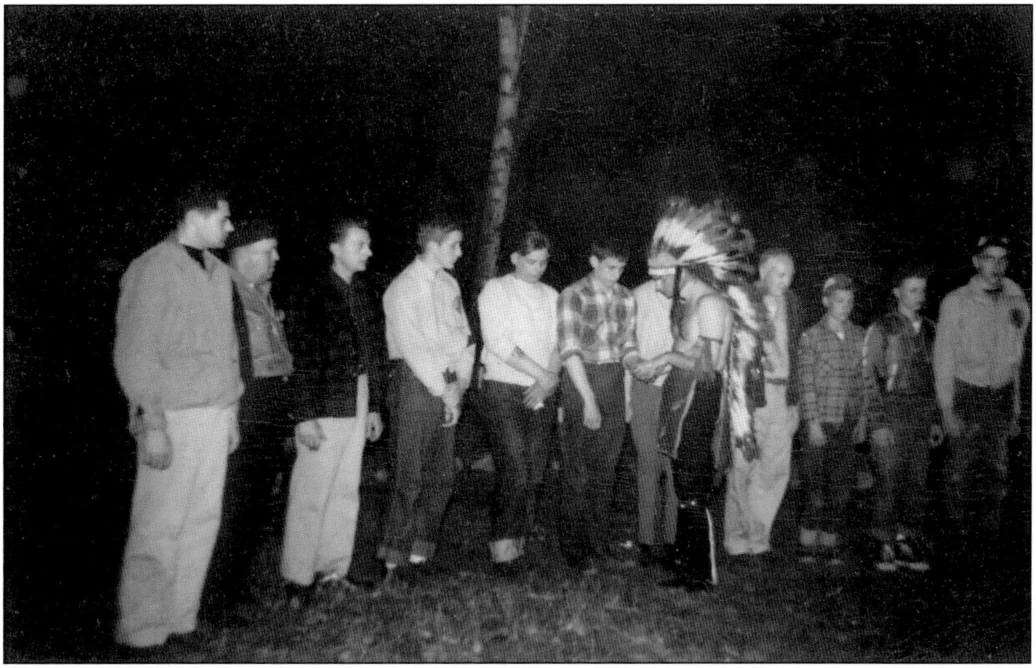

The first Ordeal of Wannalancit Lodge No. 451 was held on May 23–24, 1952. In keeping with the tradition of the Braves, all the youth chosen were members of Wah-Tut-Ca's staff. Pictured here is Charles Emerson (second from left), Alexander A. Vervaert (third from left), along with Clayton R. Lane (fourth from right). Mattatuck Lodge of Waterbury, Connecticut, would conduct the original ceremony for Wannalancit Lodge No. 451.

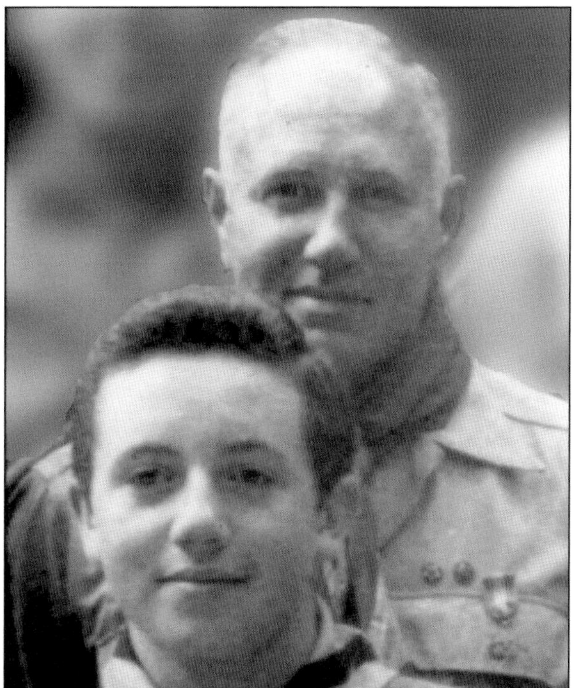

Lane would replace Vervaert as lodge adviser in 1953 and served for 15 years. He remained active in the lodge until 1977 when he relocated to Nebraska. The new lodge was named Wannalancit, who was a chief of the Pennacook Indians who lived in the Greater Lowell Area. The number was issued by the National Committee of the OA as the 451st lodge to be created.

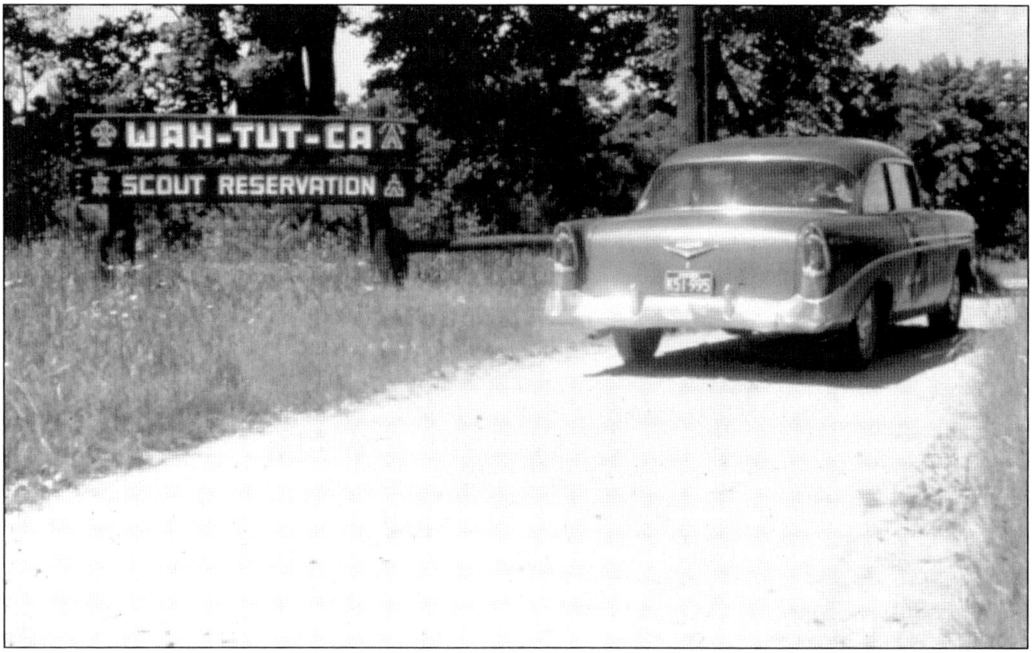

The postwar economy relieved many of the challenges associated with running the Scout camp. Cars were common, and in the 1950s, interstate highways and improved roads made the trip easier. What began as an all-day trek to camp became a trip that could be completed in less than two hours.

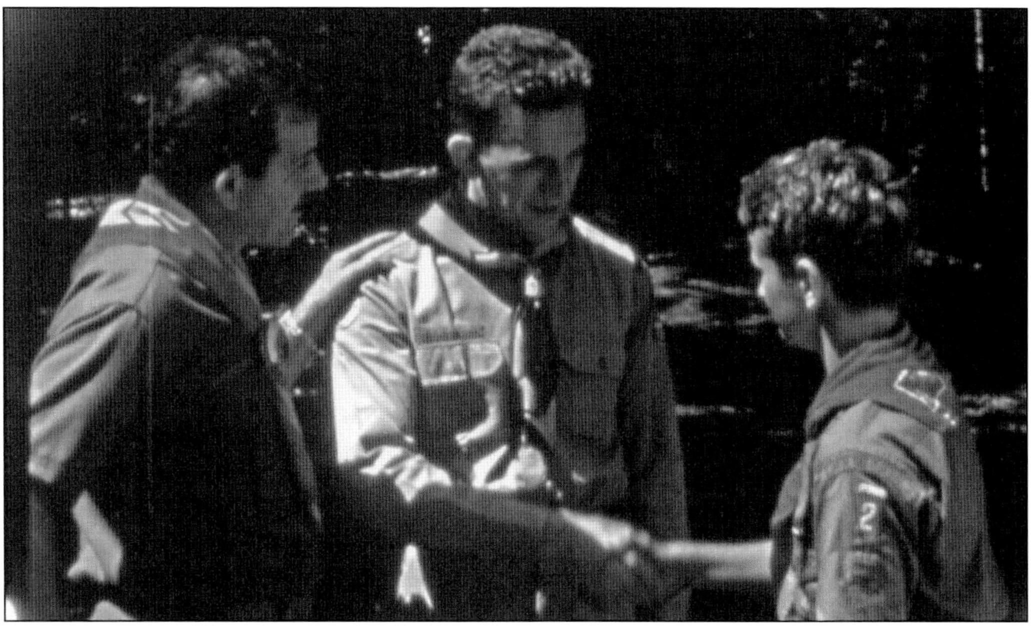

Scout executive Edward W. Butler (left) and John Vervaert (center) welcome a new camper to Wah-Tut-Ca, an event that would be repeated hundreds of times over 18 years. Butler was a distinguished volunteer before he became a professional Scouter. Butler was an Eagle Scout and Silver Beaver recipient and served as a scoutmaster in his native Holyoke, Massachusetts. His professional career would bring a period of stability to the reservation.

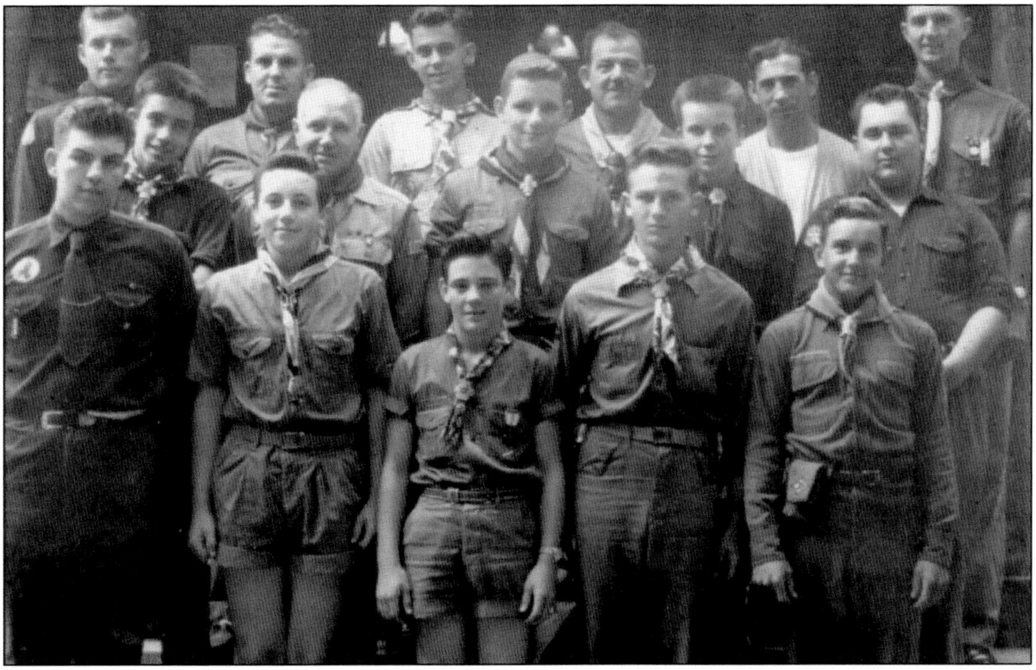

Pictured here is an early gathering of Wannalancit Lodge. Like many of Wah-Tut-Ca's traditions, the new OA program's impact would not be immediate but was a first step on a long and toilsome journey. Wannalancit Lodge was the most significant older boy program in the history of the Greater Lowell Council.

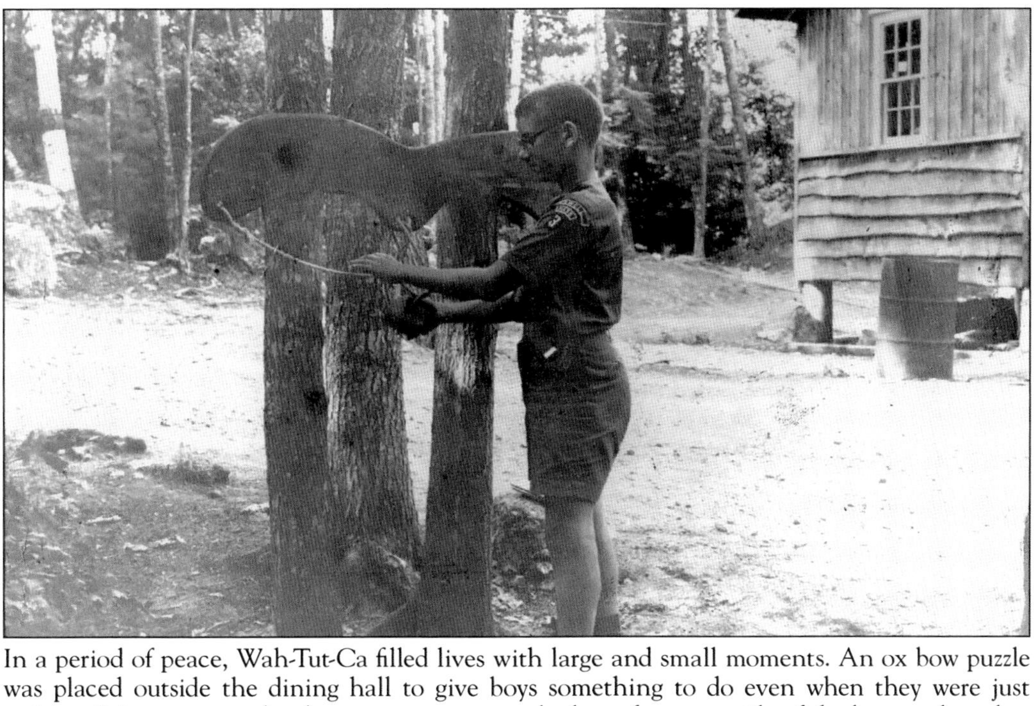

In a period of peace, Wah-Tut-Ca filled lives with large and small moments. An ox bow puzzle was placed outside the dining hall to give boys something to do even when they were just waiting. It is a rope puzzle where one must move the knot from one side of the bow to the other without going through the board. This is accomplished by manipulating the rope.

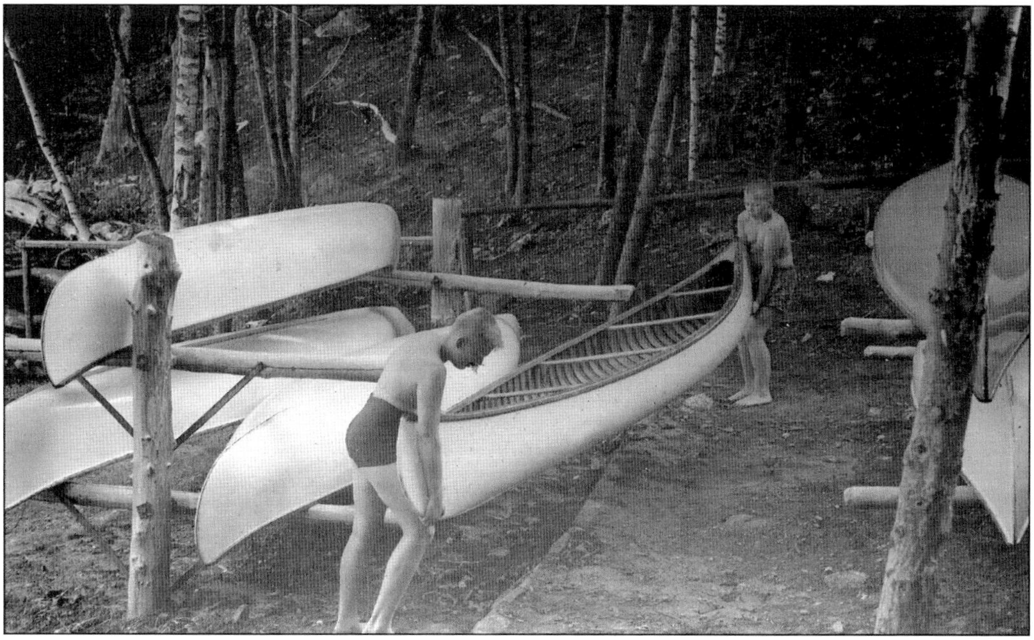

Canoeing on Northwood Lake gave a boy the feeling that he was a Native American on a noble quest. These Old Town canoes saw many seasons at Wah-Tut-Ca and are many colors. Handcrafted from cedar and canvas, their durability served camps well. They were in use until the late 1990s, when fiberglass, aluminum, and seats became desired features for Wah-Tut-Ca's most popular boat.

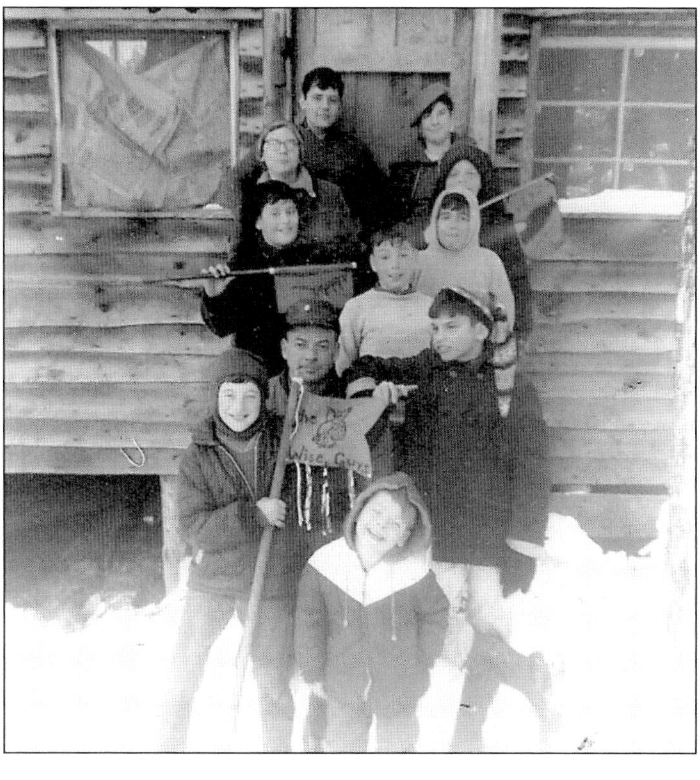

Known as "the Beaver," the scoutmaster of Troop 3, Harvey Strauss, would introduce hundreds of boys to Wah-Tut-Ca. Here he is at Wah-Tut-Ca with the boys for a winter camping trip in 1967. Many of "the Beaver's boys" would serve on the camp's staff and become leaders and innovators in programming for the next 30 years. This included his two sons, Alan and Jay, both Eagle Scouts.

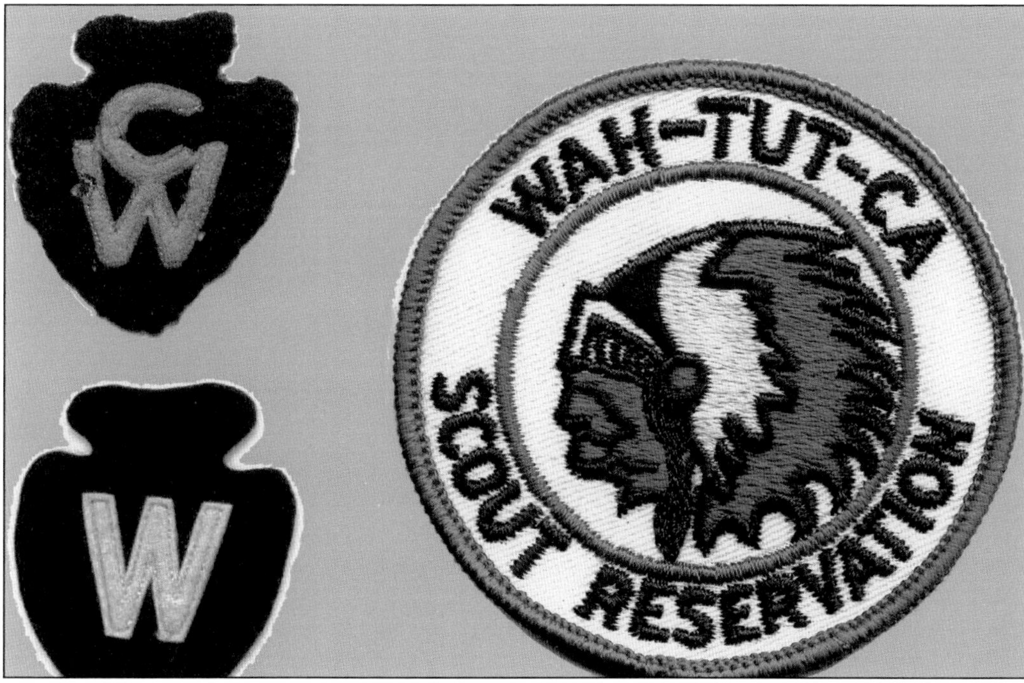

Wah-Tut-Ca's emblems have changed with the times. The first camp patches were simple felt appliqué sewn onto an arrowhead. In the 1950s, the Indian Head would replace it. Alexander A. Vervaert designed the latter, which would become the recognized symbol of Wah-Tut-Ca for over 30 years. It is the mark left by a generation who expanded and stabilized Wah-Tut-Ca during the postwar years.

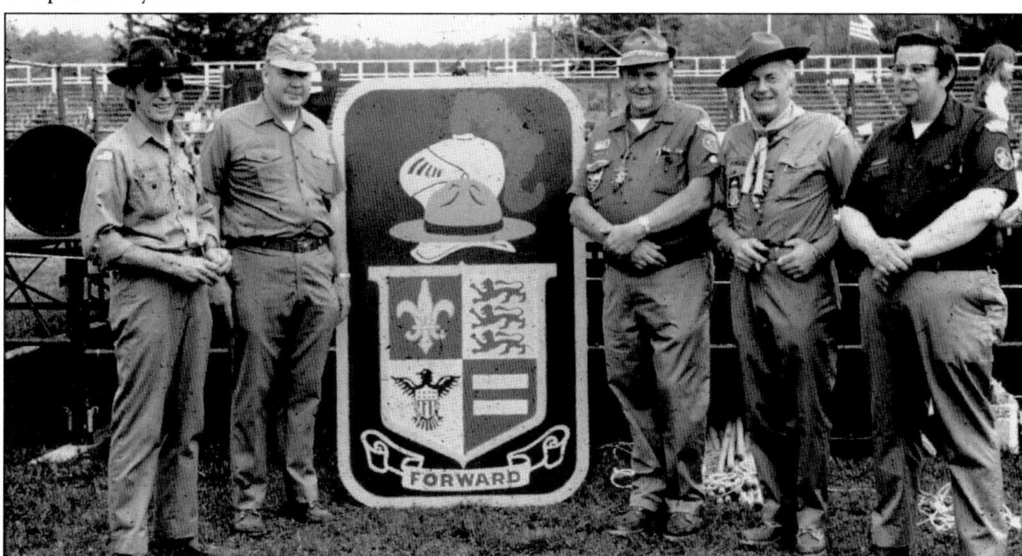

This group of Scouters came from what is now known as the "greatest generation," those who lived and fought through World War II. From left to right are Norman Trudeau, scoutmaster of Troop 49; Richard Grinder, Scout commissioner for the town of Wilmington; Harold Dow, council training chairman; Alexander A. Vervaert, council commissioner; and Blake M. Watson, camp ranger. They would prepare another generation to lead Wah-Tut-Ca.

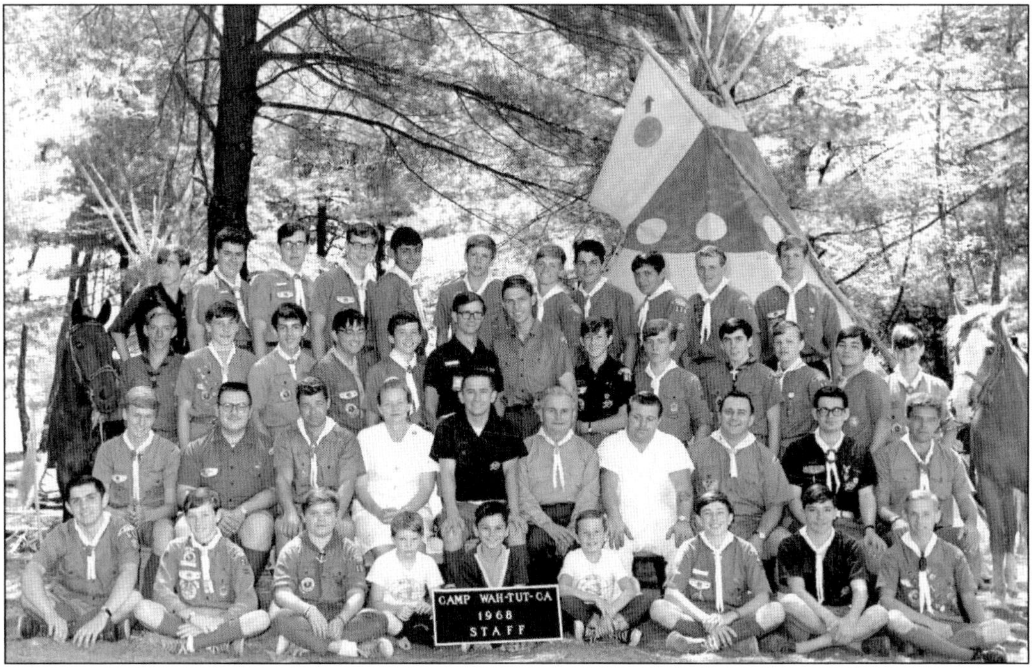

There are signs of great changes occurring at the Reservation. Two staff portraits, 5 years apart demonstrate changes in style and substance. The 1968 photograph shows a clean cut and orderly camp staff. By 1972, hairstyles were much longer and less uniform in appearance. Baby boomers had arrived and were now taking their place as leaders of Wah-Tut-Ca. Many in these pictures would be drafted into the military during the Vietnam era. It was a time of great social change and a reflection of the community as a whole. Through these years there was evidence of a widening "generation gap" between "boomers" and the "greatest generation." Yet something would always be shared between the two points of view; they both had a love of Wah-Tut-Ca Scout Reservation.

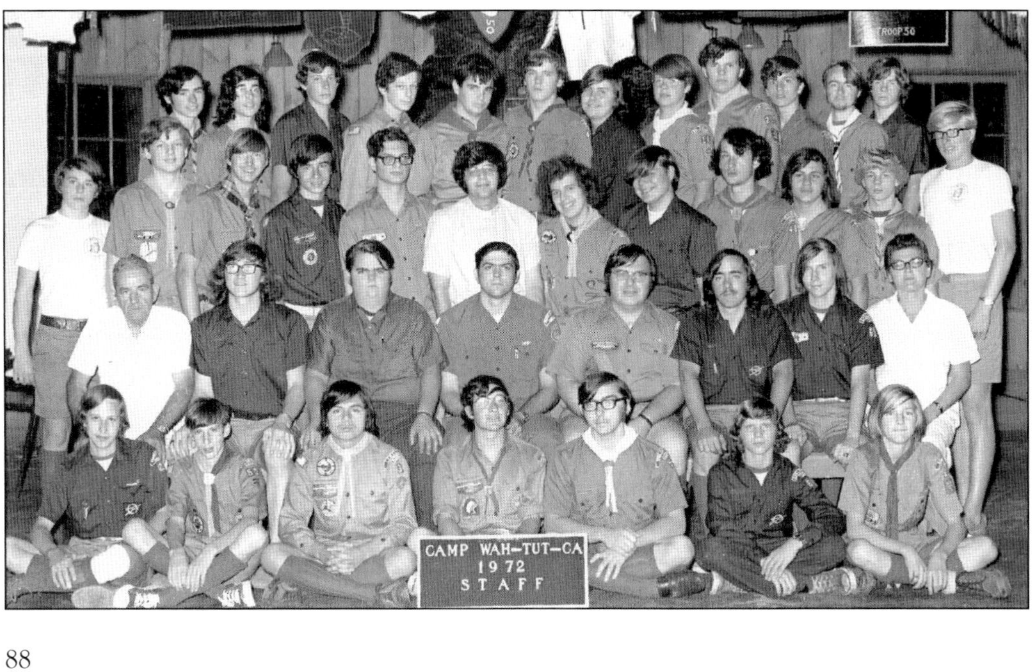

Six

"Wind for Our Sails"

Wah-Tut-Ca needed to keep pace with the tremendous social changes that occurred from the 1970s to the 1990s. Increasingly Scouting and camping had to compete against part-time jobs, video games, cable television, the home computer, and eventually the Internet. Family composition was shifting. Working mothers and single-parent families became common. No longer limited by lack of cars and roads, the escape from Greater Lowell was far from a novelty.

Wannalancit Lodge lead the way. Heavily influenced by the biannual National Order of the Arrow Conference, or NOAC as it is known, young Arrowmen staff members brought the experiences and ideas back to the reservation. Like the Wah-Tut-Ca Braves, camp staff members lead Wannalancit Lodge. Working on summer camp staff was inseparable from the lodge program.

In 1987, present and past staff, volunteers, and lodge members staged a massive celebration to mark Wah-Tut-Ca's 50th anniversary. On June 27, over 1,000 people gathered at the reservation to remember the work of the founders. A total of 26 Scouts hiked for three days from the old camp, Chadwick in Dunstable, Massachusetts, to Wah-Tut-Ca Scout Reservation in Northwood.

The introduction of the Orion Program in the early 1980s would become a signature feature to the Wah-Tut-Ca experience. Since the 1950s, most of the camp's programs centered on advancement, and campers spent their time in merit badge classes. The Orion Program was an "open program" format that ended these classes.

In 1994, Wah-Tut-Ca broke the all-time summer camping records under the leadership of reservation director Craig Ryder. A total of 1,047 campers spent the summer on the shores of Northwood Lake.

Scouting on a national level was also adapting to a changing world. Traditional funding sources where being stressed. In the 1990s, many Boy Scout councils merged to consolidate resources. After years of debate, the Greater Lowell Council finally accepted the need to merge with one of four neighboring councils.

The Greater Lowell executive board chose its eastern neighbor headquartered in Haverhill, Massachusetts. An agreement was reached where Lowell and Wah-Tut-Ca would become part of the Yankee Clipper Council. On December 31, 1999, the Greater Lowell Council ended and the question on everyone's mind was would Wah-Tut-Ca stay Wah-Tut-Ca?

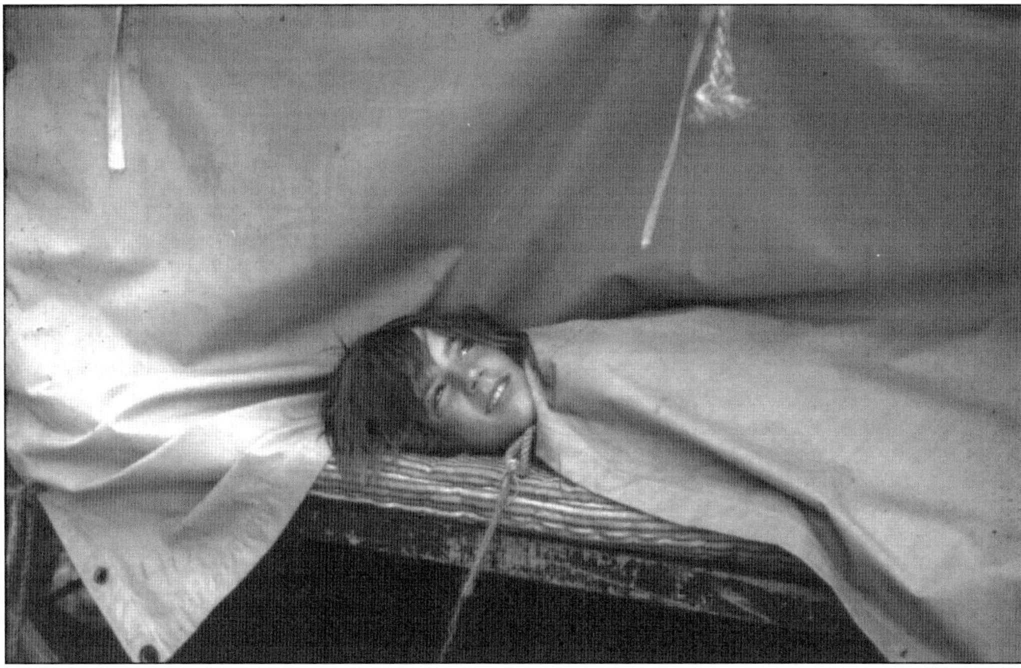

Each morning at Wah-Tut-Ca holds a promise for a new adventure. As camp entered the 1970s, a new dawn had broken. The camp would see many changes in the coming years. For Wah-Tut-Ca to remain relevant it had to adapt to a new world. Those who would make those changes did not realize that they had set out upon a new Wah-Tut-Ca adventure.

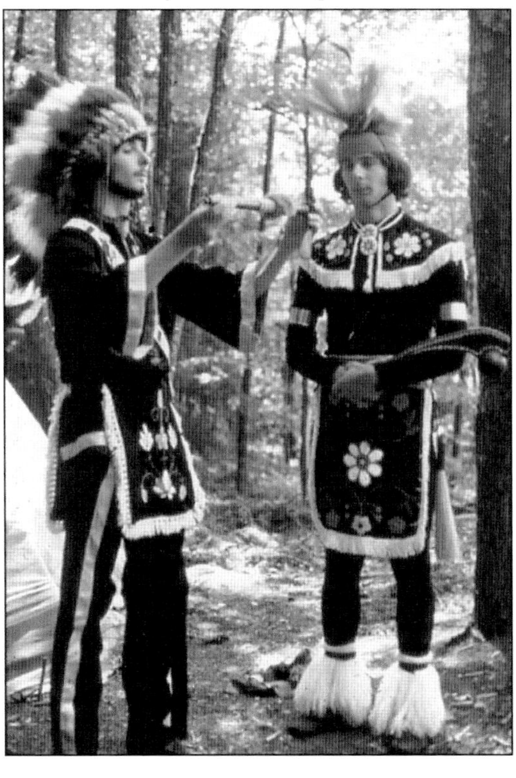

Alan and Bruce Lepore were leaders in the lodge dance and ceremonial teams. The difference between Wannalancit Lodge programs and the camp programs would become hard to distinguish in the coming years. During the summer at Wah-Tut-Ca, the Lepore brothers ran the Indian Village and would be seen in Native American regalia at campfires and other events.

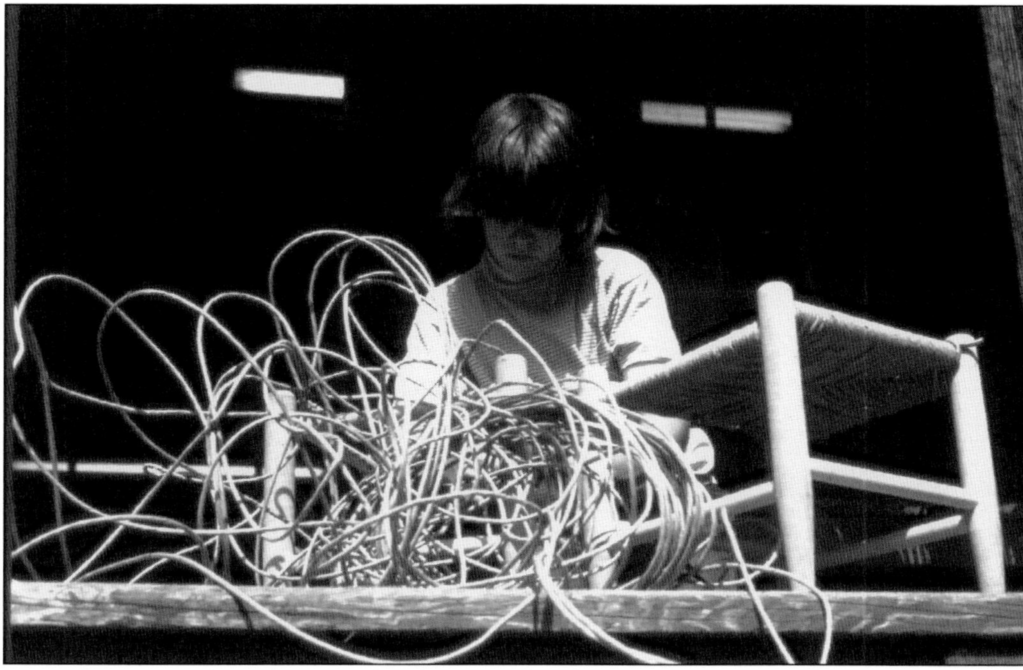

Here a Scout struggles to bring reed under control and to weave it into a stool. Steven Marchacos, who served on staff from the 1960s to the 1980s, took this photograph and hundreds of others to develop camping promotion slide shows. Marchacos's photographs were used by Wannalancit Lodge and brought to troop meeting halls to encourage boys to go to camp.

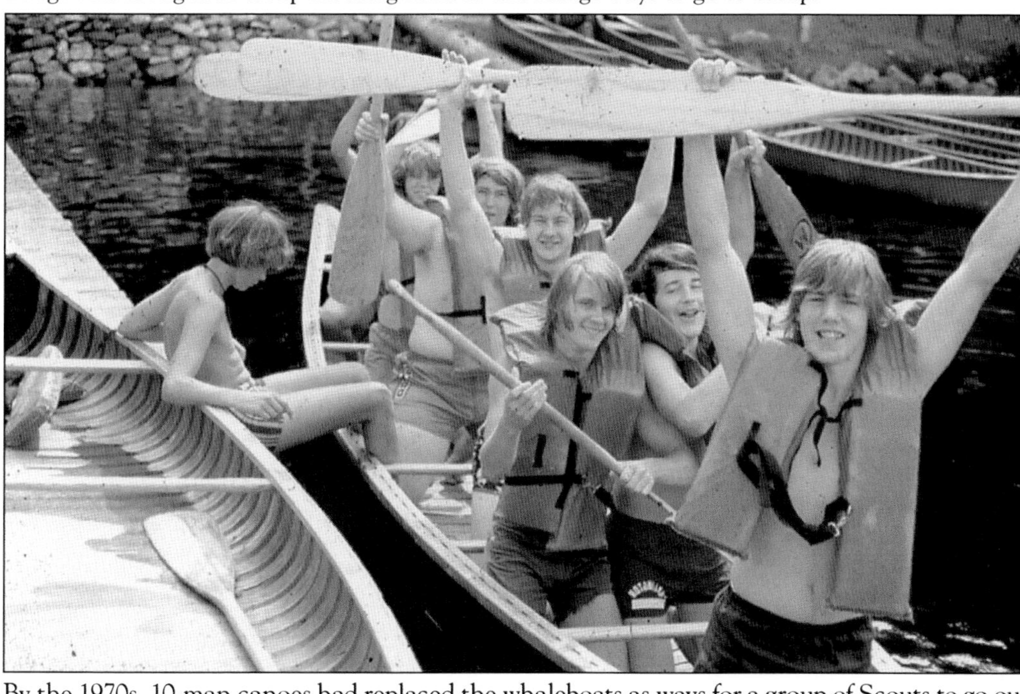

By the 1970s, 10-man canoes had replaced the whaleboats as ways for a group of Scouts to go out and explore the lake. A favorite destination at the end of Northwood Lake was Johnson's Dairy Bar. Scouts would take the boats out in a determined pursuit of ice cream.

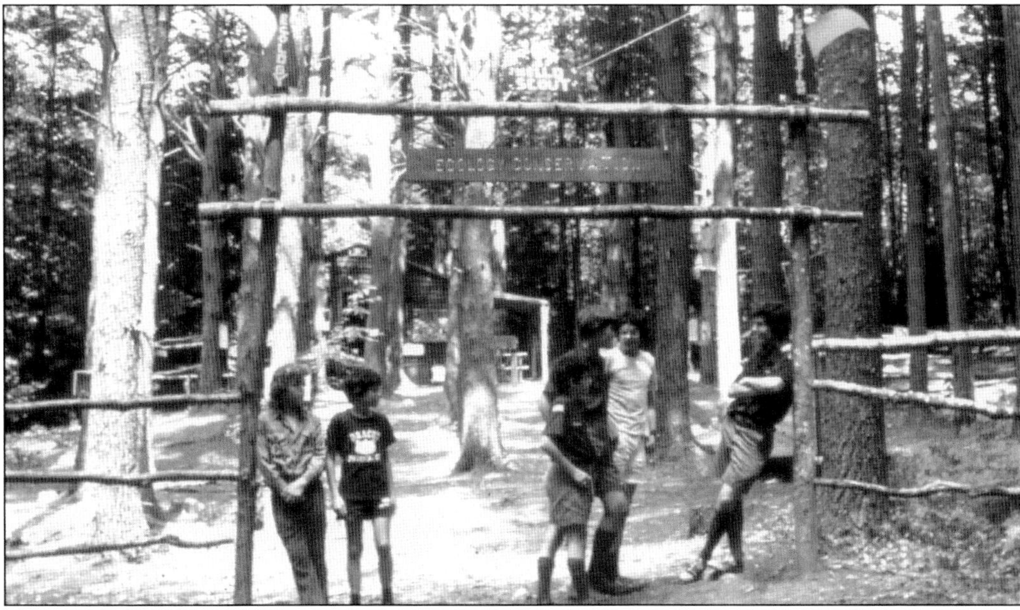

A gateway to the discovery of nature leads to one of the major program areas at Wah-Tut-Ca. The ecology conservation area would offer Scoutcraft and nature activities. The area had over a dozen working laboratories and moved beyond the merit badge program. It had a "scientific theme," no doubt due to the college student who ran the area. Scouts would conduct experiments in soil science, insect life, and engineering.

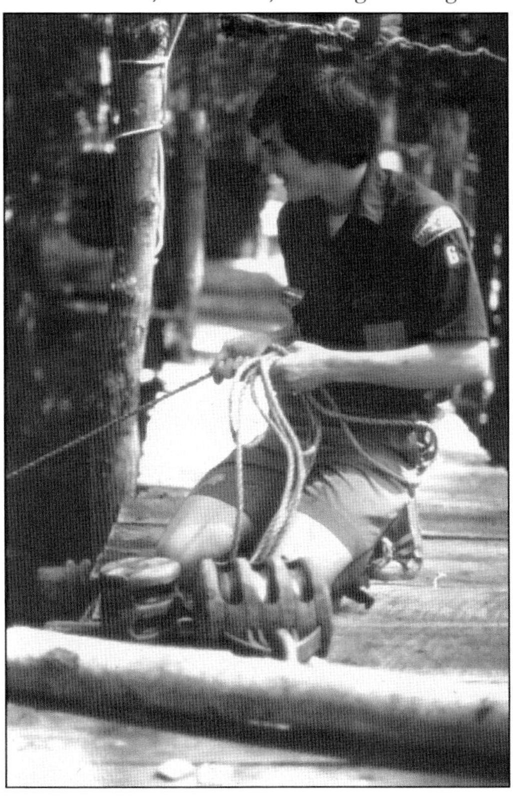

A two-year project in the ecology conservation area was the building of a bridge that would span the ravine over Wah-Tut-Ca's Northbrook. James Chandler, area staff member, pulls up another beam as the project nears completion. The staff claimed, although never verified, it to be the largest bridge built by Scouts east of the Mississippi.

Brian J. Lobao served 23 years as lodge adviser and was a major influence on the growth of the camp, the lodge, and the council. In his youth he served as lodge chief and director of the Ecology Conservation Program. His dedication to the lodge, his energy, and his spirit would help the program grow. Always striving for excellence, he would often be quoted as saying, "Good is just not good enough."

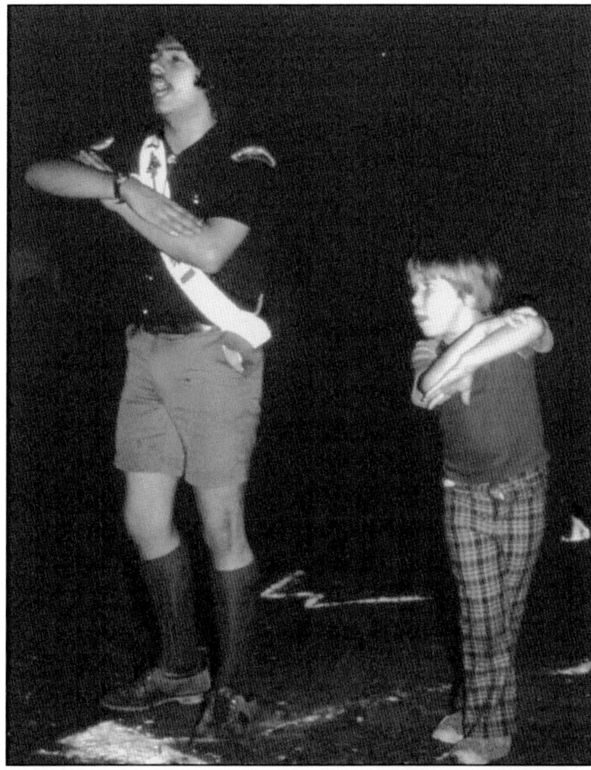

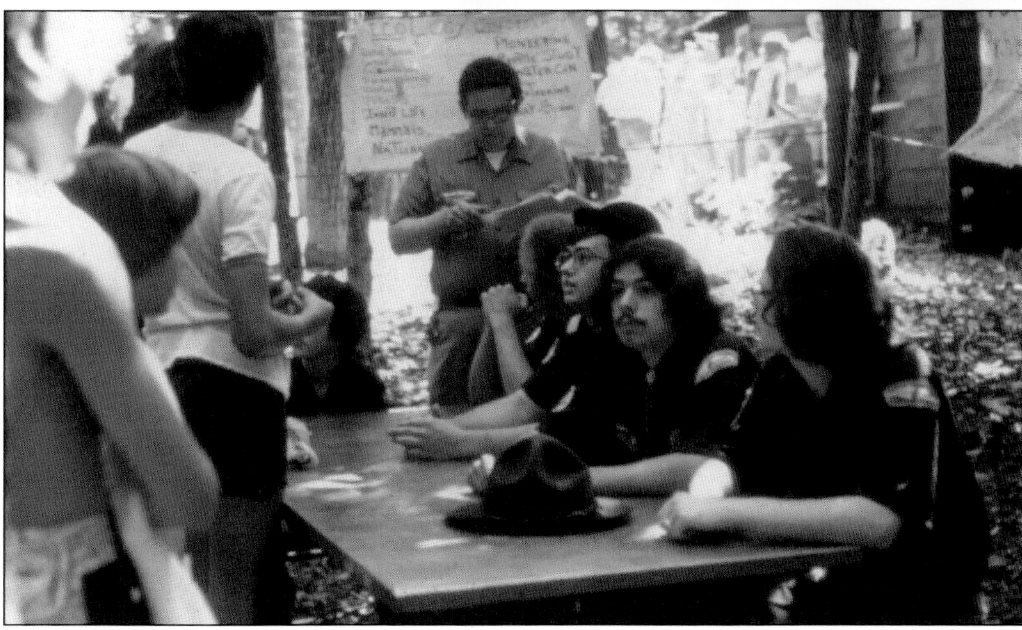

Lobao (second from right), Ken Kronlund (third from right), and Blake Watson (standing in rear) are in this photograph as Scouts sign up for merit badge classes. Wah-Tut-Ca's program was almost completely devoted to advancement with merit badge classes from morning until sundown. Many of the camp's area directors, particularly Lobao, were frustrated by the limitations placed on a boy's camp experience that would force him to spend a day in classes.

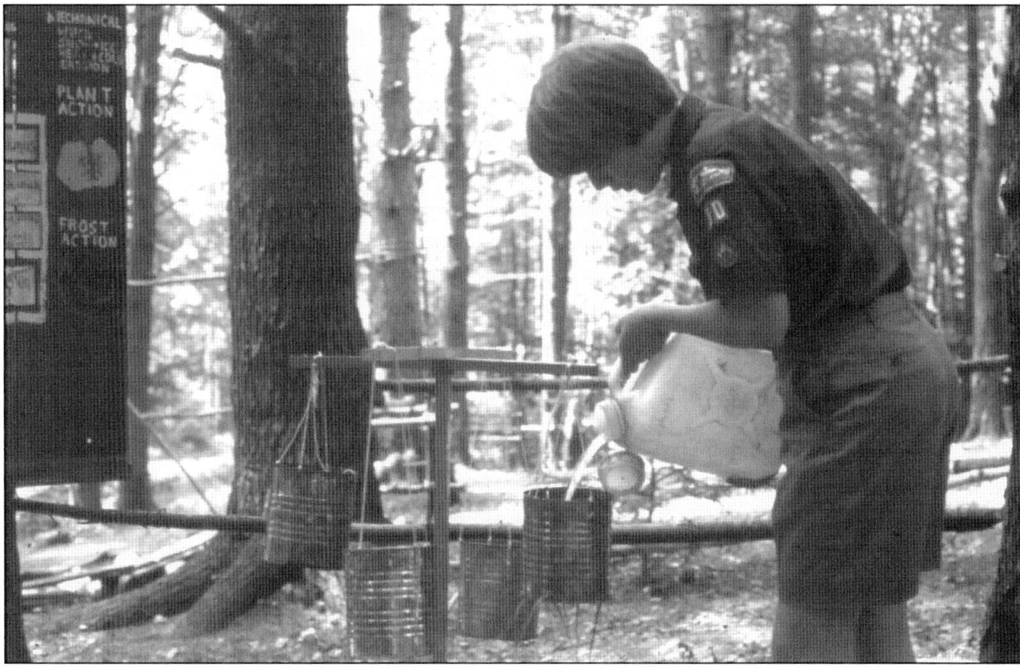

Mark D. Giguere, on his first year on staff, is working in the "dirt" laboratory demonstrating soil percolation. Giguere served as chief of Wannalancit Lodge and later the reservation's program director. Through his participation in the lodge and camp program, Giguere developed leadership and communication skills. His spirit continued to develop Wah-Tut-Ca's program sending it in new and dynamic directions.

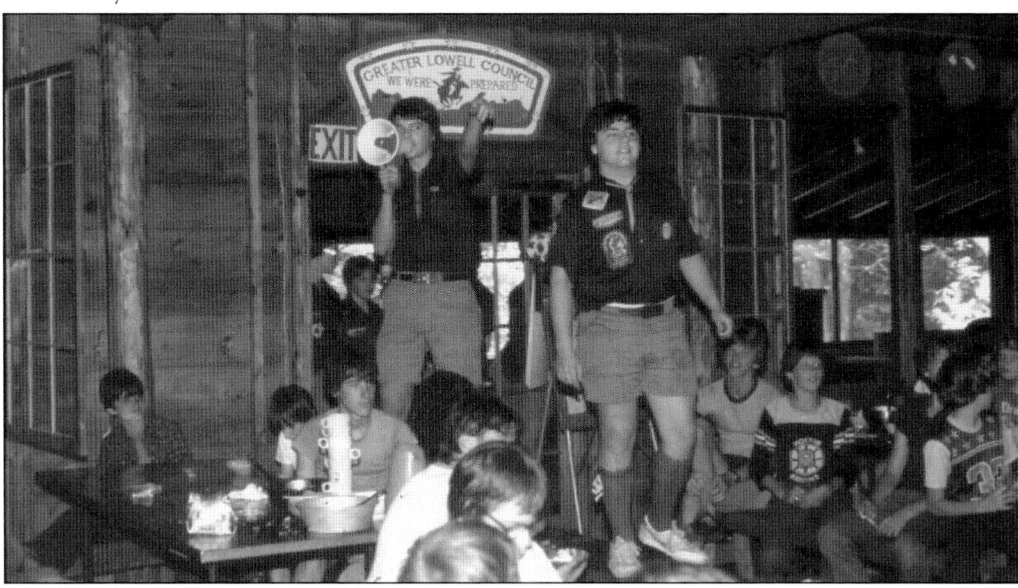

When Giguere became program director, he introduced the Orion Program. He is shown here with area director George D. Kouloheras in the dining hall. The open program ended classes at camp. Boy Scout advancement remained important but not the only aim of the camp's program. Brian J. Lobao developed the Orion Program, but it was Giguere and people like Kouloheras who sold it.

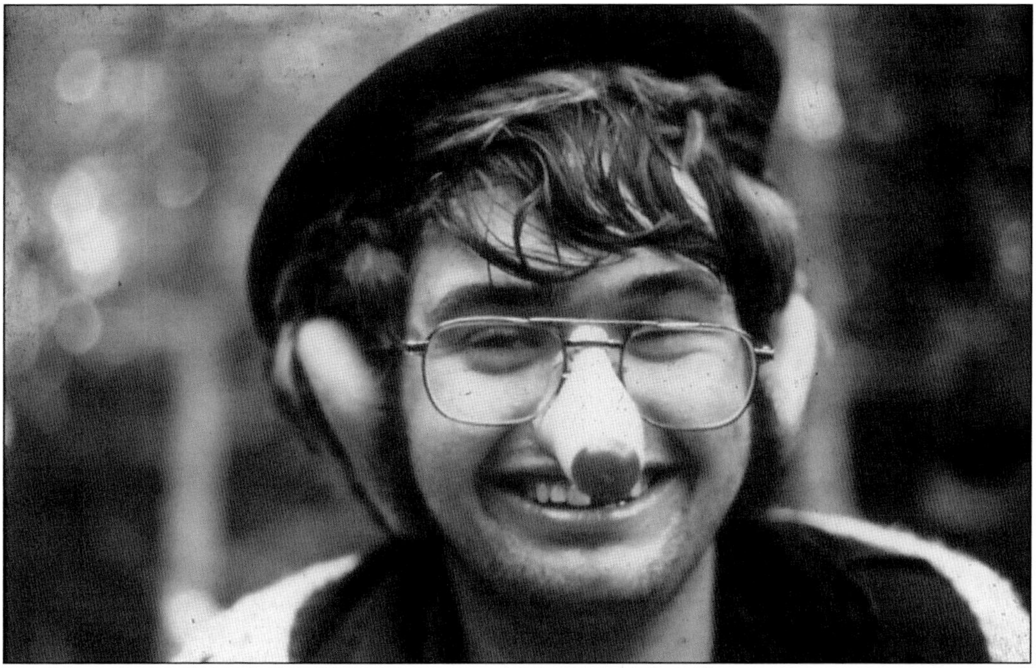

With less emphasis on advancement, a stronger focus was placed on campers having fun. The staff would put on skits, sometimes lasting days. Kenneth H. Kronlund Jr., shown here, is dressed up as a hillbilly. He would wear the costume and stay in character for a large part of the week. "Uncle Kenny" became a noted and respected physician in the Greater Worcester area.

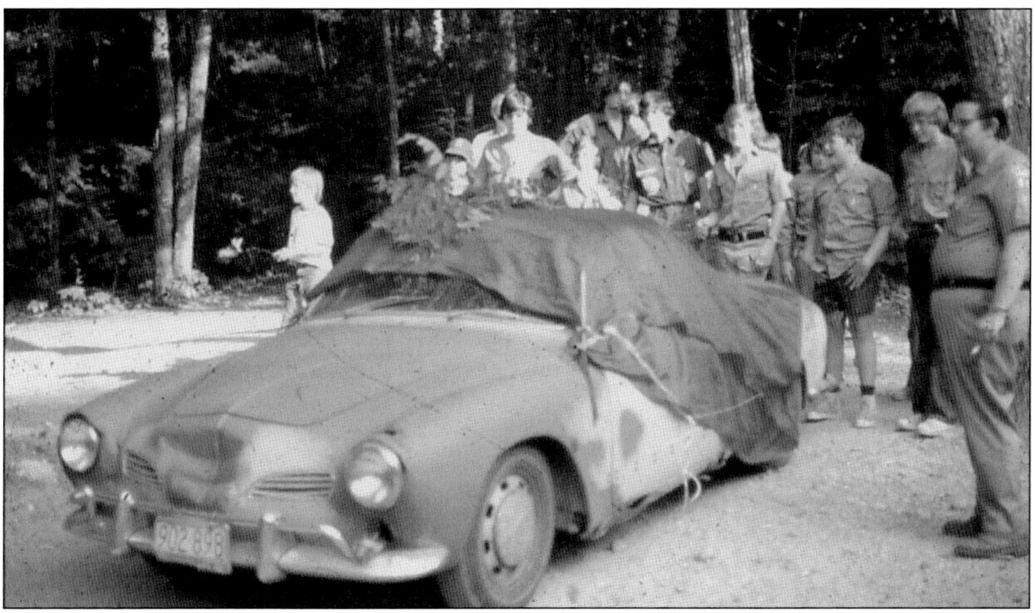

Kronlund served as an area director and later program director. Working at summer camp was not a lucrative venture. College students would often struggle to pay tuition on a Wah-Tut-Ca salary. Kronlund's Karmann Ghia was the best transportation he could afford. This Volkswagen would become part of the camp's program. It is being dressed as a giant vegetable for a "Tomato Day" celebration.

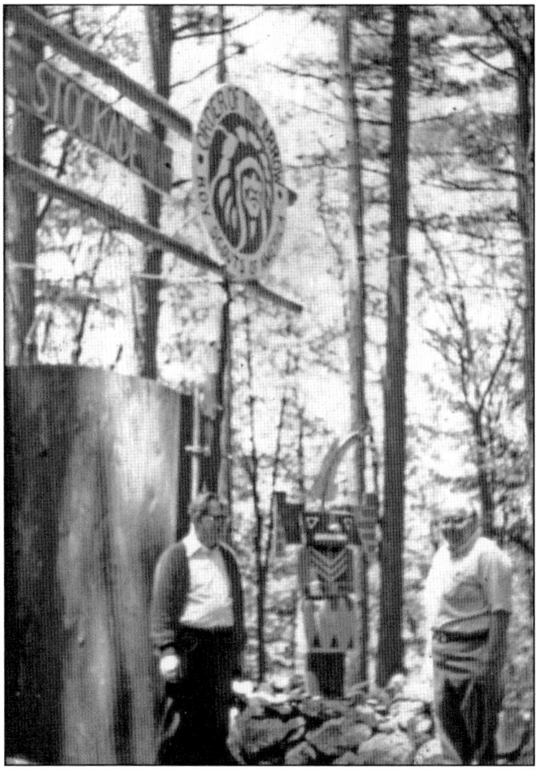

Edward A. Tomasi (right) became the Scout executive of the Greater Lowell Council in 1975. His career's greatest achievements were at Scout camps and his involvement with the OA. Tomasi chose those who would lead the camp and the lodge forward. With the appointment of Blake M. Watson as camp director and Brian J. Lobao as the lodge adviser, Tomasi's impact was felt for many years.

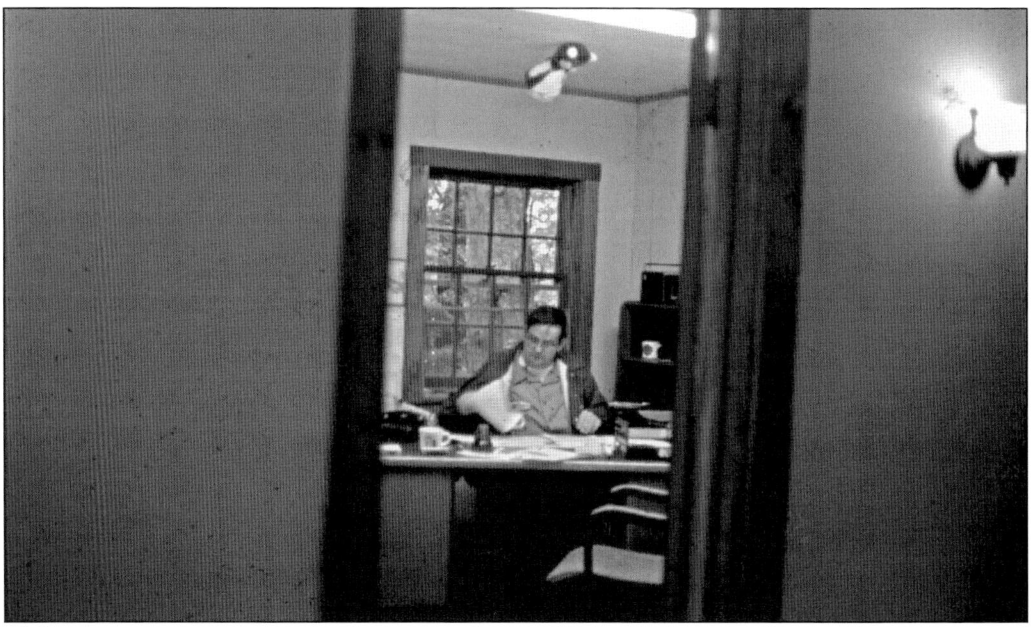

Blake Watson, scoutmaster of Troop 16 and 61 in Chelmsford, Massachusetts, became council camping chairman in 1968. In 1975, he gave up his job as a banker and moved to Wah-Tut-Ca to become the first full-time ranger. In 1979, Scout executive Edward A. Tomasi appointed Watson as camp director. Until his retirement in 1990, Watson's devotion and skill had a remarkable impact on camp operations and administration.

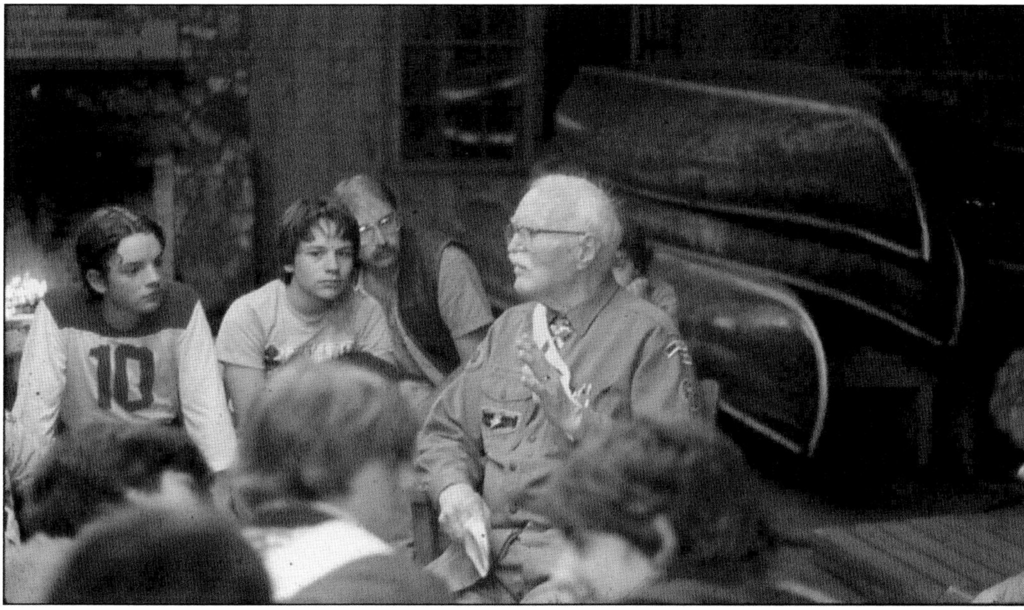

The influence of the OA on camp went beyond the membership of Wannalancit Lodge. In 1983, Col. Carroll A. Edson, the cofounder of the OA, visited Wah-Tut-Ca. In 1915, he and Dr. E. Urner Goodman began the OA at Treasure Island Scout Camp on the Delaware River. During Colonel Edson's visit to Wah-Tut-Ca, he stressed the importance of getting young Arrowmen involved in camp.

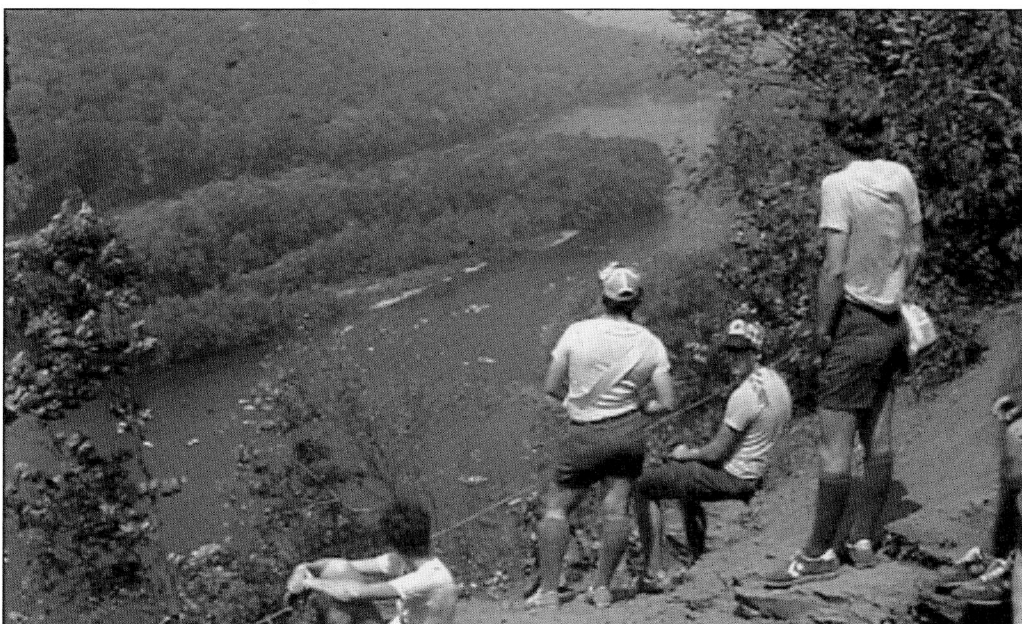

Every two years, Wannalancit Lodge would travel to an NOAC. At these conferences ideas about camp programs would be exchanged. On a NOAC trip the lodge visited Treasure Island Scout Camp, pictured here. Noticing the campfire circle at Treasure Island was named the E. Urner Goodman Stockade, after the OA's founder, they returned to Wah-Tut-Ca and renamed its campfire circle the Clayton Lane Stockade after the legendary adviser.

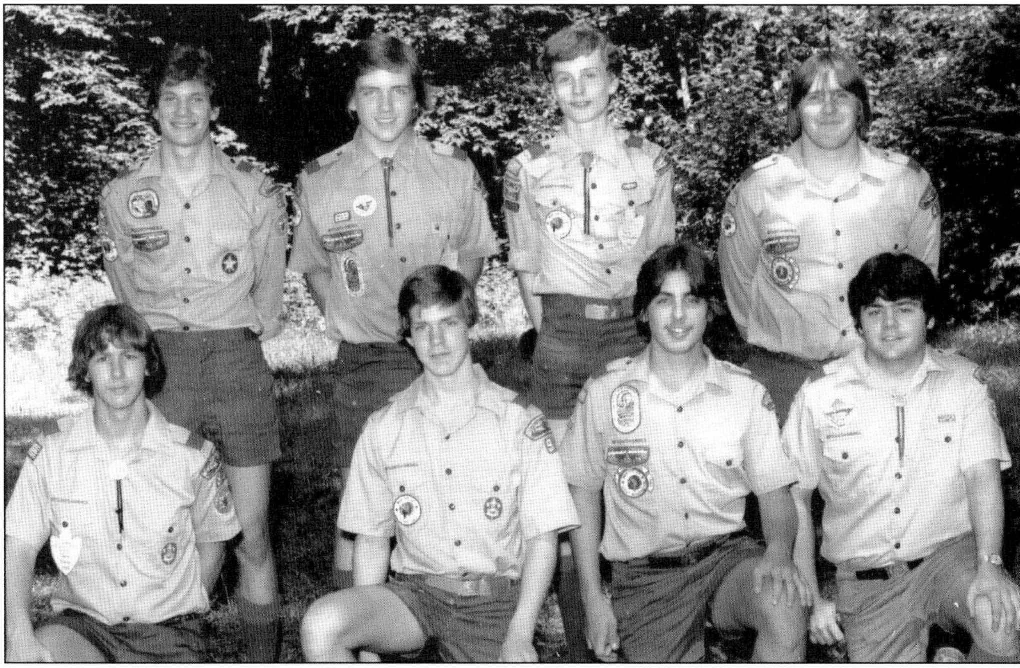

Although most of the glory of working on a camp staff goes to the program people, staff who served the camp operations developed their own traditions. In 1983, George D. Kouloheras (first row, right) was drafted into leading the kitchen crew when the cook quit. Craig Ryder (second row, second from left) would become camp director, and next to him, Peter Gallagher (second from right) would become an associate lodge adviser.

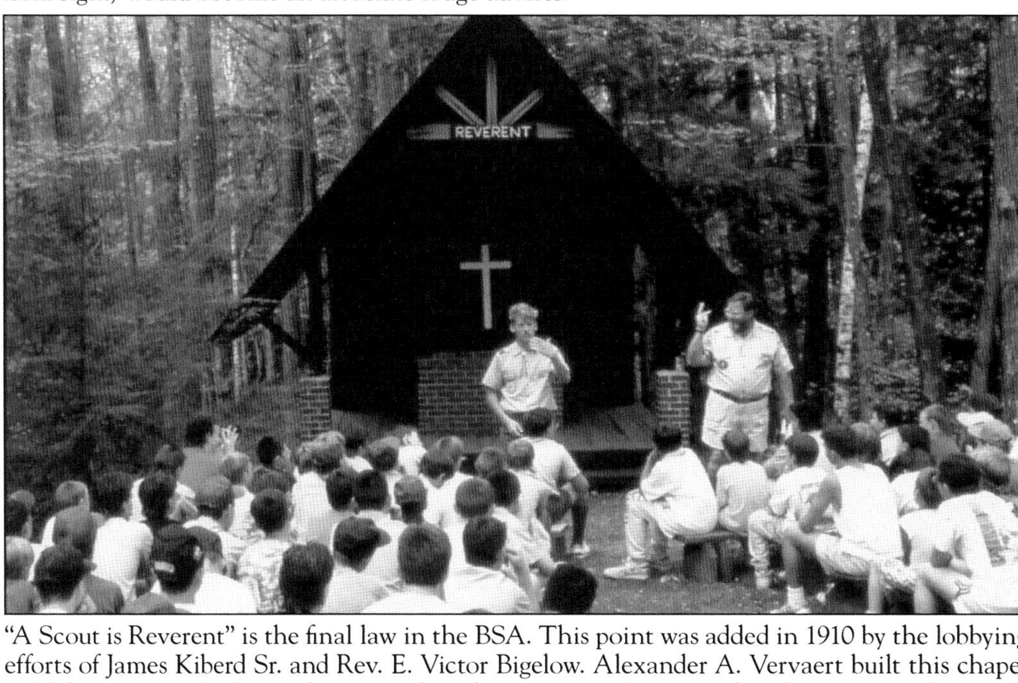

"A Scout is Reverent" is the final law in the BSA. This point was added in 1910 by the lobbying efforts of James Kiberd Sr. and Rev. E. Victor Bigelow. Alexander A. Vervaert built this chapel at Wah-Tut-Ca in 1968. His design was based upon a Scout's praying hands. Ecumenical services are held at camp once a week to remind a Scout of his duty to God.

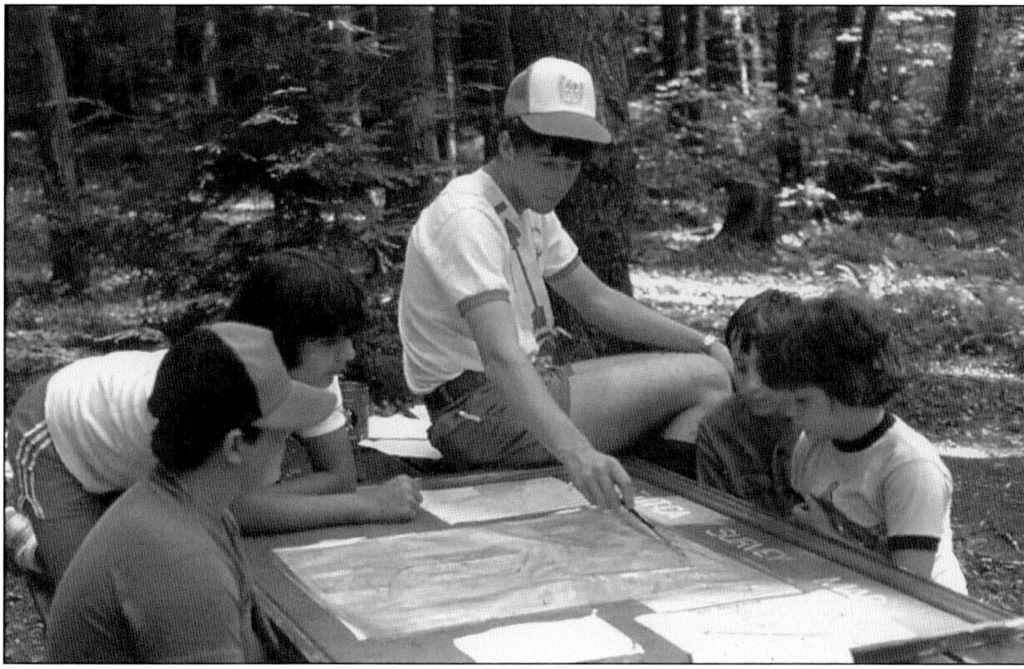

Pictured here is Thomas F. Markham III at the Ecology Conservation Program area in 1981 teaching Scouts. With great leadership abilities, Markham would become Wah-Tut-Ca's director of the outdoor adventure area and lodge chief for the 1982–1983 year. In 1988, Markham founded The Key Foundation Inc. and later became president of the Greater Lowell Council.

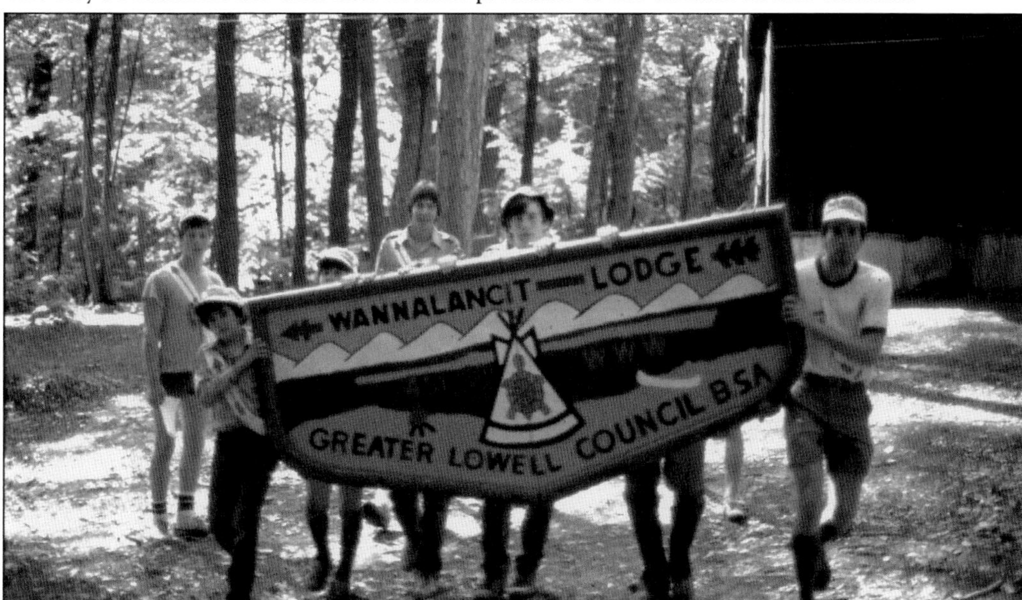

Wah-Tut-Ca was the heart of Wannalancit Lodge. In 1983, the lodge hosted a section conclave at camp. A conclave is a weekend gathering of lodges from multiple states and councils. Here lodge members carry their oversized Wannalancit Lodge flap with pride. Although not all camp staff were members of Wannalancit Lodge and not all lodge members were part of camp staff, it became impossible to separate the two stories.

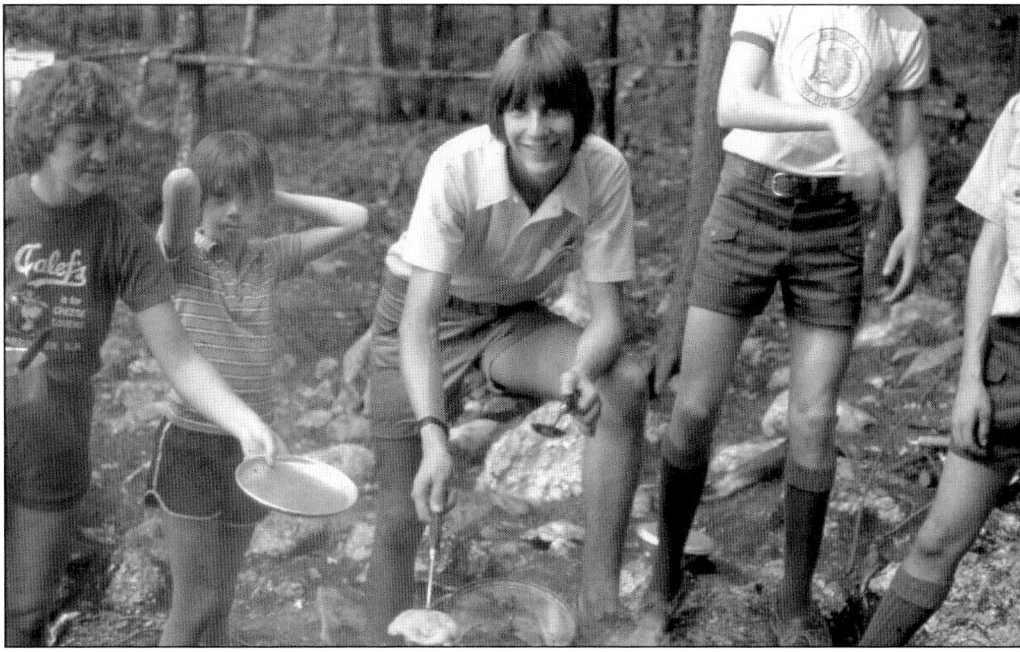

Scott H. Sughrue (center) was a lodge chief and later the program director. Known for his positive energy and enthusiasm, Sughrue brought growth, fun, and adventure to the reservation. As program director, he used a three-part plan to create a "Complete Wah-Tut-Ca Experience." His programming focused on program areas, campwide events, and small ad hoc games and activities.

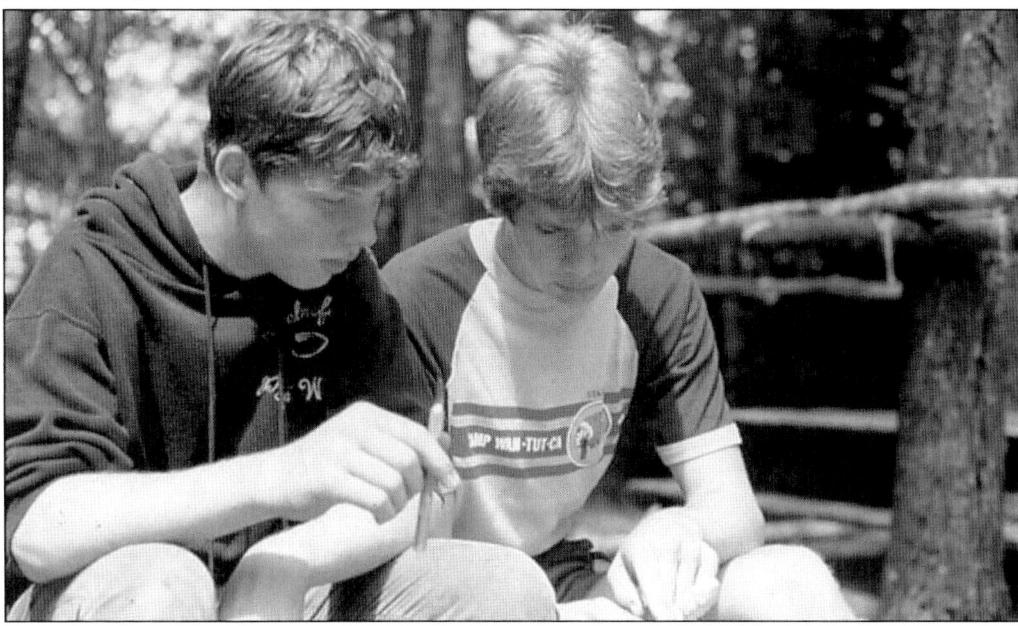

One of Wannalancit Lodge's most spirited leaders was Andrew Curry-Green. Pictured on the right helping a Scout with a handicraft project, Green was a camp staff member that boys wanted to hang around with. If one was with Green one could not help but have a great time. Tragically Green was aboard American Airlines Flight 11 on September 11, 2001. The boathouse at Wah-Tut-Ca was renamed after him to honor how he lived.

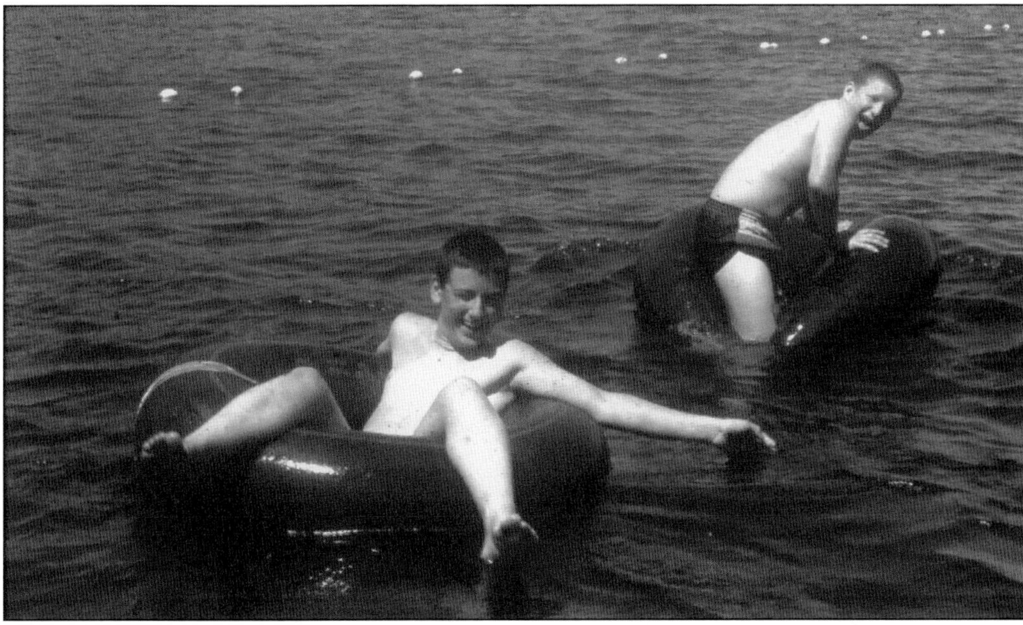

Seeing Scouts float down the Delaware River at Treasure Island Scout Camp on inner tubes in 1983, Sughrue developed an idea for Wah-Tut-Ca. Although Wah-Tut-Ca streams where not navigational by inner tube, the lake was a fine substitute. Sughrue went to trucking companies and collected as many inner tubes as he could get. With so many tubes in the water it was said one could walk to the rafts.

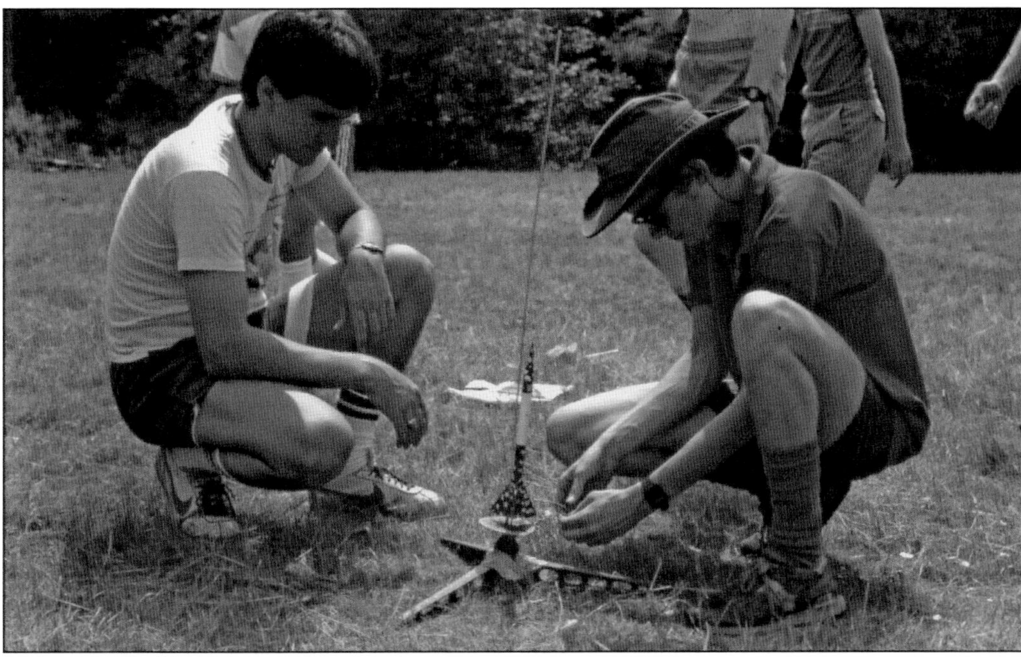

Model rocketry was introduced by Sughrue after he saw it at another Scout camp. Campers would build their rockets in the handicraft lodge and take the finished product to the field at the top of the hill. The thrill of the launch was quickly followed by the search for where it went, or as they would say at Wah-Tut-Ca, a "voyage of recovery."

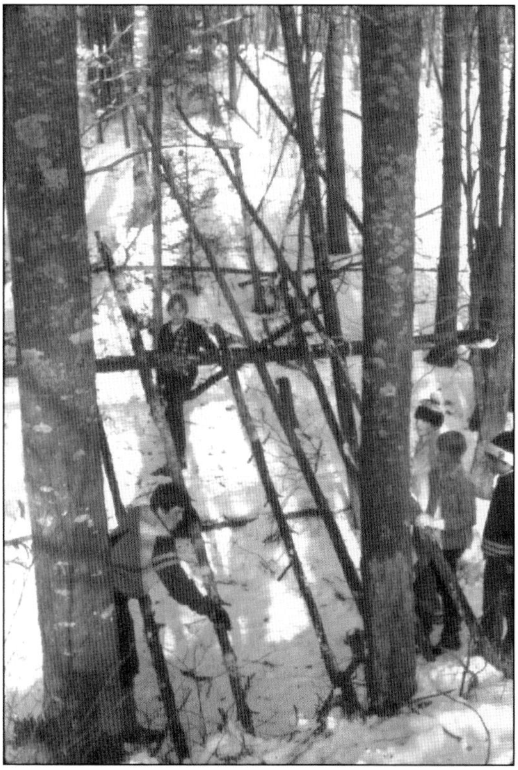

Brian J. Lobao developed the Nor-Tut-Ca program in the 1980s. Held during the February school vacation, this program used Wah-Tut-Ca as a winter camp. Scouts would spend the week on cross-country skis and have many activities based on a Nordic theme. At the end of the week, boys would ski out to the edges of camp and have a "sleep out" in the snow.

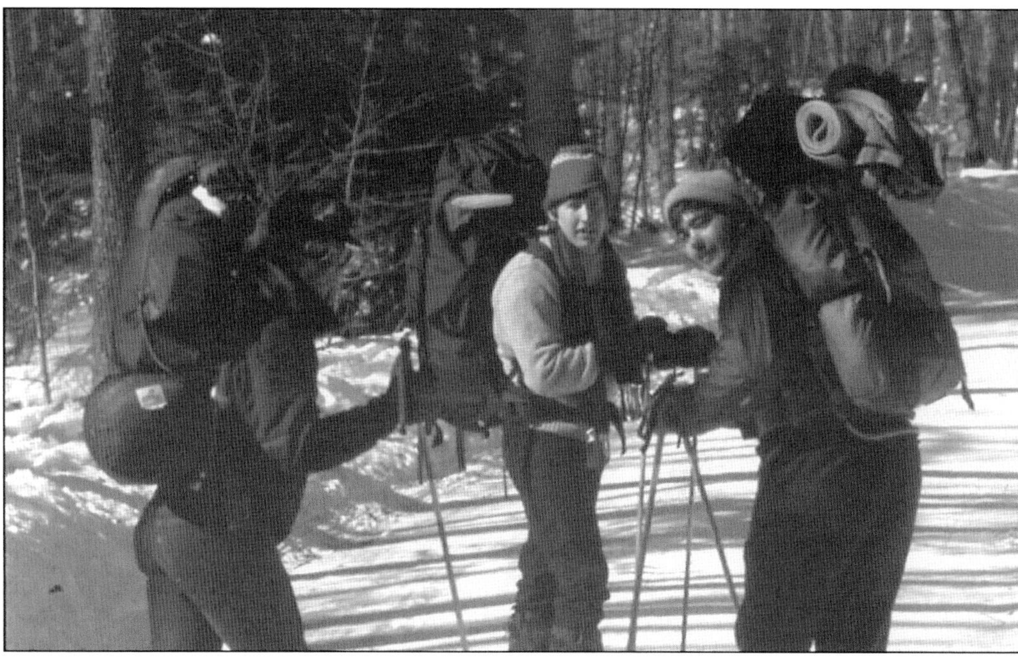

In the center, between Jeff S. Eckelkamp (left) and Daniel Farrell (right), is Christopher E. Eckelkamp skiing the trails of Wah-Tut-Ca at Nor-Tut-Ca. Chris is the oldest in a family of nine boys. He and his brothers would serve and lead the lodge and camp in many programs. Eckelkamp most recently has served as camp director of the Greater Lowell Cub Day Camp.

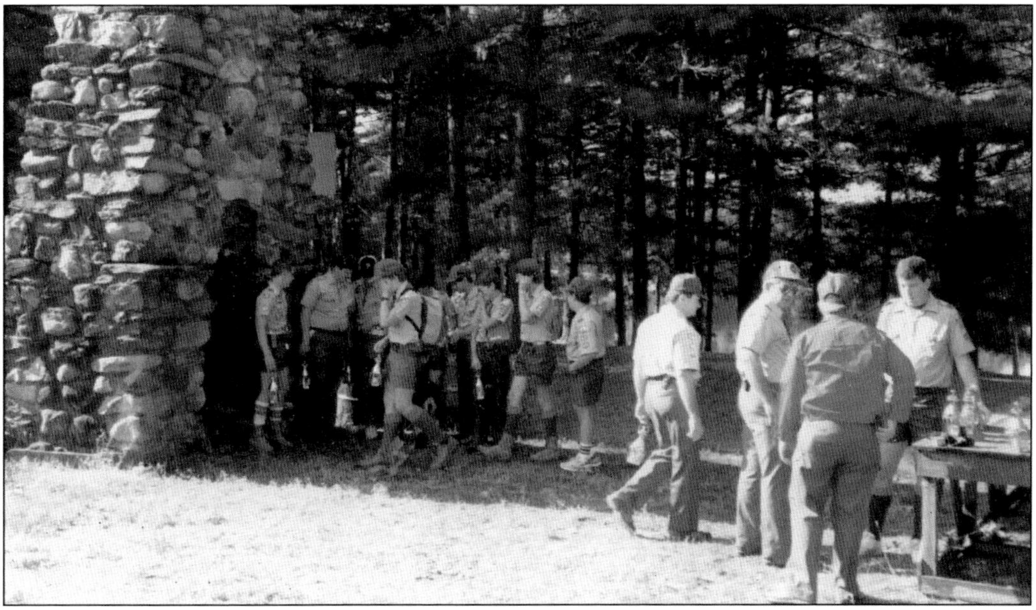

In 1987, Wah-Tut-Ca celebrated its 50th anniversary. A yearlong event, it would have many programs to commemorate the opening of Wah-Tut-Ca. Two books on the history of Wah-Tut-Ca were produced. Alexander A. Vervaert produced the *Wah-Tut-Ca Scrap Book*, and Brian J. Lobao wrote *Glow the Brighter*. Old Home Day was celebrated on June 27 with over 1,000 Scouts and their families in attendance. The most dramatic and symbolic event was lead by Albert J. Deprez. Three days before Old Home Day, 26 Scouts assembled in Dunstable, Massachusetts, at the site of the old Camp Chadwick. After lighting lanterns, they began the hike to Northwood to honor Wah-Tut-Ca's founders. At the end of the campfire, these Scouts carrying the lanterns entered the Clayton Lane Stockade. A memorial flame was lit with the words "from this spark we begin Wah-Tut-Ca's second 50 years."

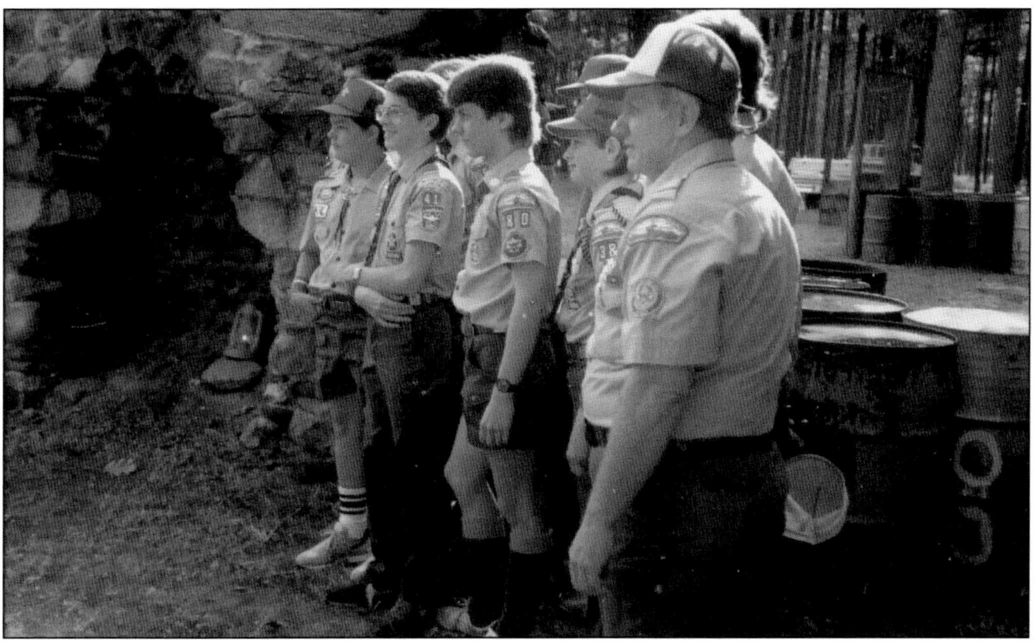

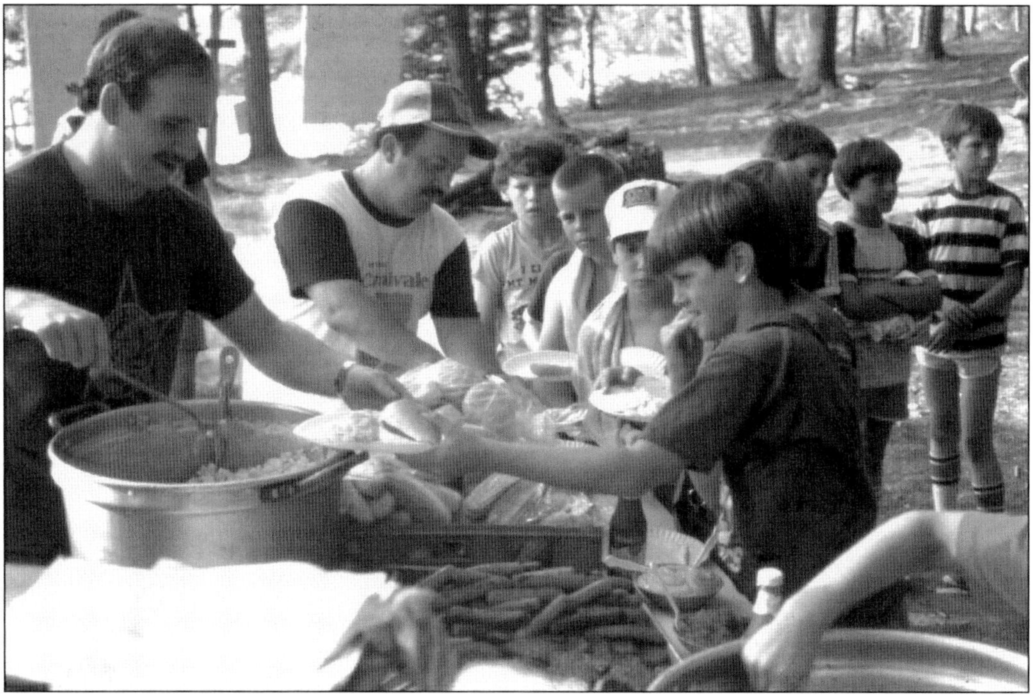

In the 1980s, the BSA developed and promoted camping programs for Cub Scouts. Barney Barbera (second from left) would lead the reopening of Camp So-Kee-Tay. This junior camp of Chadwick and Wah-Tut-Ca had been closed in the 1950s by the BSA. So-Kee-Tay was closed a second time in 1999 when the Greater Lowell Council merged with the Yankee Clipper Council.

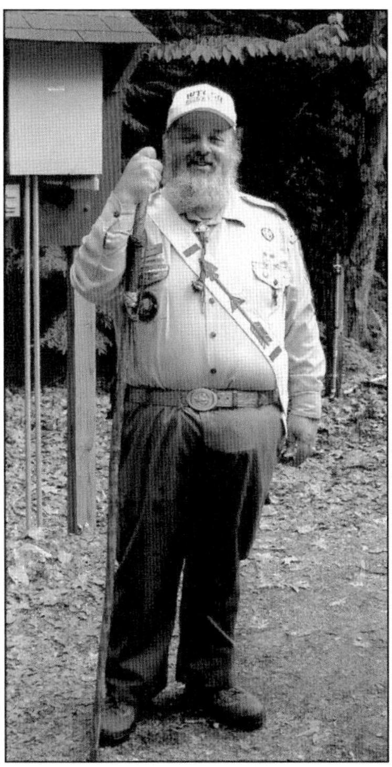

Tony Bacchi left a legacy of growth at Wah-Tut-Ca. He became the scoutmaster of Troop 74 of Chelmsford, Massachusetts, and would later serve as the council camping committee chairman. During his tenure as camping chairman, he would be one of the prime leaders in shaping an expanded camp program. Bacchi passed away in 2001, but his vision for new buildings and facilities is still being implemented.

Craig Ryder (left) came to Wah-Tut-Ca as a youth and became reservation director in 1991. Ryder was unselfish, humble, and led by example. Just by watching him, individuals would be inspired to work just a little harder and give a little more. Like many of Wah-Tut-Ca's greatest leaders, his leadership and service were rooted in a deep love of Wah-Tut-Ca and commitment to its future. He asked all to catch a higher vision.

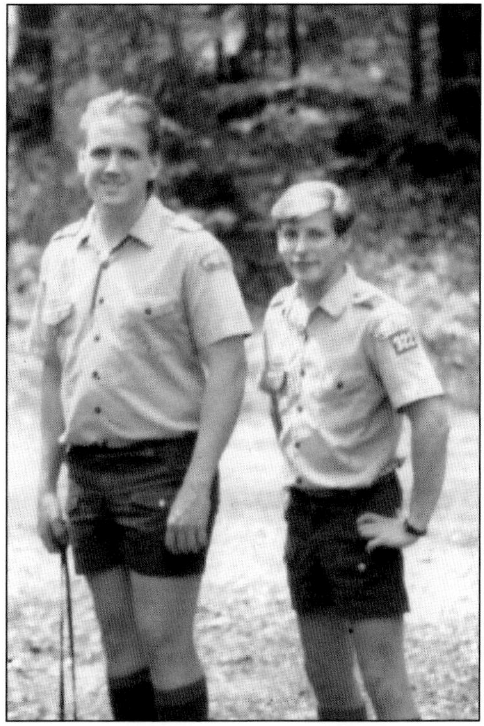

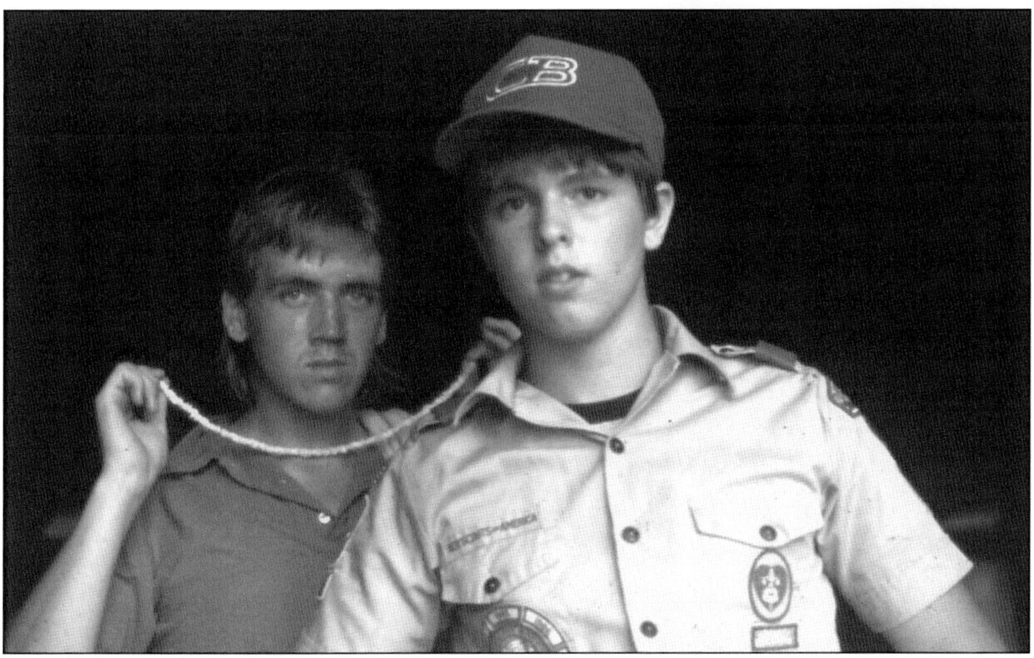

A young Craig Ryder (rear) is seen here with camper David Leonard. Ryder and Leonard would work on camp staff together and become lifelong friends. Many of the relationships developed on camp staff would last lifetimes. Together they would celebrate weddings and the births of children. Leonard would be one of dozens of Wah-Tut-Ca's alumni to hold vigil the night Craig Ryder passed away after a long battle with cancer in 2005.

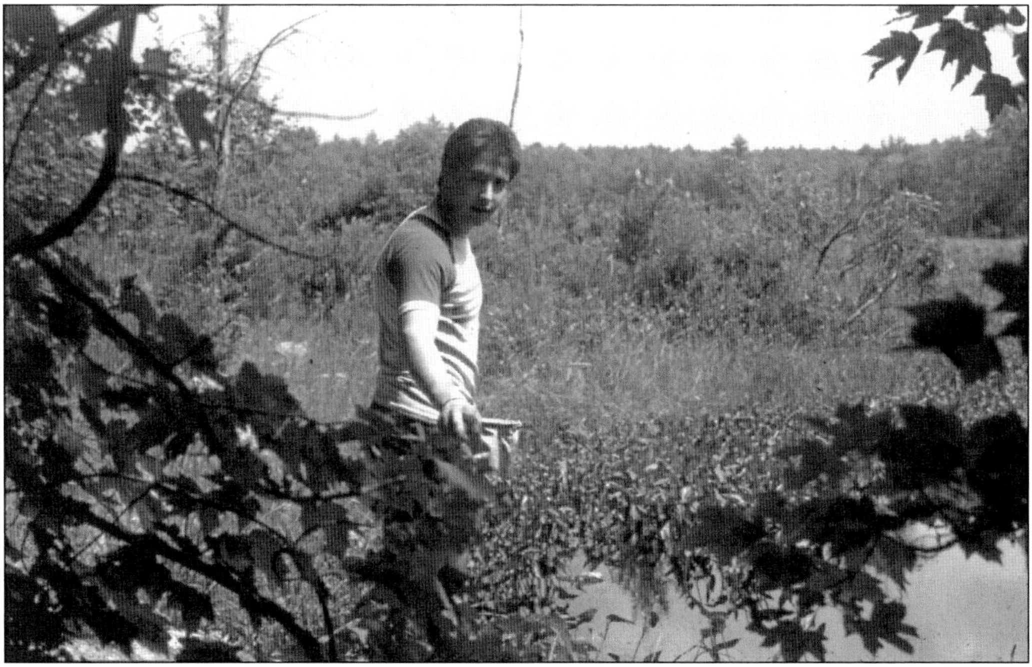

Marc "Gus" Desgrosielliers was a camp staff member with an intoxicating personality. Desgrosielliers served as an area director and lodge officer and attended several NOACs. His spirit flowed through the lodge and council programs. Here he leads Scouts to the swamps found on Wah-Tut-Ca's boarders. The Swamp Stomp would become a popular nature activity.

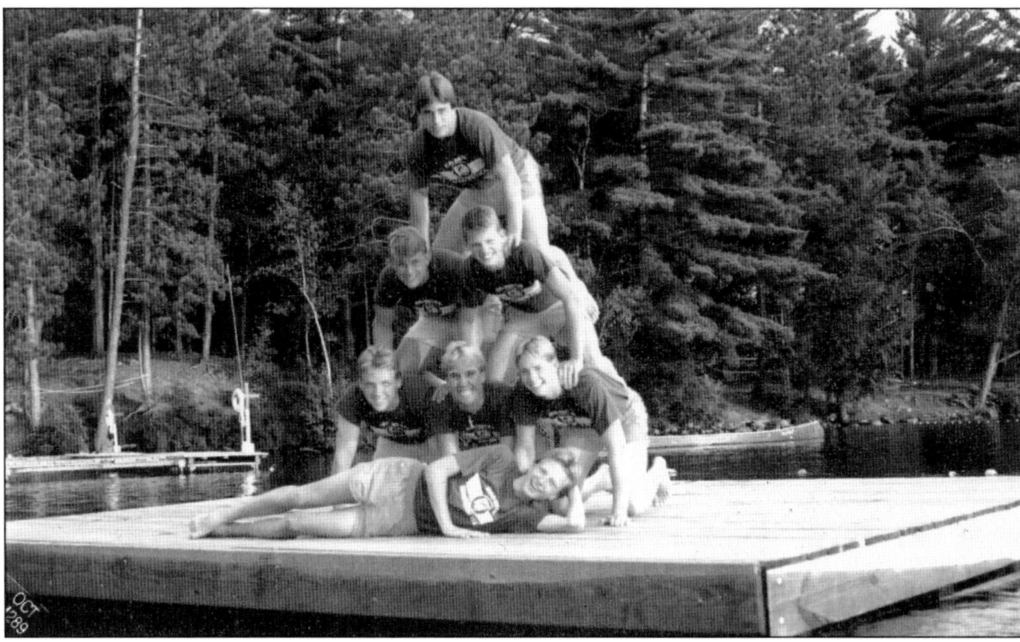

By the 1990s, being on camp staff was a quest for excellence and achievement as noted by this waterfront "pyramid of power." In this picture are three camp directors, four aquatics directors, two COPE directors, five OA vigil honor members, and three lodge chiefs. The friendships and commitment to Wah-Tut-Ca would last long after this picture was taken.

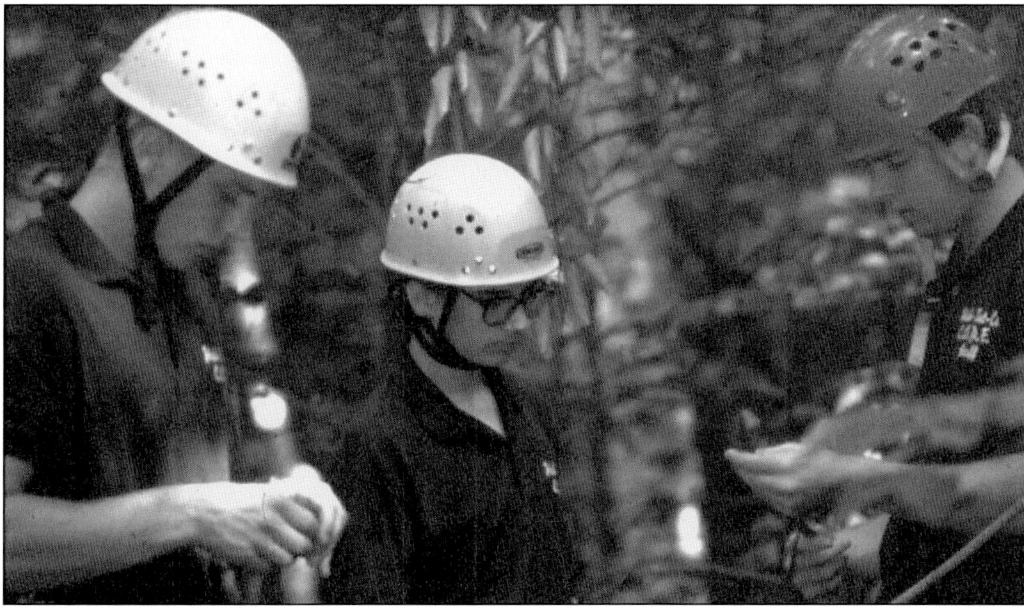

One of the features of the expansion of the camp program was the addition of a ropes program. It developed into what is called the Challenging Outdoor Personal Experience (COPE). Mark Juhola (at the far right) and Joshua Ratty (center) directed this program aimed at keeping older boys interested in camp. COPE teaches leadership, teamwork, communication, self confidence, and trust.

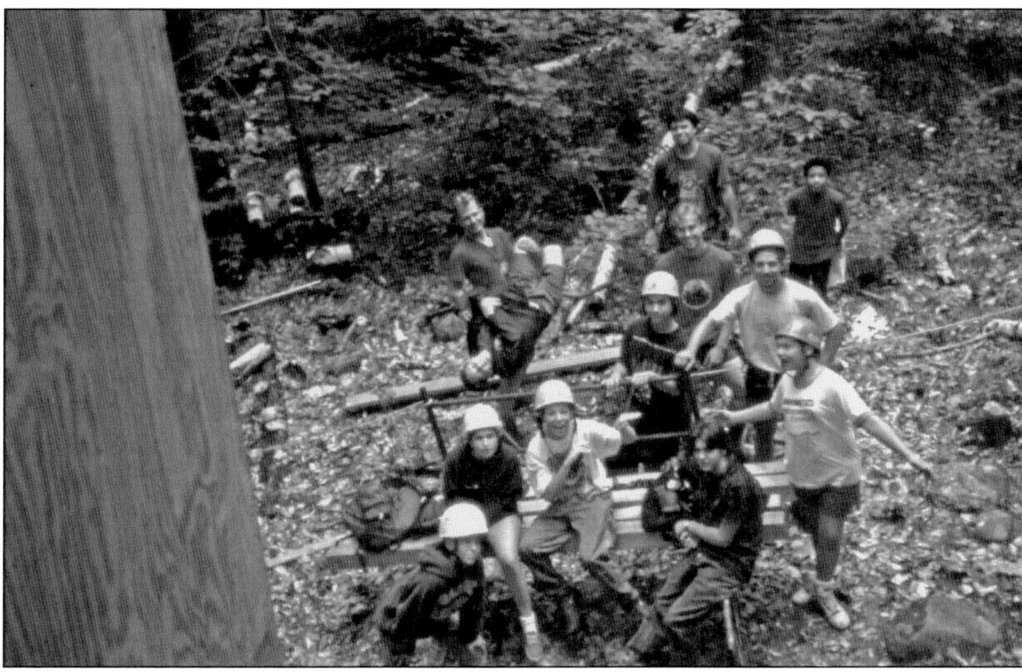

COPE was one of the programs championed by Craig Ryder and Tony Bacchi to make Wah-Tut-Ca more appealing to older boys. It was noted that after two or three years at Wah-Tut-Ca, Scouts felt that there was no longer a reason to attend. These programs were directed at that group and designed to bring another level of challenge to a Wah-Tut-Ca camper.

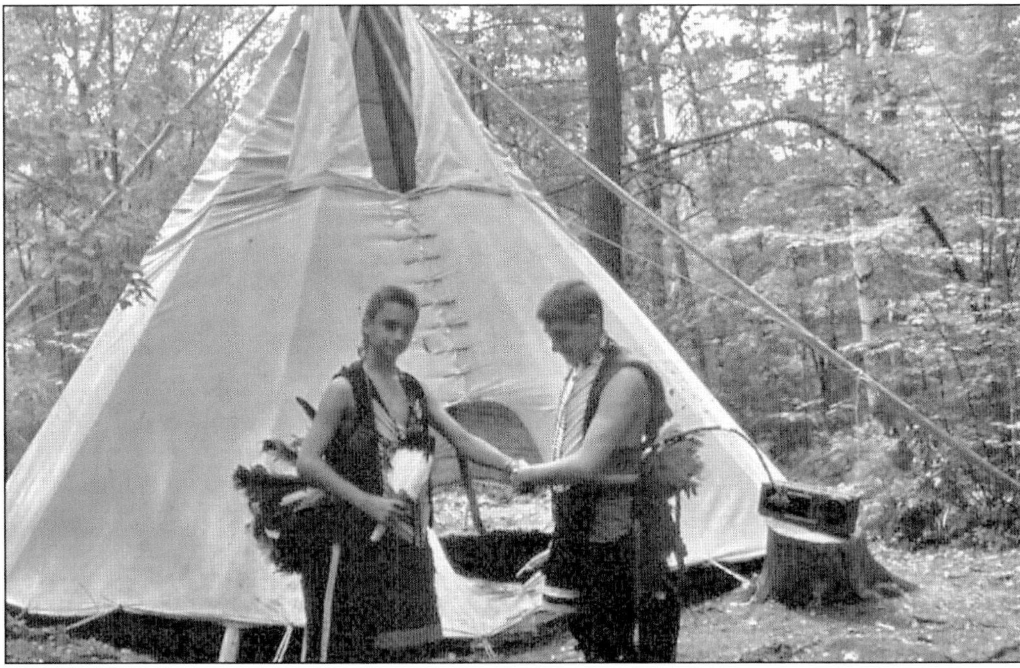

Bennett A. Sawyer (left) worked as a camp staff member. He was also a Wannalancit Lodge officer. A member of the lodge dance team, Sawyer would combine both interests at Wah-Tut-Ca's Indian Village. His positive, heartfelt spirit would be a source of encouragement and inspiration for many friends and brothers.

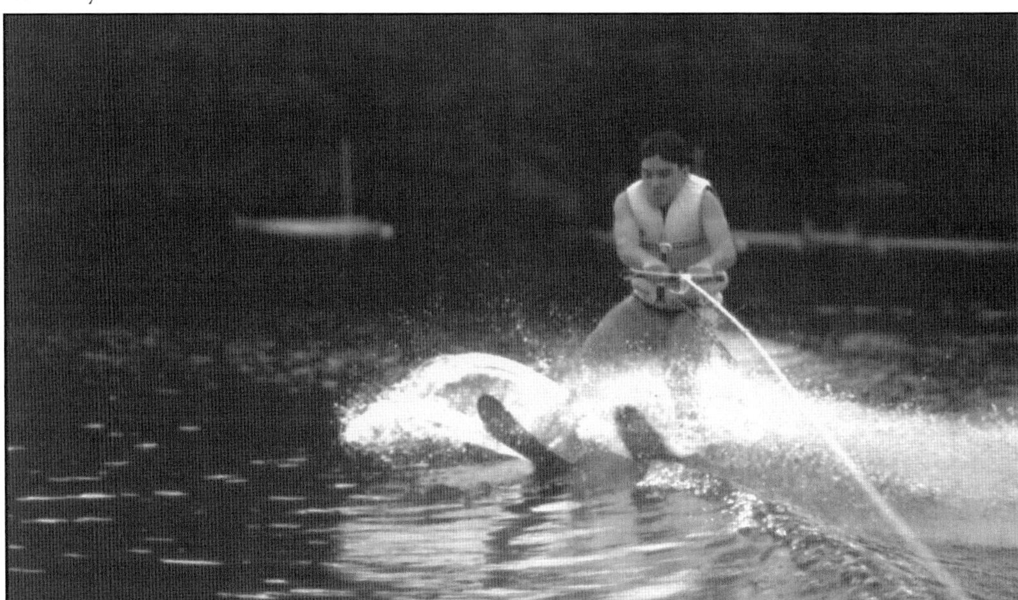

The camping committee felt that Wah-Tut-Ca, as a Scout camp, should be second to none. Noting that Wah-Tut-Ca lacked a motorboat when many other camps had one, they came up with a way to buy one. Critics of these expansion programs described them as "gilding for the camp." In fact, these efforts resulted in increased attendance and an improved financial performance for the camp.

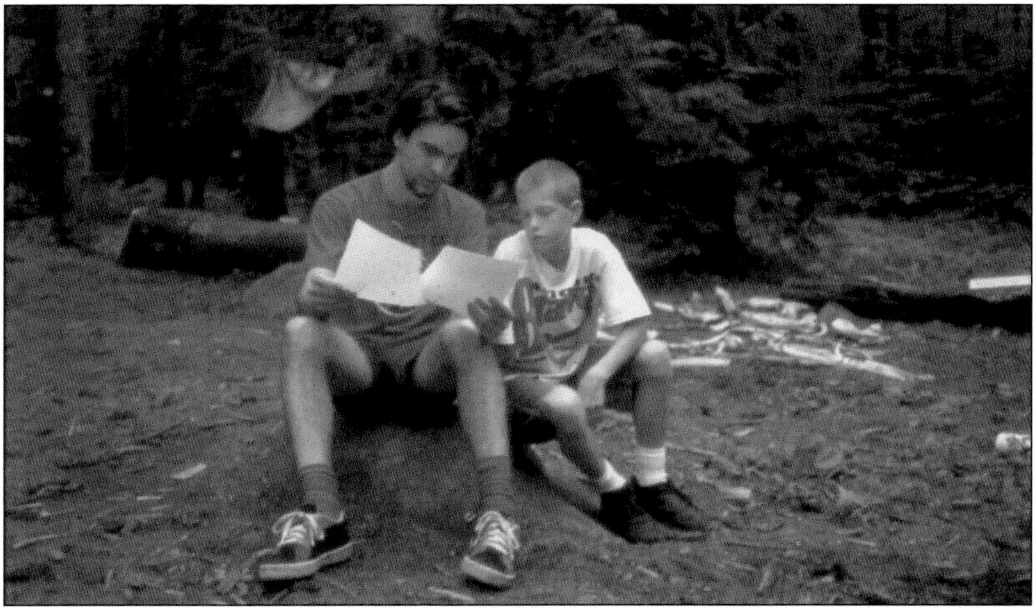

Wah-Tut-Ca has always been a place for storytellers. Michael F. Fournier is seen here teaching a scout while working on staff at Wah-Tut-Ca's Discovery Area. At Wah-Tut-Ca, histories and stories are told from one generation to the next. Each person telling the story adds his own perspective and charm. Yet everyone who tells a story does so with a sense of spirit and adventure.

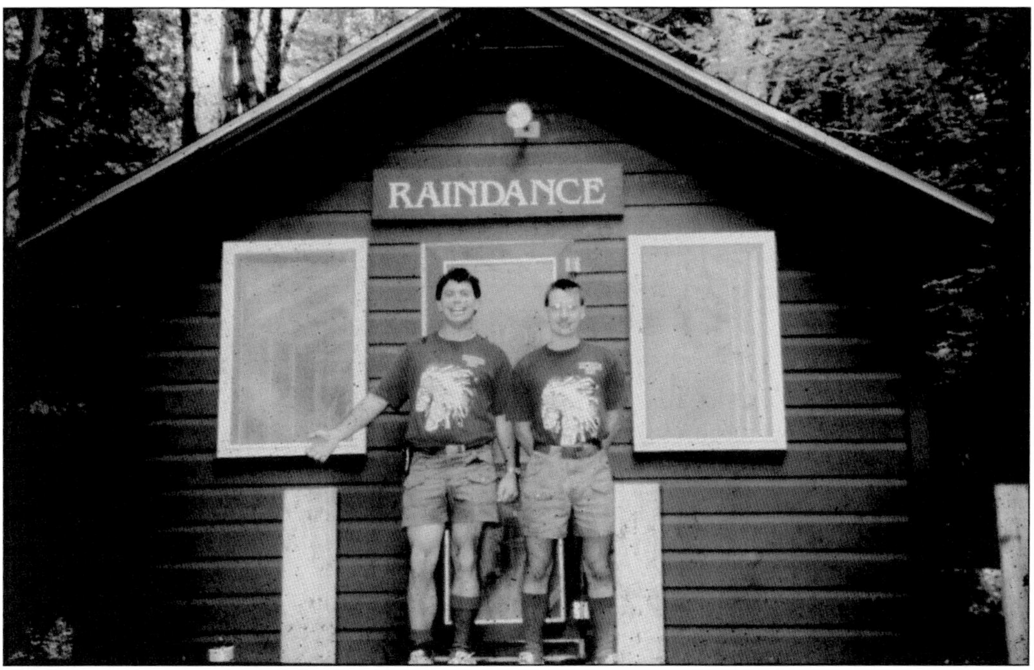

Raindance is one of the original Chadwick cabins moved to Wah-Tut-Ca in 1937. In 1991, it was moved again from the Wannalancit to the Shanawanda campsite. It would be Alexander A. Vervaert's last project at Wah-Tut-Ca. When the project was completed, Vervaert went back to do a few finishing touches. He was later found with a paint brush in his hand. He had died in the place that he loved.

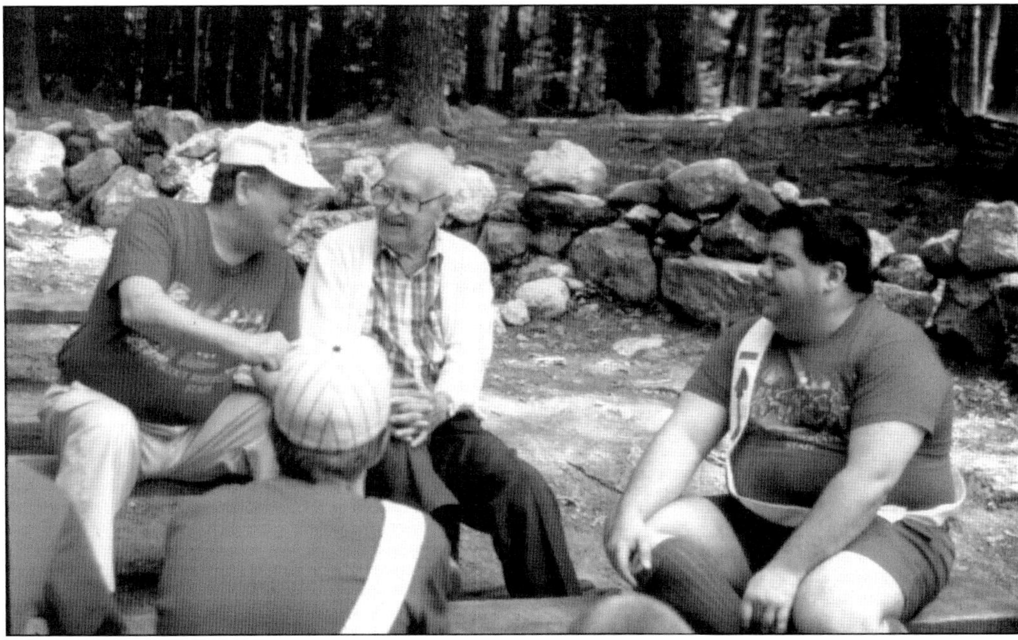

Former lodge advisers Harold R. Stevens (left) and Clayton R. Lane (center) visited Wah-Tut-Ca in 1992. They are seated in the stockade with George D. Kouloheras at Lane's last visit to Wah-Tut-Ca. Stevens and Lane shared their memories of camp and the lodge. When they passed, Kouloheras would take on the responsibility of telling these stories to another generation.

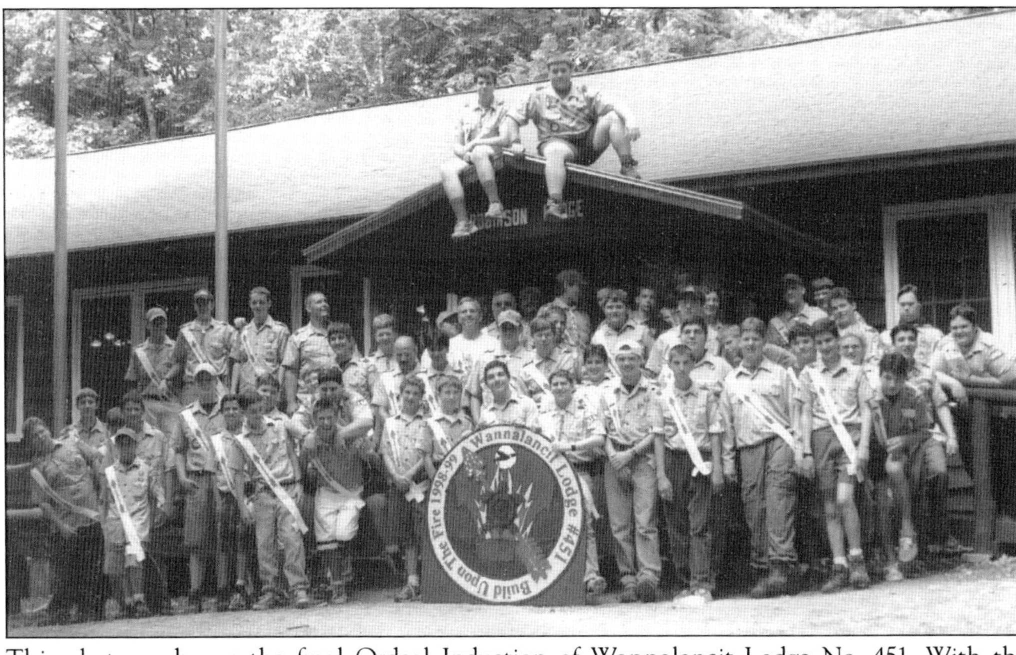

This photograph was the final Ordeal Induction of Wannalancit Lodge No. 451. With the merger of the Greater Lowell Council with the Yankee Clipper Council, Wannalancit Lodge ended. Wah-Tut-Ca would now look to a new lodge, Nanepashemet Lodge No. 158. Much of the old lodge's leadership focused their efforts on improving Wah-Tut-Ca and sharing its spirit with a much larger community.

Seven

Keep the Spirit Alive

Into the 21st century, Boy Scouting faced extreme challenges. A wider variety of youth programs and other recreational opportunities competed with Scouting. A regional survey of Boy Scout summer camps found that most camps in the Northeast were only being used to 25 percent of their capacity. Many newly merged councils across the country were selling camps in order to establish endowments to fund operations. Many Greater Lowell volunteers worried about the fate of Wah-Tut-Ca.

After the merger, there were signs of a flagging spirit. The Yankee Clipper Council already ran a fully functioning Boy Scout camp at Camp Onway and a summer Cub Scout program at Lone Tree Scout Reservation. Some asked, "Had Wah-Tut-Ca become redundant?"

Those who love Wah-Tut-Ca rallied and relied on the same sense of innovation, adaptation, and continual improvement that had motivated Wah-Tut-Ca's leadership since 1936. They displayed bold determination through efforts both large and small to improve the camp's programs. As a result, attendance began to increase. New troops in the Yankee Clipper Council and some from as far away as New York and New Jersey began to call Wah-Tut-Ca home.

In the middle of the 2006 season, an event occurred that revealed the can-do spirit of Wah-Tut-Ca. Without warning, a microburst, an intense storm with winds of over 100 miles per hour, hit Wah-Tut-Ca. The devastation was immense. The storm knocked out power, damaged or destroyed several buildings, and totaled 11 vehicles. Wah-Tut-Ca had never before suffered storm damage on this scale.

By the next morning, campers happily ate melting strawberry ice cream and cocoa puffs at tables outside the damaged dining hall and listened to announcements about the new locations of some of the program areas. That week and the rest of the summer continued on in the Wah-Tut-Ca tradition.

Today Wah-Tut-Ca thrives. Each summer, hundreds of scouts make their way up the road to Blake's Hill. The wind still fills their sails. Scouts still go on "voyages of discovery." They keep the spirit of Wah-Tut-Ca alive as the generations did before them. They know that Wah-Tut-Ca is more than a summer camp. It is a home of friends and brothers.

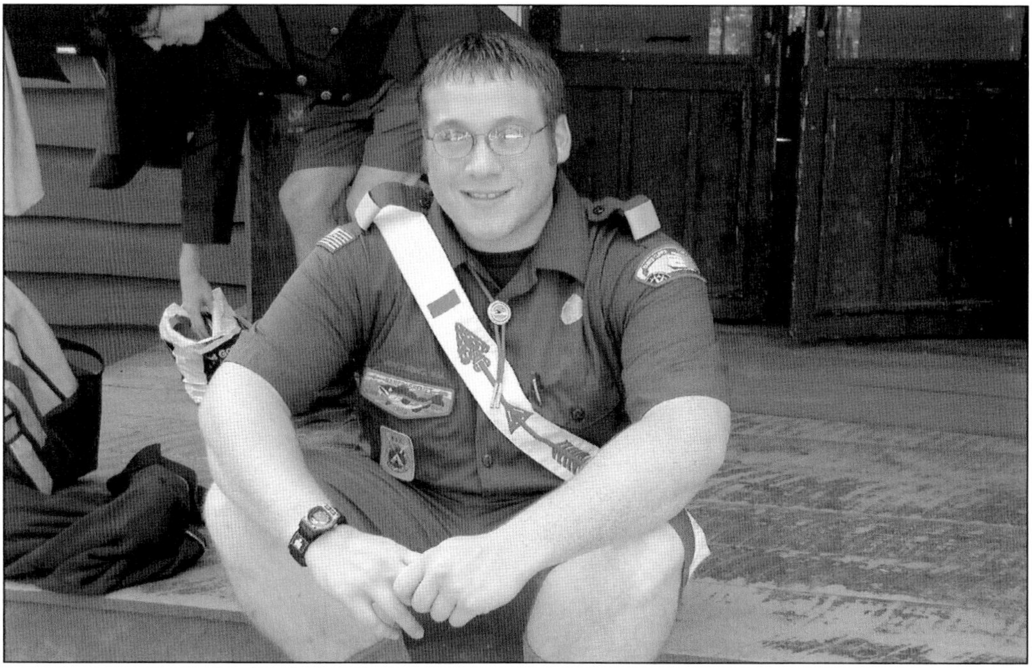

Kevin R. Dion was the last lodge chief of Wannalancit Lodge No. 451. Since the merger with the Yankee Clipper Council, he has been instrumental in keeping the spirit of Wah-Tut-Ca alive, serving as both program and camp director. His efforts resulted in further growth in attendance and expanded opportunities for all scouts that come to camp.

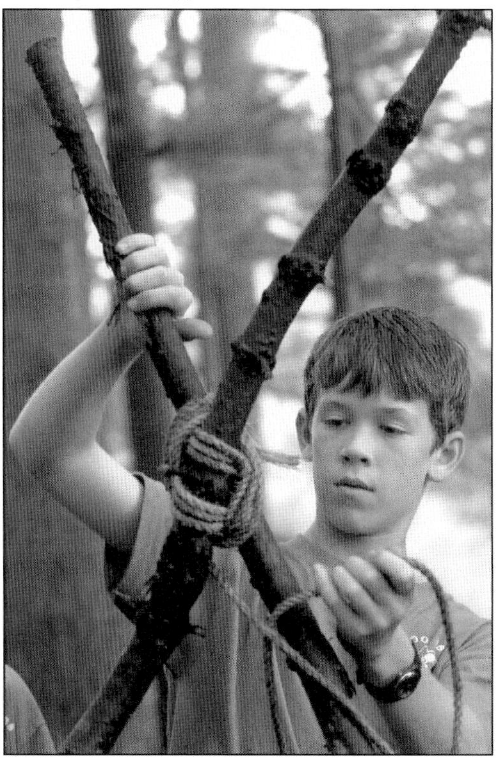

Knot tying is one of the first skills a new Scout learns. In a camp filled with several hundred people, it is easy for one person to feel lost in a crowd. The Wah-Tut-Ca staff does everything possible to recognize each individual accomplishment and to celebrate every victory.

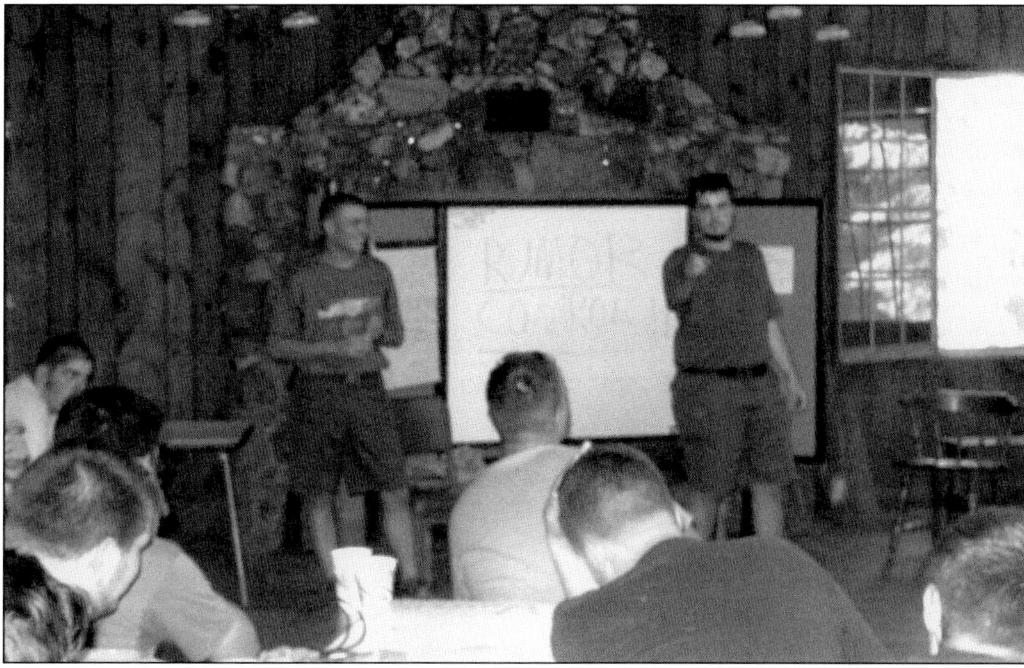

New staff members sit eager to hear the stories from older leaders of Wannalancit Lodge at staff week prior to the opening of camp. Raymond Morrison (left) and Greg Smith give a presentation passing on the skills and knowledge they learned from their involvement with the lodge and camp staff in prior seasons.

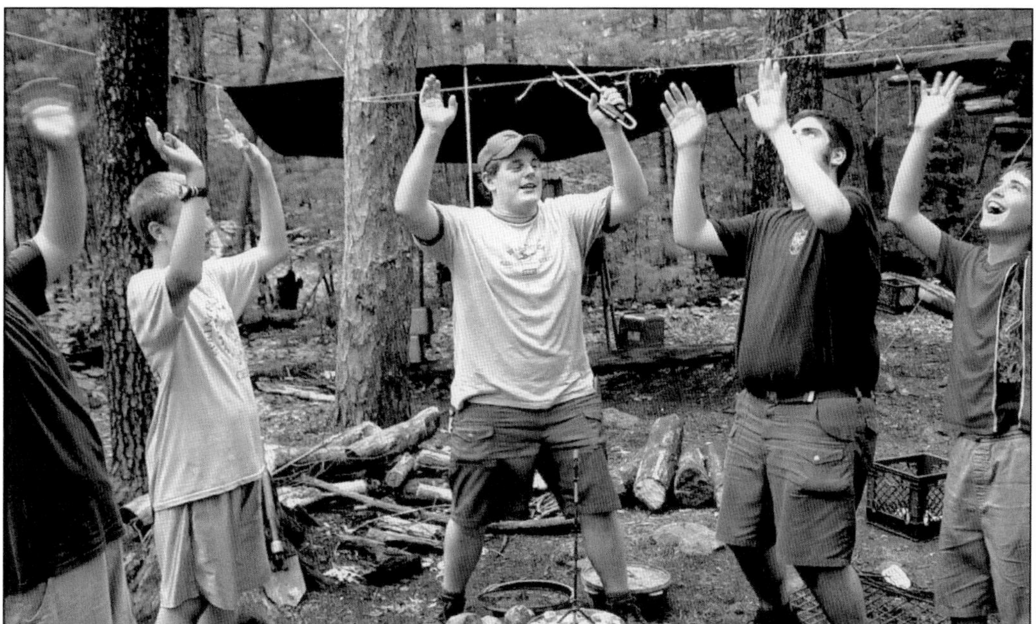

While teaching was important, staff members are always looking for a way to keep things fun and interesting. Here Ryan Kelley (center), the Frontier director in 2003, instructs campers in a practice that Dion had once passed on to him. While cooking he asks the boys to "pray to the fried dough gods" to make sure everything comes out all right.

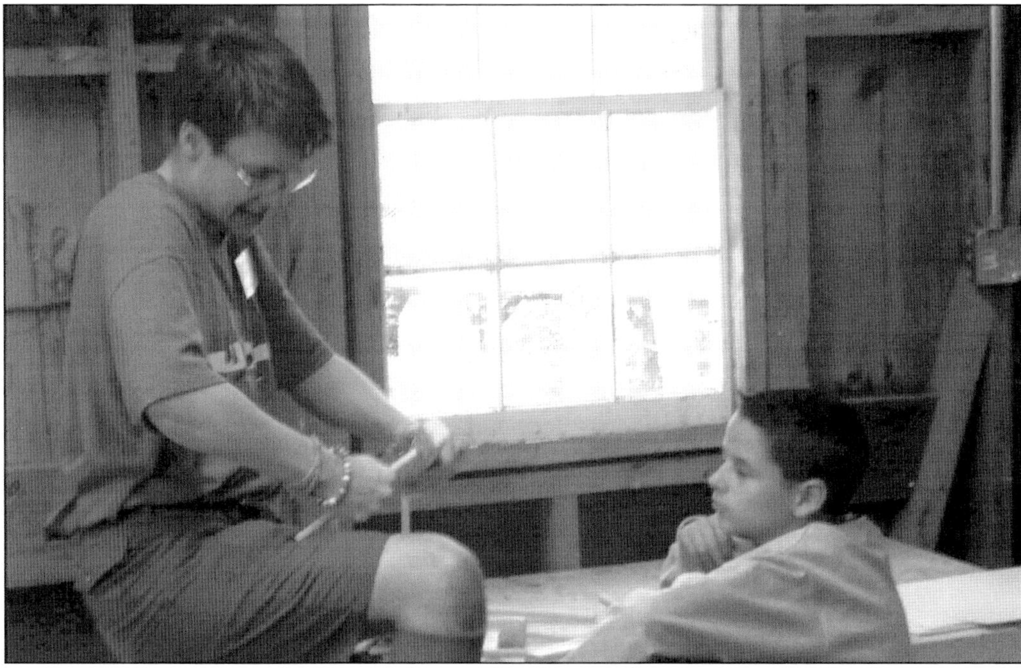

Staff members like Mike Simmons made camp a supreme adventure. Any area Simmons worked in benefited from his enthusiastic yet dry sense of humor. During his time as director of handicrafts and the Frontier, he improved the programs in both areas. Simmons is known for his dramatic and "epic" programs that excited and involved the entire camp.

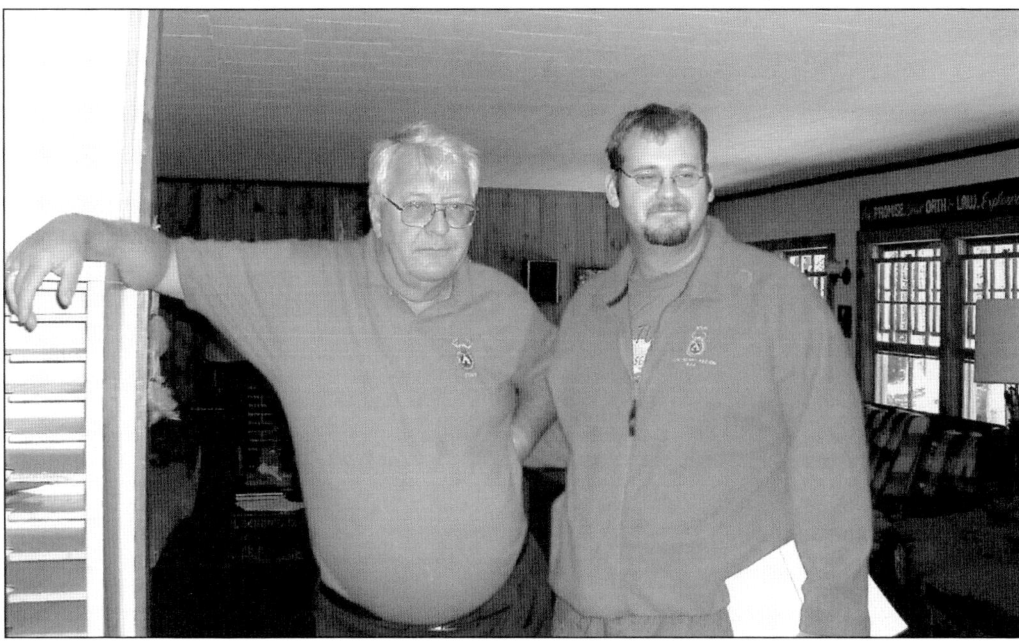

Frank Barre, Scout professional, and his son Matt are standing in Williams Lodge, the camp service center. Matt served as camp director in 2001 and 2002. From the early 1990s, Frank has been a mentor to each successive camp director. His quiet patience and love of summer camp programs were ever present as he taught each camp director to succeed in his own way.

Charles (Chad) McMurrer went to Wah-Tut-Ca as a camper in 1988. After high school, McMurrer joined the Marines, seeing action in Bosnia. Returning from the corps, McMurrer became director of shooting sports and later camp director. One of his many accomplishments was overseeing the development and completion of the new shooting sports area. Construction of the new ranges began in 2003 and was completed in 2005.

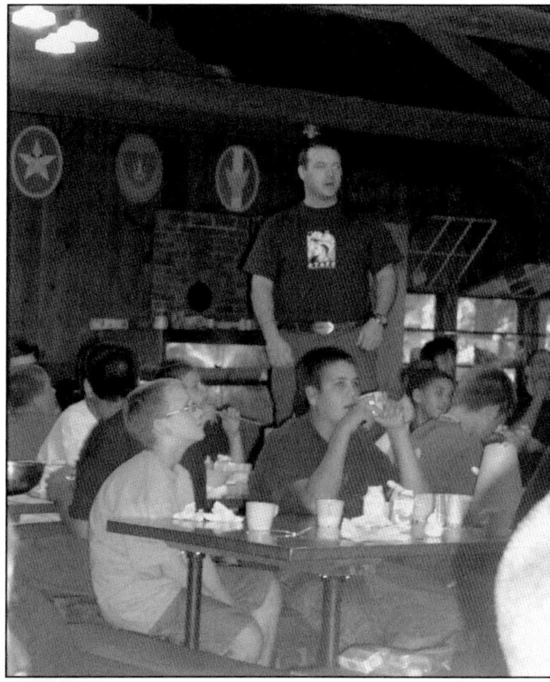

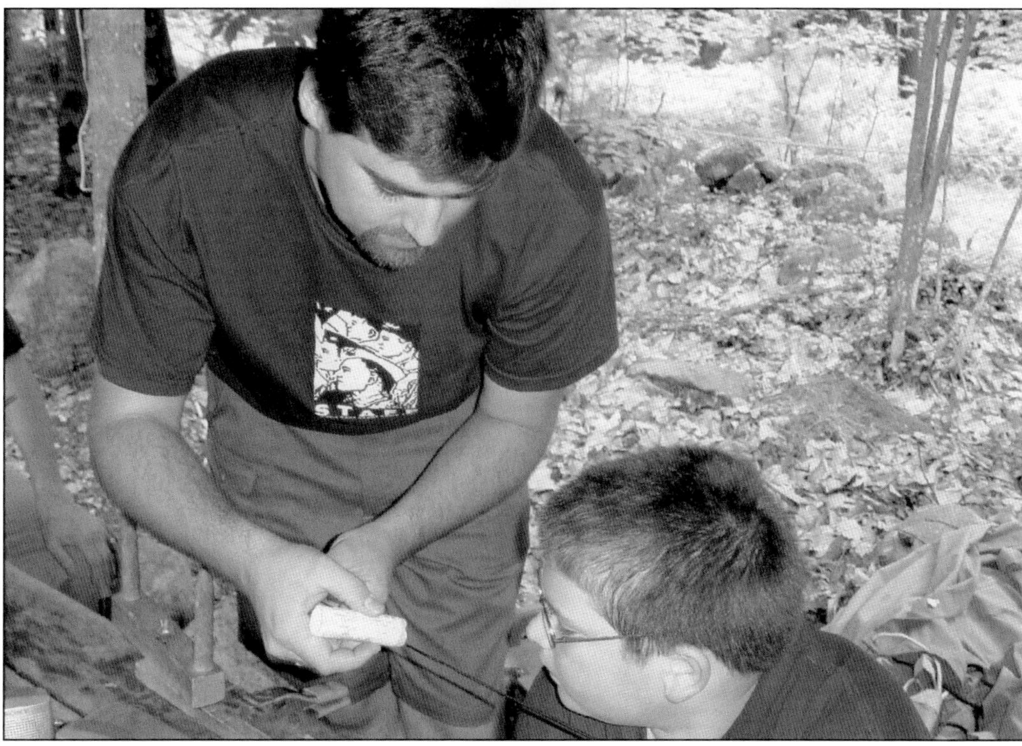

Daniel S. Smith is a former lodge chief of Wannalancit Lodge No. 451 and became an associate adviser of Nanepashemet Lodge No. 158 after the merger. Smith is known for his ingenuity in finding new ways to get things done. He is a trained engineer and truly lives the part, shown by his focus on the smallest of details. His impact is seen in every aspect of camp programs and operations.

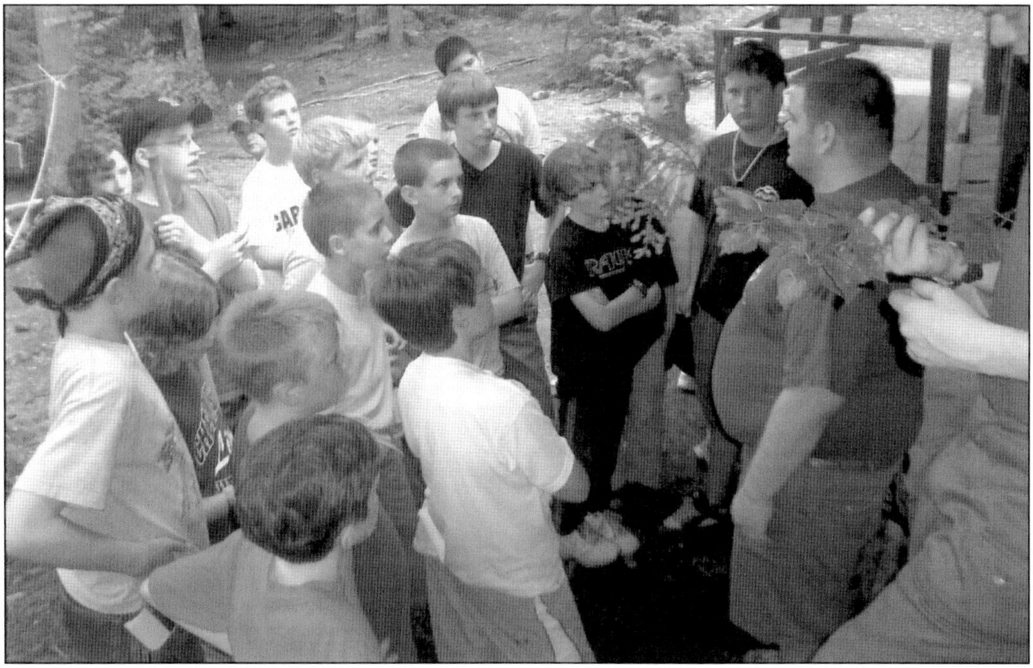

The staff placed great emphasis on ensuring that first-year campers had an amazing experience. The Project Green Program was designed specifically for the needs of these young scouts. Focusing on basic Scout skills, Project Green was instrumental in expanding attendance, as most participants would return for a second season.

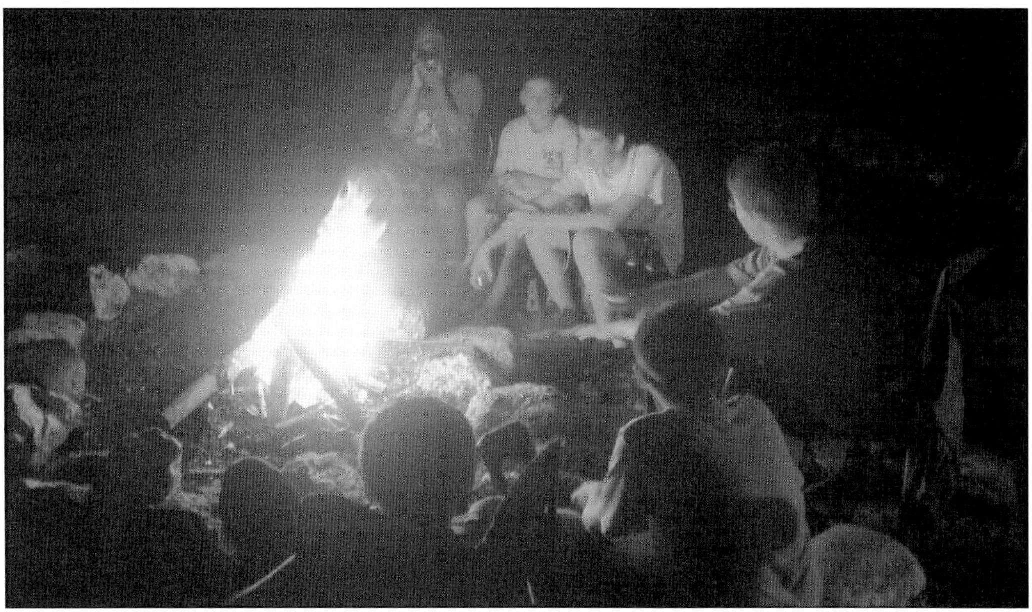

What would camp be without campfires? Thanks to the generosity and expertise of many former staff members, campfires became extraordinary productions for campers to enjoy. From the very first night in camp, campers were drawn in by these exciting spectacles. During the week, staff would take pictures and create a closing slide show that would remind everyone of their amazing camp experience.

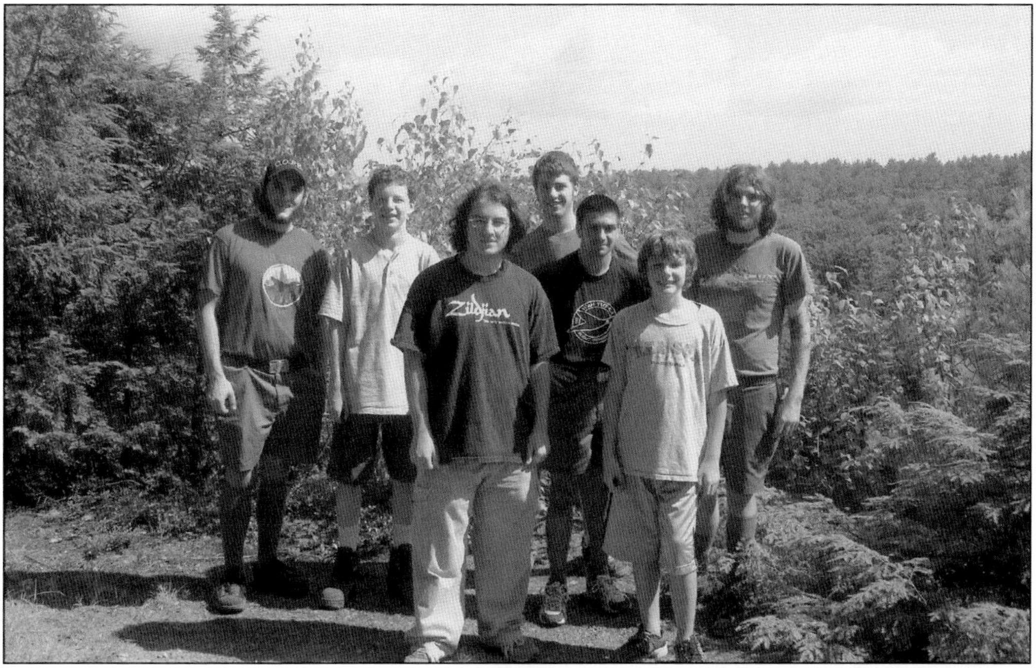

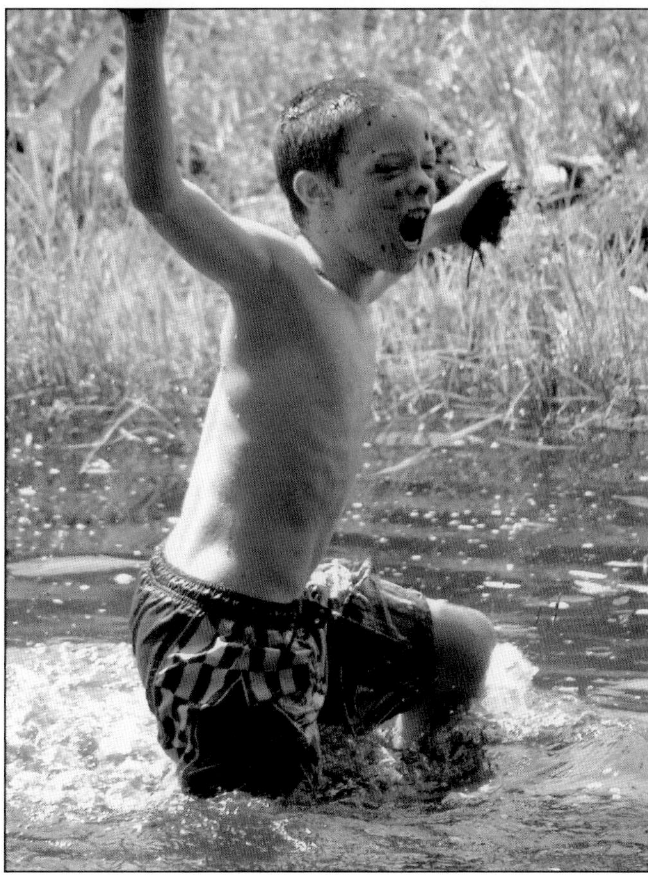

Brothers Ryan and Pat Dromgoole are pictured here with a group of Scouts they had led on a hike to Robinson Lookout. The phrase "voyage of discovery" is spoken often at the beginning of each summer during staff training. Those words would repeatedly ring in each staff member's ears. The brothers embodied a passion for getting kids out to where they could see the amazing aspects of nature. The Swamp Stomp, often led by Pat, continues to be an opportunity for Scouts to learn a little about nature and have a lot of fun at the same time.

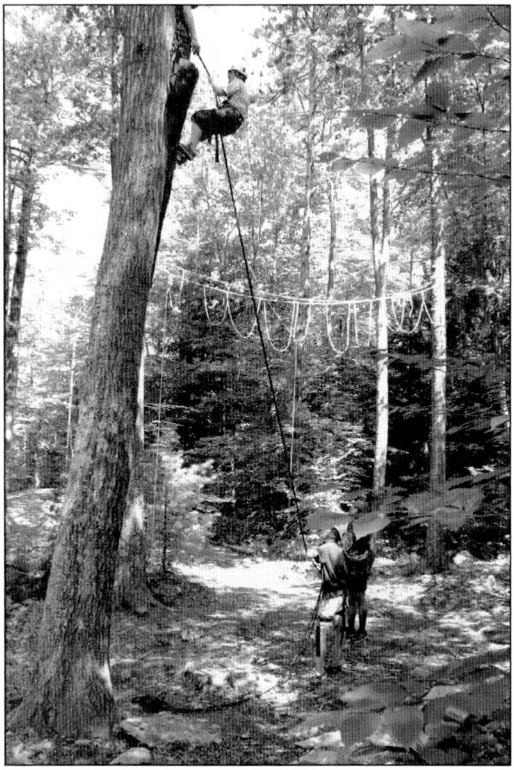

Nate Tobey, director of COPE, taught scouts to push themselves through team-building activities and leadership training. The COPE course would be rebuilt by Keith Garvey, Ryan Dromgoole, and other volunteers to meet the new required safety standards. It remains one of Wah-Tut-Ca's most popular older boy activities.

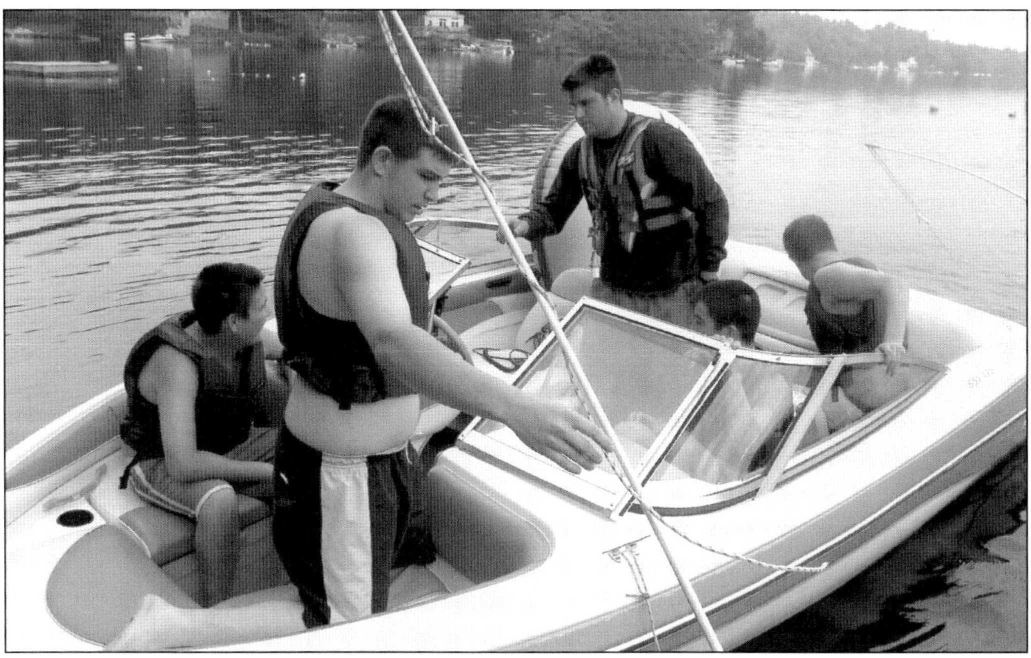

Aquatics II, the advanced waterfront activity, under directors such as Jim Ploski and Jon Keating continued to grow. With Dan Smith's engineering skills, Wah-Tut-Ca's fleet of boats would be improved. An effort of the camping committee championed by Carl Silvia, Wah-Tut-Ca would gain dozens of kayaks. Today Wah-Tut-Ca has more boats afloat than any other time in its history.

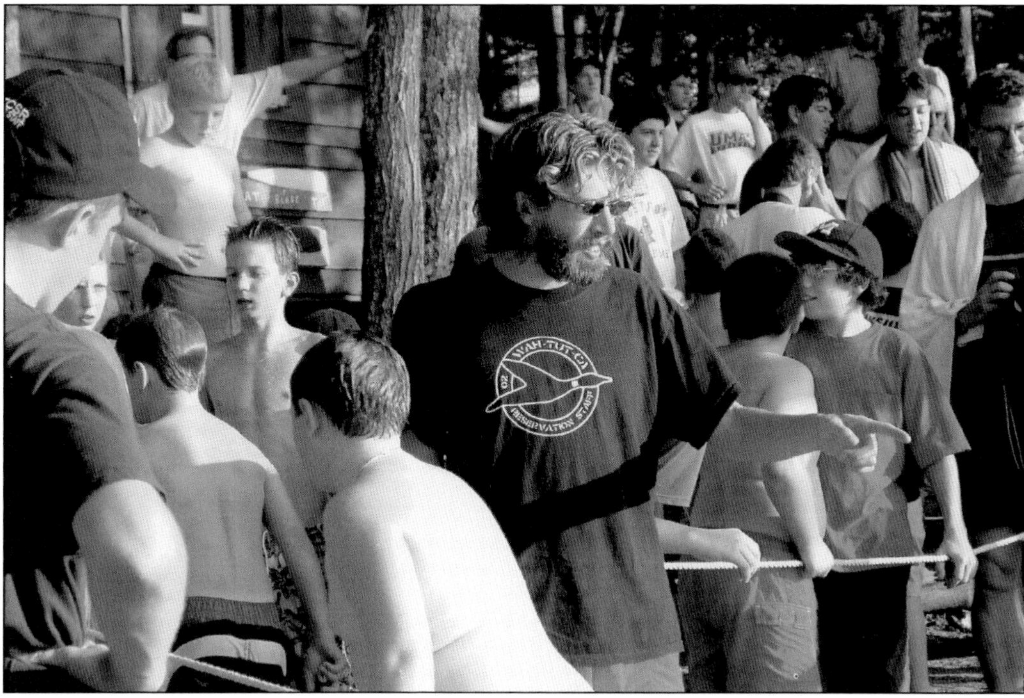

Jonathan J. Keating is associated with the aquatics program at Wah-Tut-Ca. He improved the program by establishing standards of excellence in safety and oversight. Always concerned with the needs of individual campers, he focused the waterfront program so that it was meaningful for each boy. Many campers join the staff because of his influence and example.

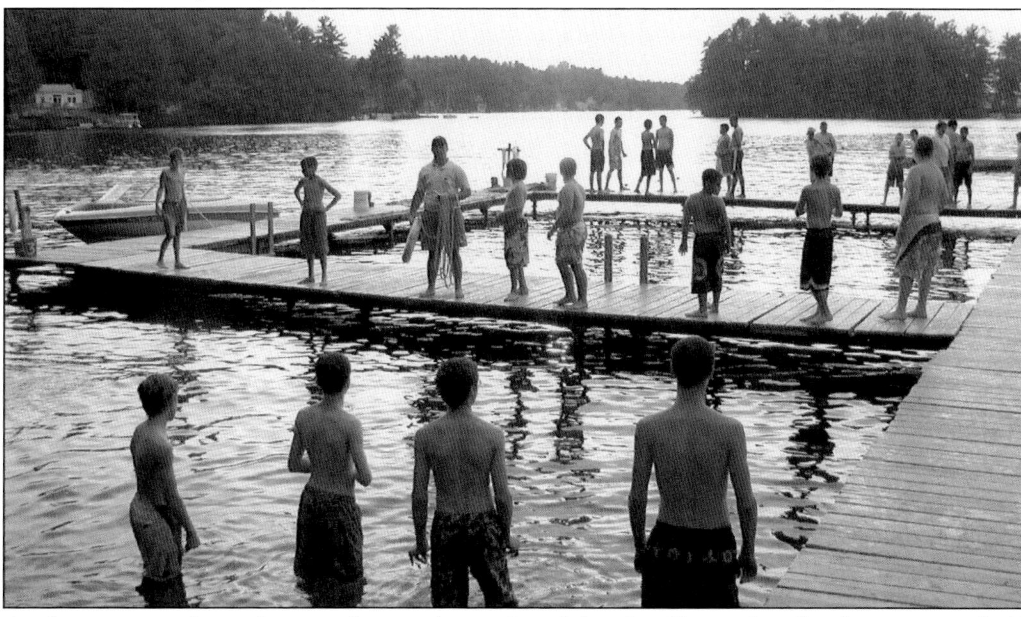

As the sun goes down, boys go for one last swim of the day. Scouts beg for the sunset to hold out a bit longer, for they know that sunset means the end of the day's activities. The end of each day brings them one day closer to the end of the week, the end of the summer, and the start of longing for the next one.

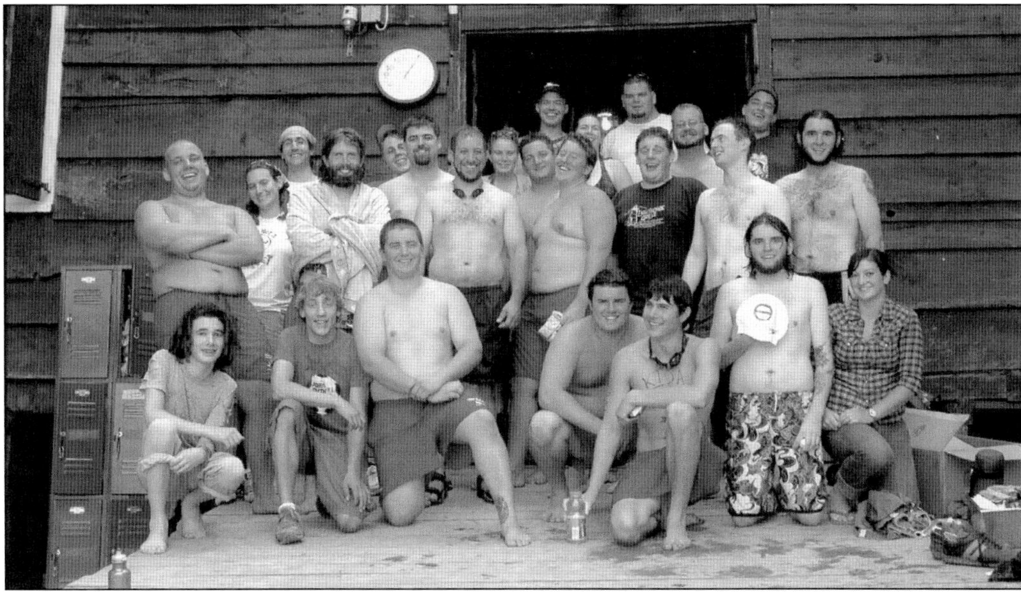

After the tragic death of former staff member Andrew Curry-Green on September 11, 2001, The Key Foundation Inc. began a project to construct a new boathouse as a memorial to his life. In 2005, in an event organized by Jonathan J. Keating, 14 people, in a swim-a-thon, swam three miles across Northwood Lake to raise money for the project. Although many of the swimmers had never met Green, they rallied around the project to pay tribute to a "brother." The event reminded everyone that no matter what year one worked on camp staff one is always a friend and brother. In 2006, the event was repeated with Green's widow Shannon Curry-Green swimming the distance. Matt Bowler, shown here at the end of his swim, encapsulated the feelings of all who participated—Keep the Spirit Alive! The swimmers' purpose was clearly to honor one of their own.

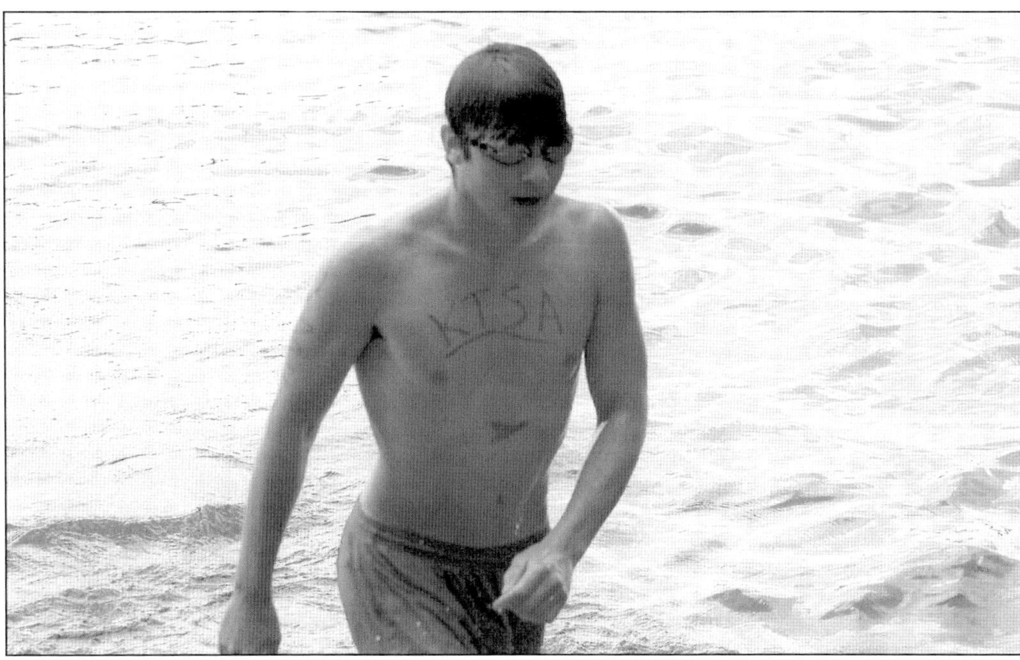

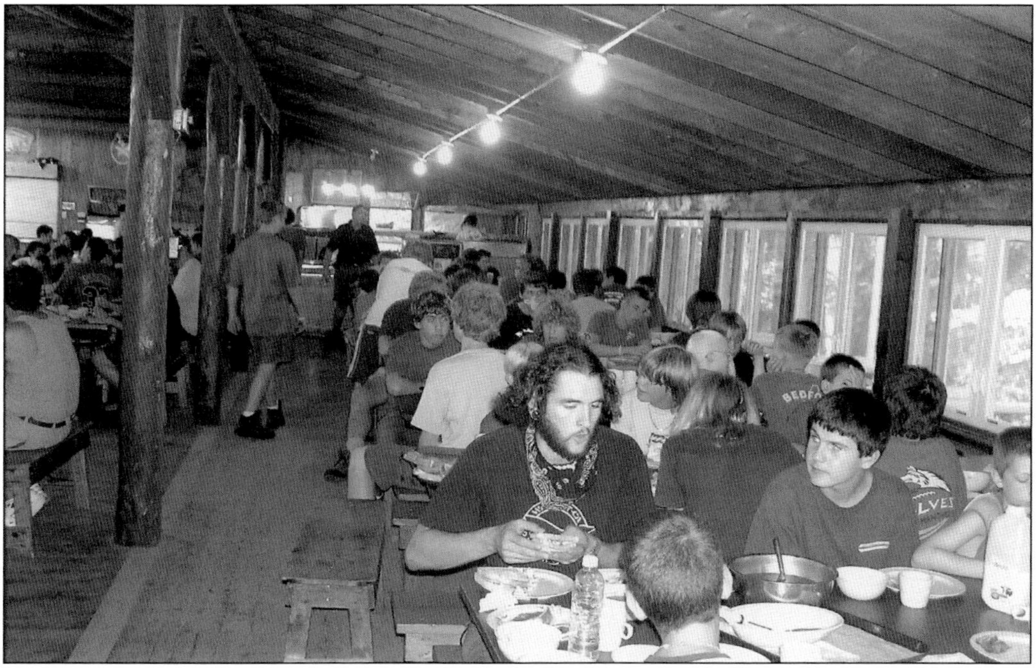

With more scouts in camp each week, many troops had to dine on the back porch of the dining hall. They often felt isolated from the songs, announcements, and antics that are a part of every meal at camp. In an effort to give all troops a common experience, the camping committee removed the wall that separated the porch from the main room in 2005.

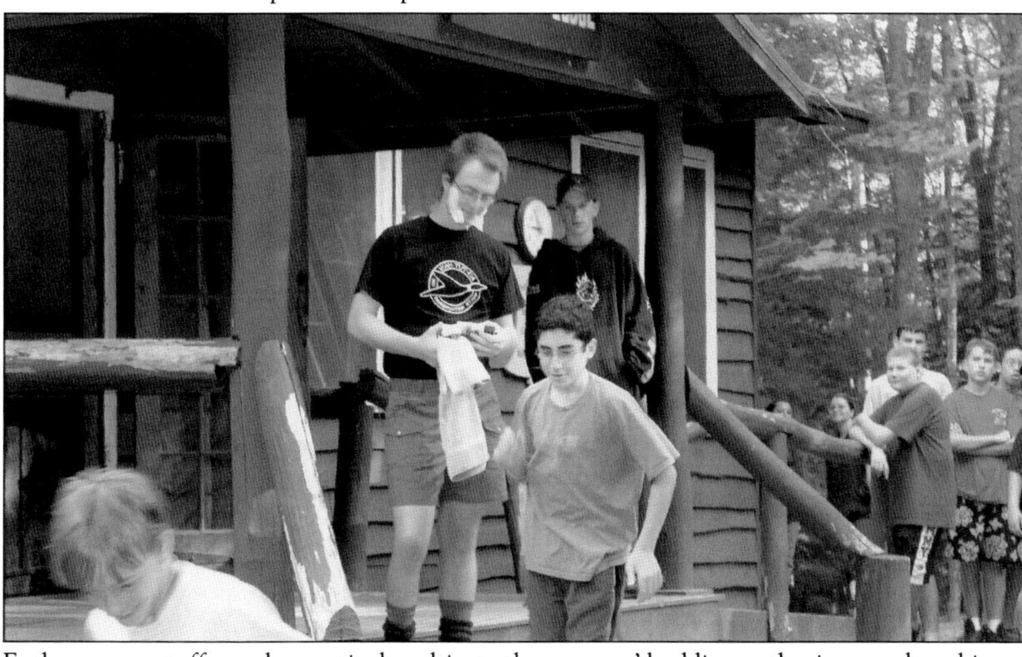

Each summer, staff members actively cultivate the campers' budding enthusiasm and wackiness. Here commissioner Howard (Howie) Martin plays along with a prank by two campers who would both go on to become staff members. Each staff member hopes that he has inspired a camper to join the ranks and carry on the traditions and spirit of the camp.

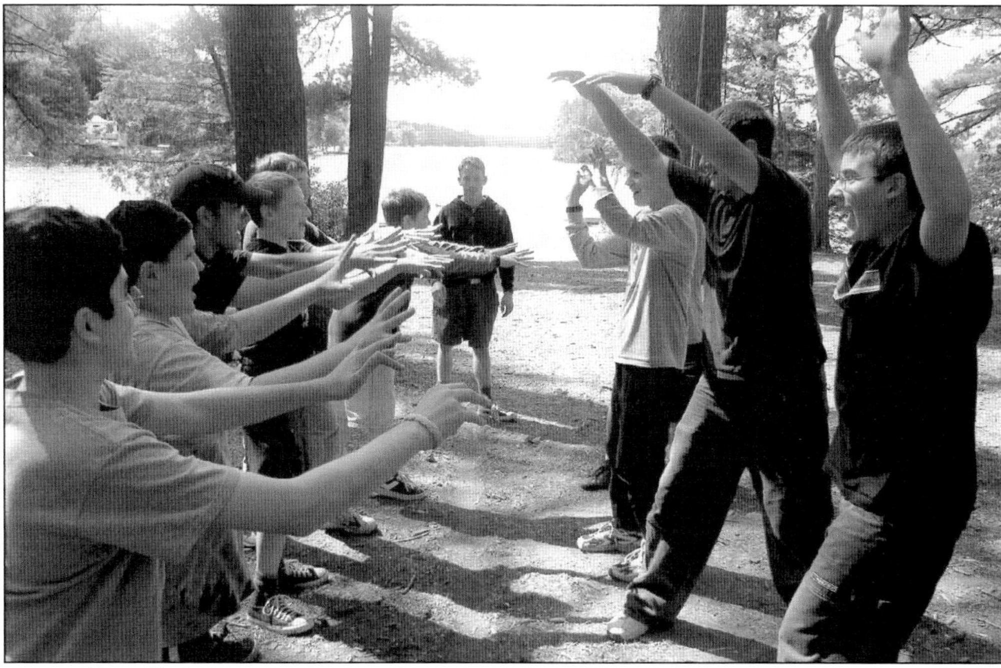

Originally called Discovery Point, the area now known as Pawtucket, located just past the waterfront, became a place for games, gatherings, and the family barbecue at the end of the week. Taking time out for fun, Scouts enjoy a staff favorite. This classic game of Giants, Wizards, and Elves has only just begun.

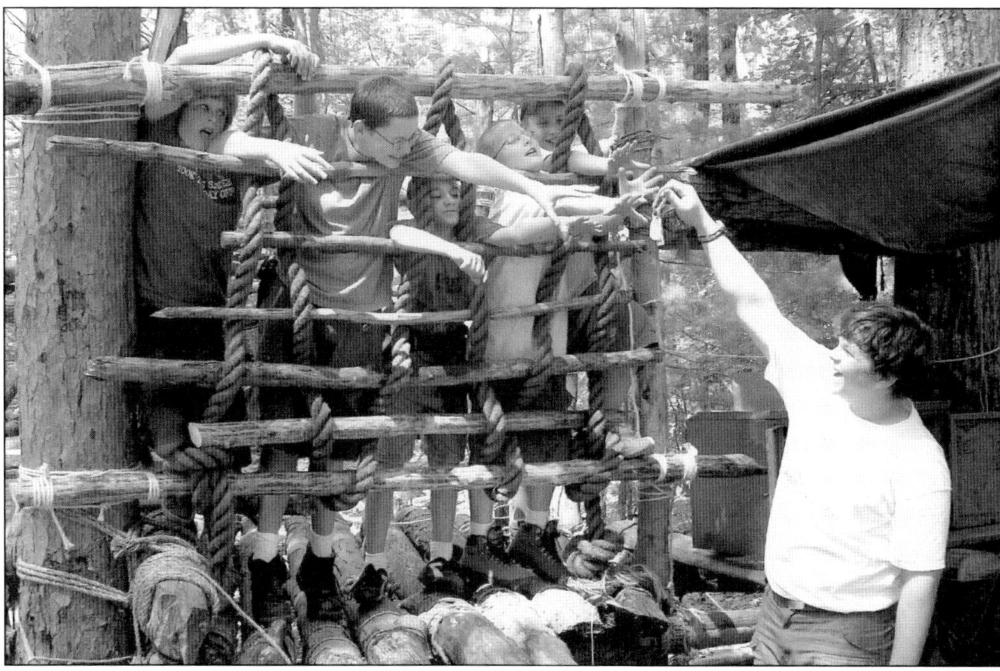

Kevin Latina (right) is representative of the new post-merger generation of Wah-Tut-Ca staff. He would spend all of his summers on staff in Wah-Tut-Ca's Frontier area. Known for his spirit and wit, Latina knows how to keep Wah-Tut-Ca's most time-honored tradition. Wah-Tut-Ca is fun!

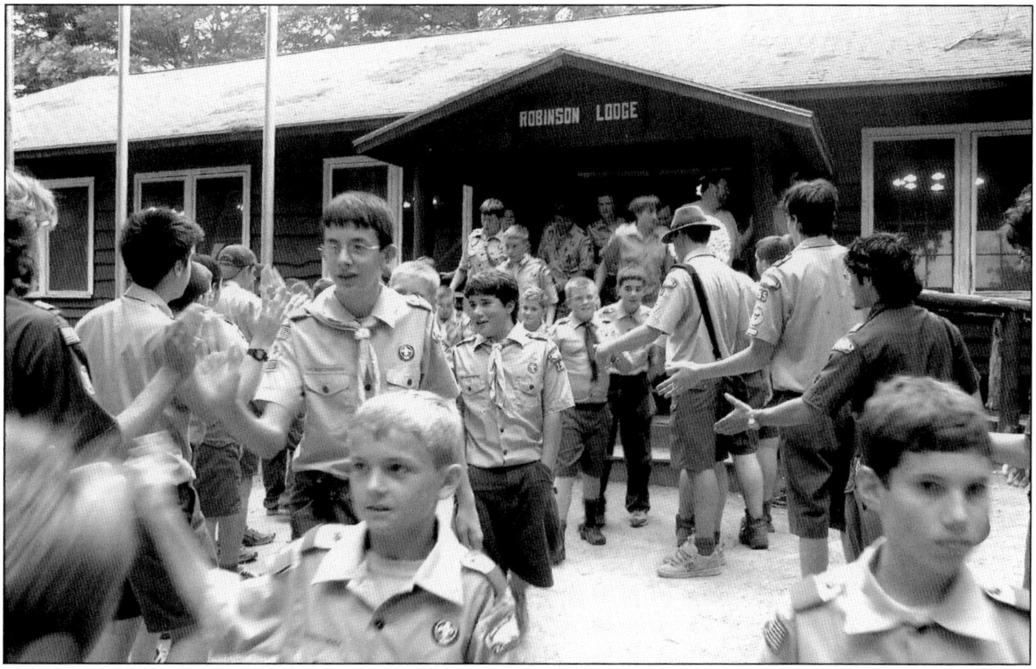

In 2006, under the leadership of Kevin R. Dion as camp director, Wah-Tut-Ca would have record Boy Scout numbers. Summer attendance had seen peaks and valleys over the years, but now Wah-Tut-Ca was seeing consistent growth. Being part of a larger council was proving to be advantageous. As a Yankee Clipper Council camp, Wah-Tut-Ca now has thousands of additional potential campers. In the age of the Internet, Scouts from all over the Northeast can learn of the opportunities that Wah-Tut-Ca offers. Most of Wah-Tut-Ca's projects are now based on expanding the capacity of the camp to hold more campers.

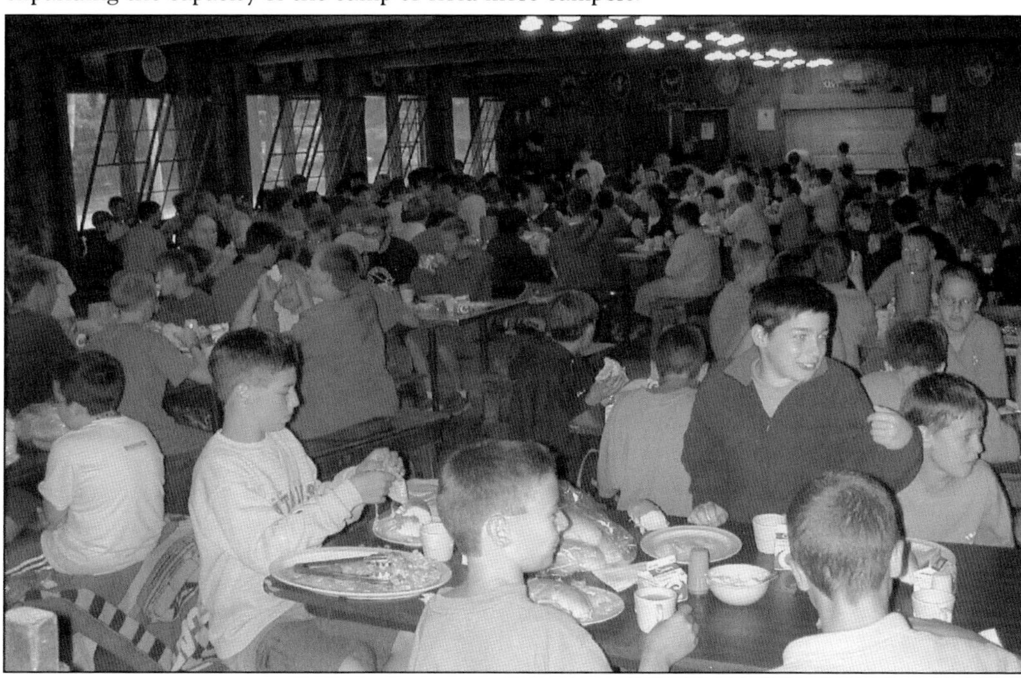

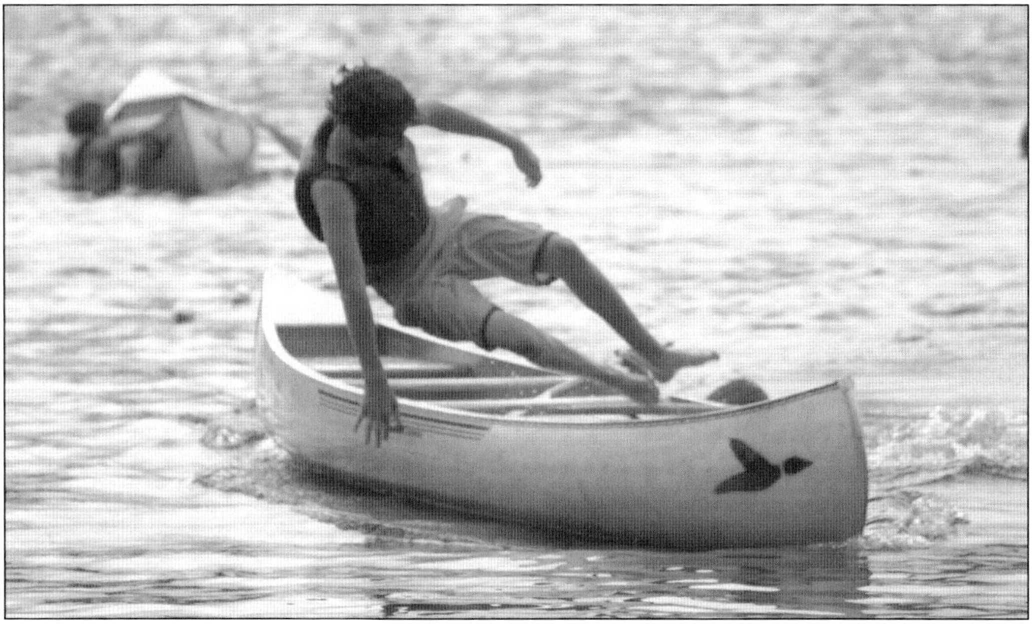

During a canoe "In and Out Race," one team shows its prowess. The water carnival gives troops an opportunity for some friendly and inevitably ridiculous competitions. Each team leaves with its own fond memories even though no one really remembers who has won from one year to the next.

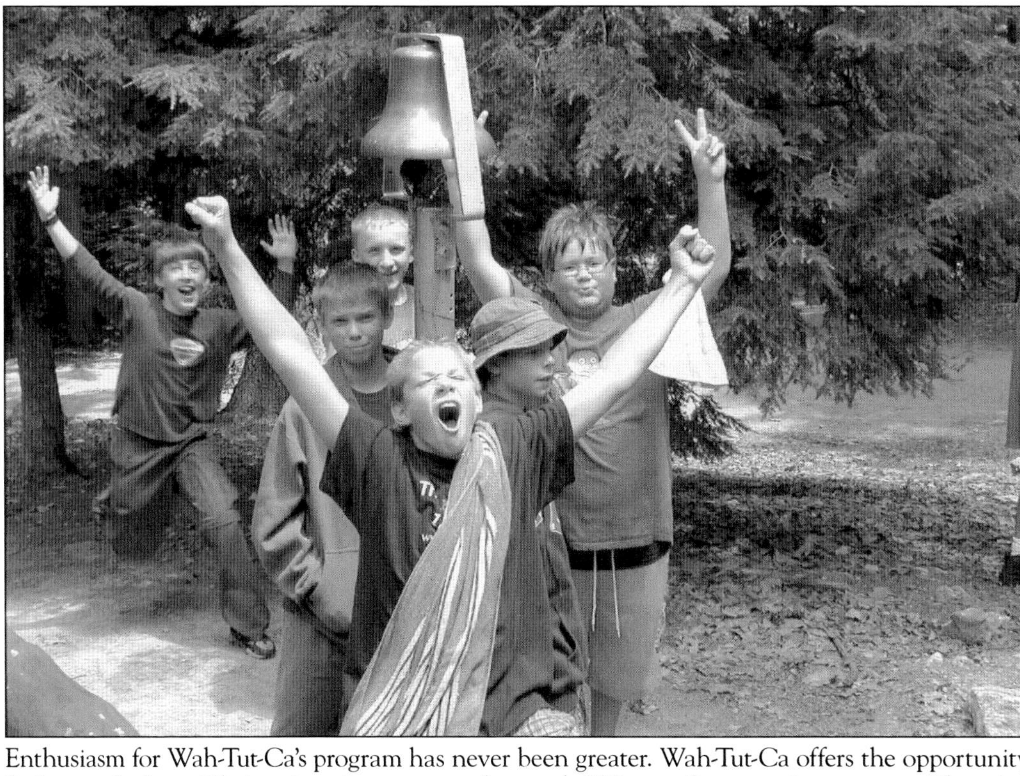

Enthusiasm for Wah-Tut-Ca's program has never been greater. Wah-Tut-Ca offers the opportunity for boys to be boys. Their voices ring out over the nearly 300 acres from sunrise to sunset. There is a sense of tradition, a sense of purpose, and a sense of optimism every day a Scout walks the trails.

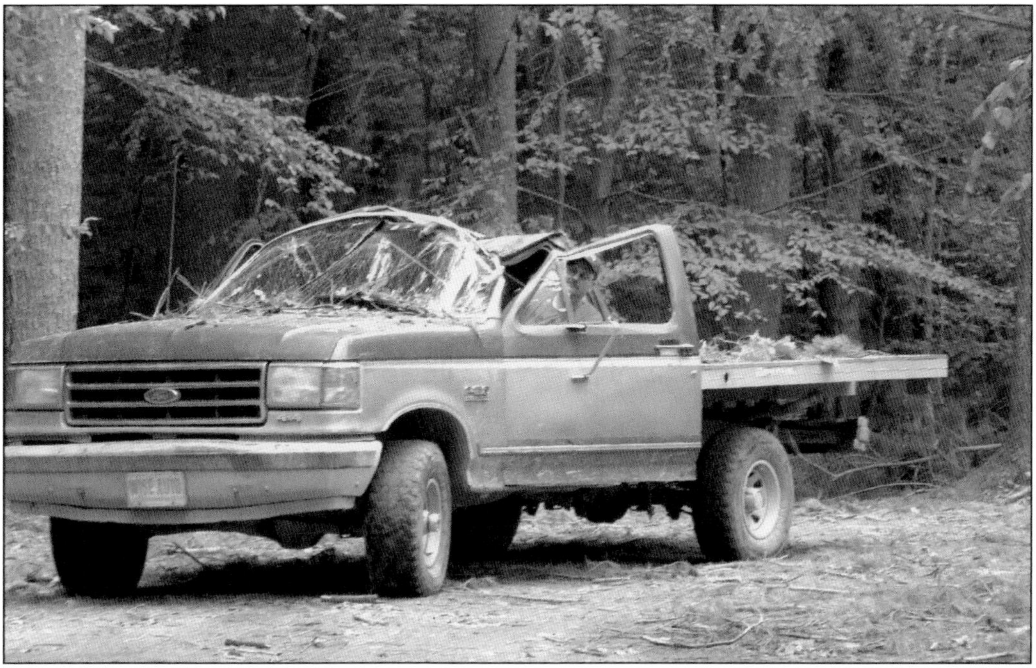

In 2006, Wah-Tut-Ca was hit by a powerful storm with winds over 100 miles per hour. It is likely that any other camp would have closed after taking a hit of this magnitude. Other Yankee Clipper Council camps could have taken in the remaining campers as well as provided a camp for those scheduled to attend the one remaining week of the season. No one would have blamed them for closing down. It would take more than trees to crush the spirit of Wah-Tut-Ca. The staff and volunteers showed that they have the same spirit that had inspired all those who had come before them. Their can-do attitude is a direct and worthy succession from the founders of Wah-Tut-Ca. They overcame obstacles and did what was needed so a Scout could have his week at Wah-Tut-Ca.

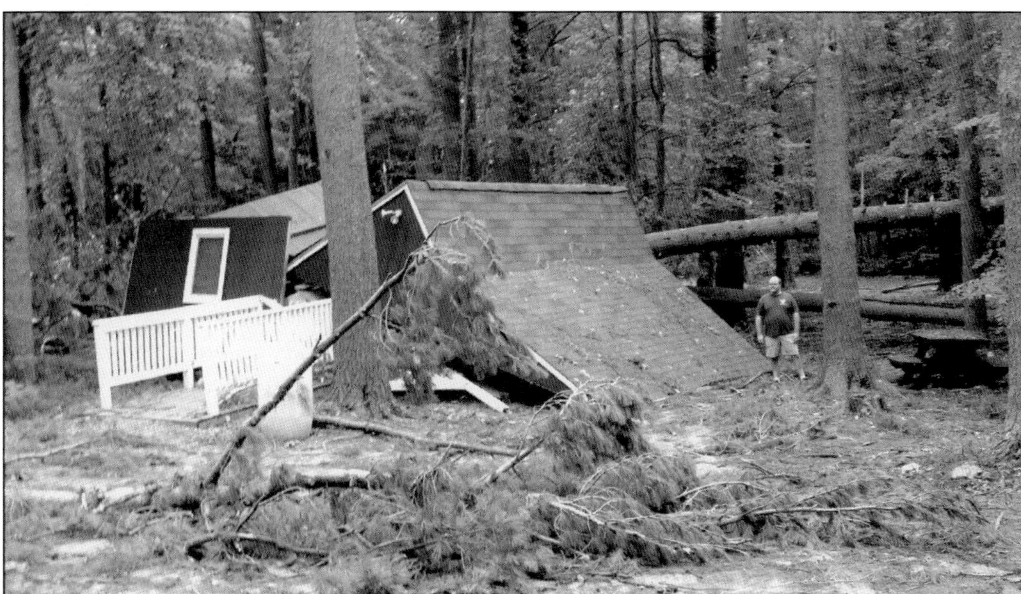

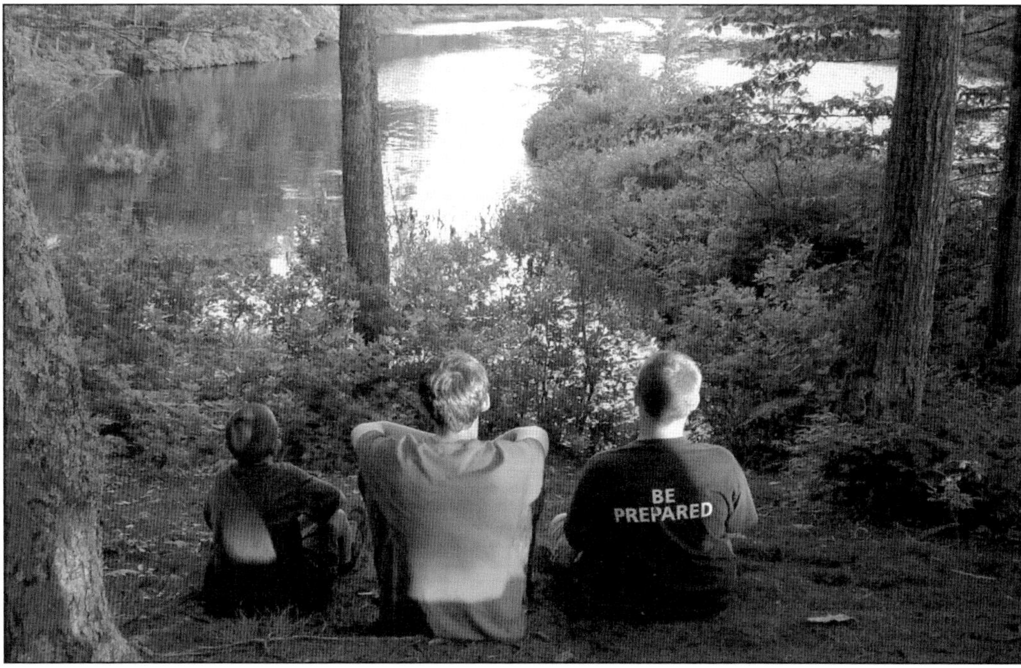

Wah-Tut-Ca has quiet moments filled with thoughts and introspection. Boys certainly enjoy the natural beauty of the forest and the lake. Some 70 years later, the sunsets still give reason to pause and reflect. With each sunset, a hope is given that the next day's adventures will surpass the experiences that are now shared.

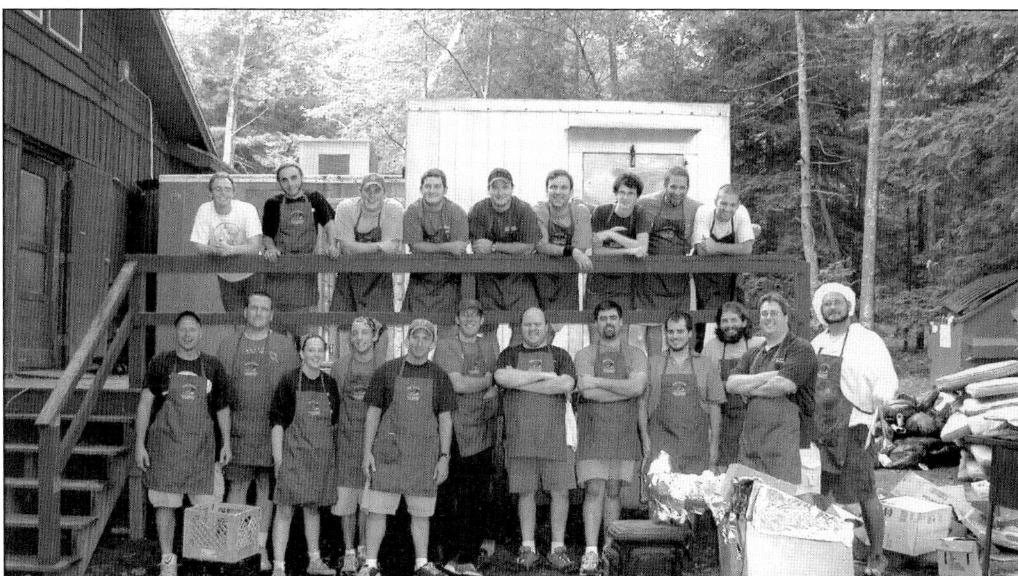

The camp staff reunion is a tradition that was started by Dennis Livoli. Held at the closing camp staff banquet the Wah-Tut-Ca alumni come home to recognize and show appreciation for the current staff by preparing their meal. For the alumni it is a chance to honor those who have taken their places. For the current staff it reinforces and adds importance to their role in Wah-Tut-Ca's history.

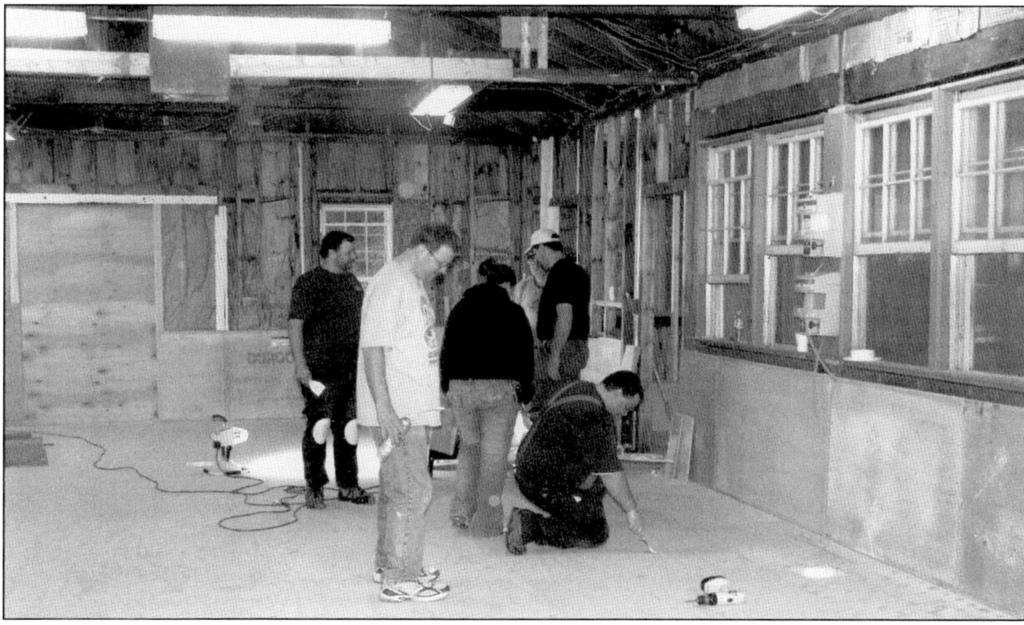

John Bushway, properties and maintenance chairman of Wah-Tut-Ca, leads the committee in renovating the kitchen area. With the growing number of Scouts attending Wah-Tut-Ca, this project is necessary to expand the capacity of camp. Bushway and his committee continue the tradition began by Charles A. Robinson, who accurately predicted, "Wah-Tut-Ca will never be completed."

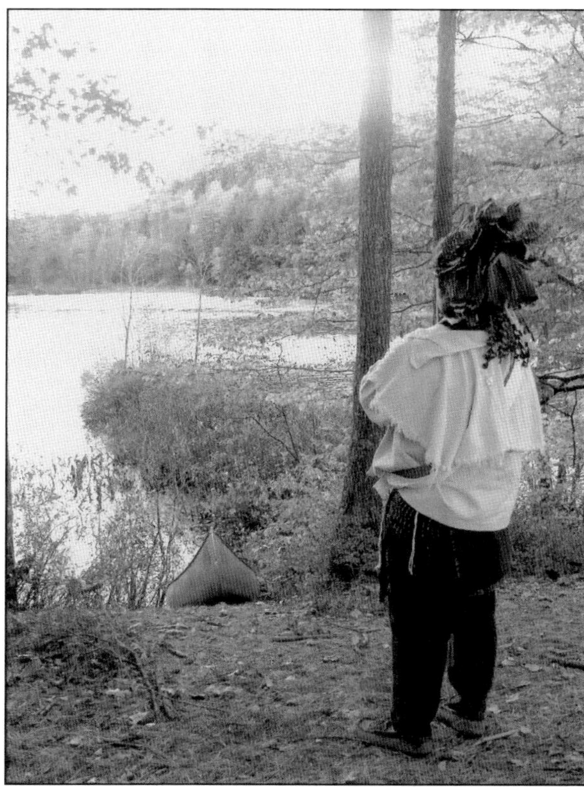

Bobby Garrahan, camp staff member and chief of Nanepashemet Lodge No. 158, awaits the start of an OA ceremony on a crisp fall morning. Voices from the past still can be heard by another generation living the adventure and beginning yet another chapter in Wah-Tut-Ca's "voyage of discovery."